LAS VEGAS

LAS VEGAS

Deke Castleman

Photography by Michael Yamashita

ODYSSEY GUIDES
Hong Kong

First published in Great Britain in 1991

© 1991 Compass American Guides, Inc.
Maps © 1991 Compass American Guides, Inc.

Distribution in the UK, Ireland, Europe and certain Commonwealth countries by
Hodder & Stoughton, Mill Road, Dunton Green, Sevenoaks, Kent, TN13 2YA

Contributing Editors: Barry Parr, Peter Zimmerman and Kit Duane
Designer: David Hurst
Map Design: Bob Race
Cover Concept: Raquel Jaramillo and Aubrey Tse
Photography: Unless otherwise stated below, all photography is by Michael
Yamashita. The picture on page 208 is by Michael Freeman. The photo on pages
210-211 is by Richard Lee Kaylin. Photos on pages 21, 29, 35, 64, 80, 83, 87, 93,
173 and 204 courtesy of the James Dickinson Library Special Collections,
UNLV. Photos on pages 52, 61, 73, 94, 106 and 119 courtesy of the Las Vegas
News Bureau.

ISBN: 962-217-180-X

British Library Cataloguing in Publication Data has been applied for.

Produced by Twin Age Ltd
Printed in Hong Kong

Cover: The world's biggest jackpot

This book is dedicated to Benny Siegel, Davie Berman, Gus Greenbaum, Moe Dalitz, and all the Jewish gamblers who helped build Las Vegas in the 1940s and 1950s.

ACKNOWLEDGMENTS

TO MY WRITER-EDITOR COUNTERPARRT BARRY PARR, who never lost sight of the orchard while pruning the trees, and fell in love with Las Vegas in the process; to big line editor Peter "Not in Webster's" Zimmerman, who saw every little bug in the bark; to designer Dave Hurst, who, after 10 years of producing books with him, requires mercifully few words; and to Michael "Tough Life" Yamashita, who embodies not only the essence of the consummate travel photographer, but also of the ultimate Japanese tourist—I owe my deepest thanks.

I'm also much obliged to these fantastically accommodating Las Vegans: Denyce Tuller and Eddie Brown of the Riviera; Barbara Love and Ira Sternberg of the Tropicana; Carolyn Merriman and John Mueller of the Sands; Heidi Borchar of Fitzgerald's; Charlotte Richards of L'Amour Chapel; Kerry Mead of YESCO; Bruno of the Liberace Museum; Stephen Allen and Don Knepp of Las Vegas News Bureau; Jackie Brett of the Nevada Commission on Tourism; Virginia and Fred of Fun City; and especially Kathy War and the gang at UNLV Special Collections. Also to Bob Blesse and the staff at UNR Special Collections in Reno; and 55 years of *Nevada* magazines.

Bravo to Anthony Curtis of *Las Vegas Advisor*—gambler, writer, and publisher; and Dennis McBride of UNLV Special Collections—archivist, copy editor extraordinaire, and dark humorist. Encore!

I'm also indebted to Jeffrey Bubman Castleman, Jewelen Ribowski Bennett, and Naomi Bagel-belly Strauss for never failing to reanimate a word-weary spirit.

And to Virginia Michaels, for hanging in there through the months and years of thick and thin, goes my love.

CONTENTS

MAPS

INTRODUCTION

HOW DO YOU TURN ONE OF THE HOTTEST, driest, and most unlivable valleys on the continent into a cool moist oasis that's accessible, hospitable, and profitable?

That was the question facing a handful of entrepreneurs and gamblers over the last century who surveyed a godforsaken patch of desert in southern Nevada and foresaw, somehow, a booming metropolis. Their answer was first to reach the valley with transcontinental railroad track and establish a service stop to put it on the map. Later, to erect a monster dam on the nearest, mightiest river to provide unlimited power and water. Next, to build dozens of skyscraping pleasure palaces where rooms were opulent, food bountiful, drinks free, entertainment round-the-clock, and casino gambling legal, and to illuminate them with a spotlight so bright that it could be seen from everywhere in the world. Then, to lay down long highways and wide landing strips to handle the hordes drawn to its rare diversions.

And finally, to call it Las Vegas.

Railroad magnates William Clark and E.H. Harriman chose the site at the turn of the century. Publisher Charles Squires, water czar Walter Bracken, and politician Ed Clark promoted the valley's settlement in the early, surly days. Secretary Herbert Hoover, administrator Elwood Mead, and engineer Frank Crowe dammed the Colorado River and blessed Las Vegas. Casino pioneers like J. Kell Houssels, Guy McAfee, and Tony Cornero set up tables and shop, into which moved racketeers like Ben Siegel, Gus Greenbaum, and Moe Dalitz with money, muscle, and management. Tom Young dressed the town in neon, while Donn Arden imported nude French dancers. Billionaire Howard Hughes and high-financier Kirk Kerkorian applied a veneer of legitimacy, paving the way for today's corporate control.

But what does it all mean?

What unique product has resulted from the mingling of these fertile imaginations and extraordinary elements?

Here is a city that attracts 20 million visitors each year, who leave behind 10 billion dollars in the pursuit of pleasure. The pastimes are legendary and legion: gambling, shows, meals, sightseeing, escorts, lights, people-watching, cruising, golf, amusement parks, tanning, and shopping. Even the variations of each are enough to Mickey Finn the mind.

You want to gamble? You've got slots, craps, keno, blackjack, roulette, sic-bo, pai-gow, Red Dog, poker, Big Six, baccarat, races and sports. Slots? Three reel, four reel, nickel, quarter, dollar, Quartermania, Megabucks, multipliers, Berthas, video poker, keno, blackjack, roulette, bingo, greyhounds. Video poker? Straight draw, deuces and sevens, and jokers wild, second chance, high card.

You want shows? How about extravaganzas, major revues, mini-revues, headliners, lounge acts, topless, bottomless, comedy, erupting volcanoes, motion-simulated movies, dancing waters. Revues? Ice, water, magic, illusion, dance, stunts, juggling, gimmicks.

Golf? Eight country clubs, three golf clubs, and two golf courses. Restaurants? Seven hundred of them. Hotel rooms? Seventy-five thousand to choose from. Side trip to the Grand Canyon? Six air services, including a helicopter tour.

Etc. etc. etc. . . .

The average out-of-towner stays only four nights. So how is he or she to understand this place, to put the experience into perspective, or even catch a glimpse of the Big Picture?

The following Las Vegas stories are The Story of Las Vegas.

DESERT ROOTS
FROM THE PRECAMBRIAN TO THE PAIUTE

HALF A BILLION YEARS AGO OR SO, NEVADA RESTED UNDERWATER. At least twice during the mysterious 340-million-year Paleozoic era, violent and titanic episodes of uplift raised the ocean floor, drained the sea, and left towering mesas and alluvial plains. Over the next 160 million years, cataclysmic extinctions, megashears, volcanism, and climatic crises, punctuated by long stoic periods of erosion, continually altered Nevada, several times obliterating its life and landscape. Seventeen million years ago, today's familiar basins and ranges were created by the colossal jostle of tectonic forces. More than 250 separate ranges have been named in Nevada. Ninety percent of them are oriented northeast-southwest, and on a map look like a herd of earthworms marching toward Mexico. The southwest-trending cavalcade of ranges, however, jams up at a southeast-trending dead end, at the northern edge of Las Vegas Valley. To geologists, this phenomenon is known, without apparent irony, as the Las Vegas Zone of Deformation.

Beginning nearly two million years ago, four great ice ages advanced into and retreated from history. Nevada's Basin and Range Physiographic Province, which had been shuffled by earthquakes, tilted by crustal adjustments, and whittled by erosion, was now alternately drowned, drained, and ground down by glaciers. By the end of the last ice age, roughly 12,000 years ago, Las Vegas Valley had finally taken the shape it remains in today: relatively long and flat, cutting a diagonal 18 by 26 miles (29 by 42 km) across Clark County at Nevada's southern tip. Except for the Las Vegas Wash which drains into Lake Mead to the east, the valley is an enclosed system, cradled by eight or so mountain ranges. The Spring Mountains to the west embrace Mt. Charleston, highest point in the area at 11,918 feet (3,633 meters), and Red Rock Canyon, petrified red sand dunes standing sentinel in front of limestone cliffs. To the north are the Spotted, Pintwater, Desert, Sheep, and Las Vegas ranges, all pointing southward at the valley like accusing fingers. South of the Vegas Valley are the McCullough Mountains. And to the east are Frenchman's and Sunrise peaks, which form a lumpy backdrop to downtown Las Vegas.

Alluvial fans of stone, gravel, and cobble spread down from these mountains onto the valley floors, beneath which lies a concrete-like lake-bottom hardpan

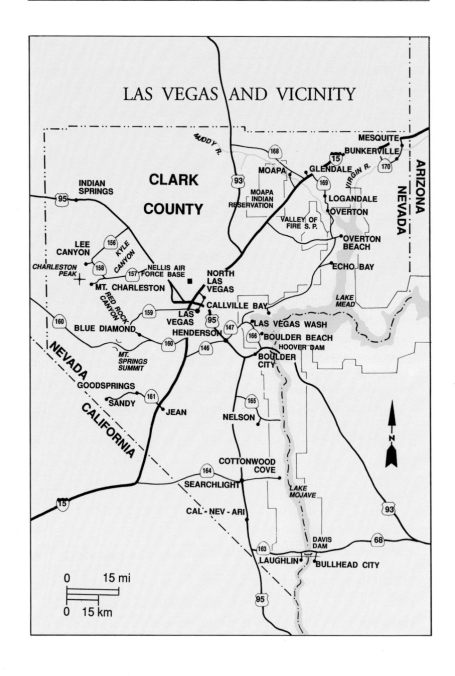

LAS VEGAS AND VICINITY

known as caliche—the scourge of construction companies and swimming-pool installers. Underneath the valley is a major system of artesian aquifers. Groundwater has been tapped at levels as shallow as 40 feet (12 meters) and as deep as 1,000 feet (300 meters). This underground lake is recharged by rain running off the ranges. Prior to the drastic depletion of the reservoir by the 1930s, artesian pressure forced this water up into the valley as a series of springs, creating an oasis of tall grasses, mesquite, and cottonwoods, with several short creeks flowing through. The first Spanish explorers stumbled upon this life-saving lea and named it *Las Vegas*, "The Meadows."

■ PALEO-INDIANS

People lived in Las Vegas Valley as early as 11,000 B.C., at the cold and wet tail end of the Wisconsin Ice Age. These Paleo-Indians lived in shoreline caves and hunted the large Pleistocene mammals—woolly mammoth, bison, mastodon, and caribou—which would disappear from the area within a few thousand years. Several expeditions to Tule Springs, an archaeological and paleontological site in east-

A peek at Las Vegas at sunrise, from Sunrise Peak.

ern Las Vegas Valley, have uncovered prehistoric hearths, fluted arrow and spear points, scrapers, and scarred and charred animal bones.

Human habitation in the valley varied with the climate. Between 7000 and 3000 B.C., the area was too arid for settlement. After 2500 B.C., however, the cli-

CLIMATE

The most famous and flamboyant gambling and resort city in the world is a neon oasis blaring brashly on the eastern edge of the Mojave Desert, on the northern edge of the Sonoran Desert, and the southern edge of the Great Basin Desert. Thus situated on a spot where three deserts merge, it's the driest and one of the hottest urban areas in the United States.

Though Las Vegas is now a large city (750,000 population) with every amenity you could possibly want or imagine, it is still located in the center of some of the most inhospitable terrain imaginable. For at least half the year, the single most important miracle of technology that makes the Mojave bearable, let alone livable, is air conditioning. Average summer temperatures fluctuate between 80 and 105 degrees F (26-40°C), with a record high of 116 (July 5, 1973). True, it's a *dry* heat, which ostensibly reduces the discomfort. But even lounging poolside in the summer can be problematic—unless you take off your flesh and sit in your bones.

Wintertime temperatures are mild, averaging 45 degrees F (7°C) occasionally dropping into the 20s (-6°C) at night, and often hovering daytime in the 60s (15°C). Las Vegas's mean annual temperature is a comfortable 66 degrees, making this resort city a definite year-round destination, with no extended off-season (quietest weeks in Las Vegas are the first three in December, last three in January, and the last three in June, in that order).

Las Vegas has the least precipitation (4.2 inches/10.6 centimeters) and lowest relative humidity (20 percent) of all metropolitan areas in the country. It's a desert out there, dry as Death Valley sand, and after the first day you'll know every water fountain in your range of operations. Cyclonic storms in summer are accompanied by cloudbursts which can drop an inch of rain in an hour, rendering the danger of flash flooding real and worrisome. In the summer, winds that carry storm fronts have been known to shift all the sand from the west side of town to the east, and vice versa. But any time of year, the winds can be so strong that a giant 30-foot (9-meter) flag on West Tropicana Avenue stands proudly at a perfect right angle to the pole; you have to hang on tight to the people mover at Caesars Palace to avoid getting blown off; and miniature golfing at Sandia Fun Center is *hysterical.*

mate changed again to nearly what it is today: cool and damp enough, relatively speaking, to support a newly arrived and evolving Indian society. Known as the Archaic or Desert Period, this era hosted a forager culture, whose members adapted to the use of such high-quality but limited resources as the desert tortoise, bighorn sheep, screwbean mesquite, canyon grape, and cholla fruit. These new settlers lived in small groups, scattered from the valleys to the peaks, the number of their members growing or shrinking according to abundance or scarcity. They built rock shelters, circular stone campsites, and roasting pits, and used the *atlatl* (a primitive but remarkably efficient arrow-throwing stick), mortars and pestles, flaked knives, and hammerstones. These Archaic Indians could be considered the behavioral ancestors of the later Paiute people.

■ THE ANASAZI

Whether the Archaic people evolved into, were absorbed or evicted by the Basketmakers is unclear, but around 300 B.C., a new people appeared in the Las Vegas area. Also hunter-foragers, the early Basketmakers were more sophisticated than their predecessors in only one respect. They lived in pit houses: three- to four-foot-deep (one-meter) excavations, with mud floors and walls, brush roofs supported by strong poles, and a central fireplace. By about A.D. 500, the Modified Basketmaker period had arrived, perhaps introduced by Pueblo pioneers migrating to their western frontier. Within a couple of hundred years, these Anasazi (Navajo for "Ancient Ones") were settled permanently in the fertile river valleys of what is now southeastern Nevada. They cultivated maize, beans, squash, and cotton, wove intricate baskets, fashioned handsome black-and-white pottery, constructed large adobe pit houses, and hunted with bows and arrows.

As their agricultural techniques became more refined and their population increased, the Anasazi entered the peak of their civilization: the Classic Pueblo or Lost City Period (850-1000). Living in a sizable urban metropolis known as Pueblo Grande, the Anasazi were intricately linked to trading centers throughout the Southwest. These centers in turn were integrated into the Meso-American system of political and economic relationships. For example, Anasazi were present at productive turquoise mines in the Amargosa Range in eastern California and near Searchlight, Nevada, 60 miles (96 km) south of Las Vegas Valley. Anasazi traders

traveled to southern and Baja California to barter salt and soft cotton for sea shells and pottery. Trade for woven textiles, parrot feathers, and copper might have been carried on with other Anasazi outposts, such as those at the Grand Canyon and Canyon de Chelly (Arizona), Chaco Canyon (New Mexico), Grand Gulch (southeastern Utah), and possibly Mesa Verde (Colorado). Travelers carried back not only products but new agricultural, technological, religious, and social ideas. Las Vegas Valley and its "Big Springs" made an excellent staging area for these excursions west and south. During the population explosion of the Pueblo Grande period, the fertile and watered valley supported an outpost of Lost City Anasazi—the only known prehistoric architecture at Las Vegas.

By the year 1000, Pueblo Grande had become Nevada's first ghost town. The Anasazi simply packed up and headed out, dispersing throughout the Southwest. They probably returned to the center of their civilization, becoming the ancestors of today's Hopi and Zuni Indians.

Why would such a sophisticated and successful civilization abandon a major city? Theories include stress from overpopulation, natural disasters (such as several seasons of drought followed by flooding, which would strip the topsoil), and encroachment by the Southern Paiute. One eminent archaeologist insists that the swampy river bottomland was a prime breeding ground for malarial mosquitos; after too many deaths, the people simply moved. A recent, provocative explanation holds that the disintegration of this extensive Southwestern society coincides with the collapse of Mexico's vast Toltec Empire. This would have severely disturbed the "global" economic foundation, such as the lucrative turquoise trade between the Pueblo Grande and Chaco Canyon Anasazi. Deprived of primary links, and suffering urban and ecological stress, the Anasazi confederacy unraveled.

■ LAS VEGAS BAND OF THE SOUTHERN PAIUTE

For the next 700 years, the nomadic Paiute occupied the territory in southern Nevada abandoned by the Anasazi. These Indians called themselves *Tudinu*, "Desert People," and spoke an Uto-Aztecan variety of the Shoshonean language, which indicates that they probably arrived from the northeast. The Paiute had some contact with the Anasazi—the squatters learned a few horticultural skills, and the property owners fortified their dwellings with walls and gates. But the Paiute seem to have been peaceful; there's no evidence of confrontation between the immigrants and emigrants.

The territory of the Las Vegas band encompassed the whole of Las Vegas Valley. It reached as far as Indian Springs in the northeast, Ash Meadow in the northwest, the Colorado River to the east, and included a couple of mountain ranges in California. This was the largest and most bountiful territory of any Southern Paiute band. The Las Vegans were bordered by the Shoshone to the north, the Moapa Paiute to the northeast, the Hualapai to the east, the Mojave to the south, and the Chemehuevi, to whom they were closely related, in the west.

One view from along US 95 in the Mojave Desert.

Today, traveling from Beatty to Las Vegas on US 95 through the Mojave Desert, this territory might seem horribly barren and inhospitable. But the hunter-forager Tudinu were blessed with great ecological variety—elevation change alone covered from 450 feet (137 meters) at the Colorado River to nearly 12,000 feet (3,650 meters) atop Mt. Charleston. And because the Paiute knew the land and its resources, they developed a suitable and successful culture. In the center of their range, Big Springs gushed out of Las Vegas Valley; creeks flowed through lush grassland and thickets of mesquite. The Paiutes established base camps of semi-permanent wickiup shelters (conical brush and pole structures), cultivated squash and corn at the springs and creeks, and traveled seasonally to hunt and harvest wild foods. Their diet consisted of whatever game was available: snakes, lizards, rodents, rabbits, desert tortoises, birds, deer, and bighorn sheep. In addition, they collected pine nuts, screw beans, agave, cholla fruit, grasses, berries, and Indian spinach to supplement their crops, stockpiling supplies for the short but lean winters. They ground seeds, pine nuts, and white mesquite beans into flour which they baked into long cakes over hot stones in their tightly woven baskets.

By nature, the Paiutes were independent and free-spirited. They roamed on foot in small, flexible family units. They had no chiefs, only heads of families. No formal structures linked the families, though annual spring and fall game drives and pine-nut harvests united villages for several days. At these times, the Las Vegas band might number up to 100 individuals. Courtships were conducted and marriages consummated at these festivals. The Paiute practiced a form of polygamy, a man taking his wife's unmarried or widowed sister, within a tradition generally attributed to the need for survival. But who knows what other reasons there might've been?

SOME PAIUTE VOCABULARY

ankle:	towinwichachang
basket:	yoo-ahts
crazy:	numpicant
cactus:	o'si
desert:	yuavi
rattlesnake:	toxo'avi
raven:	tap'puts
sin:	sangwav
spirit:	moxoam
star:	tava
sun:	tava
sun in sky:	tava puts
virgin:	cach-kumai it mama'its
white man:	marukats

Las Vegas Paiutes in dance dress on July 4, 1889.

The Paiutes' first contact with Europeans occurred in 1776. At the same time General Howe's 32,000 British troops were forcing General Washington's 19,000 irregulars into retreat from Brooklyn, New York, two Franciscan friars were establishing both ends of the Old Spanish Trail. On exploring and surveying trips into the northern hinterlands of Spain's Mexican colony, Father Silvestre Escalante blazed the eastern end of the trail from Santa Fe, New Mexico, to the southwestern corner of Utah. From the other end, Father Francisco Garces traveled toward him through California and Arizona. Garces encountered Southern Nevada Paiute, who by all accounts treated him hospitably. But it was another 50 years before further Paiute-European contact.

Before Mexico gained its independence from Spain in 1822, the Spanish goverment had enforced strict laws against trespassing. After independence, the first wave of Eastern fur trappers and mountain men penetrated the previously unknown Southwest. In 1826-27, famed trader and explorer Jedediah Smith became the first American explorer to travel through what is now southern and central Nevada, and he too made contact with Paiutes. Three years later, Antonio Armijo, a Mexican trader, set out from Santa Fe on the Spanish Trail. An experienced scout in Armijo's party, Rafael Rivera, discovered a shortcut on the route by way of Las Vegas's Big Springs, thereby making him the first non-Indian to set foot on the land that would become Las Vegas—and at the same time decisively sealing the doom of the Southern Nevada Paiute.

After 1830, the warring Utes used the northern Las Vegas cutoff of the Old Spanish Trail, blazed by Armijo, to raid the peaceful Paiute, kidnapping children and women for the slave markets of New Mexico and California. In addition, Spanish and American trading caravans began camping at Las Vegas's Big Springs and creeks; their grazing stock destroyed the precious grasses; their guns killed the limited game. At first the Indians carefully avoided the interlopers, but as natural resources were depleted, they were reduced to sneak thievery, stealing horses and cattle to butcher for food. That was when traders and travelers began shooting at the Paiute themselves.

In his excellent and moving *The Las Vegas Paiutes—A Short History*, John Allen writes, "Whites invaded the area, pushed the original occupants to the side, disregarded their rights and interests, neglected their needs, and even ignored their existence. Whites preserved only a fragment of Paiute history, often distorted by insensitivity and a lack of understanding." Indeed, this is a euphemistic way of saying that, within 25 years of initial contact, the Las Vegas Paiute band's spirit was broken, self-reliance was shattered, and dependence became a new way of life.

In 1844, surveyor and cartographer John C. Frémont noted the Las Vegas Paiutes' sunflower and pumpkin patches by the Big Springs, and watched them fish lizards out of holes. Frémont considered them "humanity in its lowest form and most elementary state." He couldn't understand how they could live with no possessions, no houses, and hardly any clothes. Frémont also noted that they stole everything and ate anything. "Diggers" became their derogatory name.

In 1848, the Las Vegas Paiute initially ran "like wild deer" from trader and traveler Orville Pratt, but he eventually managed to buy beans and corn from them. By 1851, the portion of the Old Spanish Trail from central Utah to Los Angeles had been so tamed and improved by Mormon-guided wagon trains that it became known as the Mormon Trail. This was all part of Mormon president Brigham Young's master plan to establish the great State of Deseret, with boundaries he hoped would eventually enclose the Southwest from the Rockies to the Pacific. To this aim, he sent missionaries to colonize Las Vegas Valley, and to convert and civilize the Paiute.

DESERT SURVIVAL TIPS

Las Vegas is surrounded by some of the most inhospitable terrain in the continental United States. Even nearby daytrips and short hikes in the desert can, unless proper precautions are taken, turn into dangerous experiences. Before heading into the Mojave, a few simple preparations might spell the difference between a routine and a life-threatening situation.

First, make certain that your trusty steed has had the best care. Fuel and fluids should be full. Carry at least a gallon of antifreeze, along with spare belts and hoses, spare tire and jack, tool kit, flashlight and flares, and shovel. Baling wire and super-glue often come in handy. Don't forget a rag or two. And a well-stocked first-aid kit is essential.

If the car gets hot or overheats, stop until it cools off. Never open the radiator if the engine is steaming. After a while, squeeze the top radiator hose to check the pressure; if it's loose, it's safe to remove the radiator cap. Never pour water into a hot radiator. You could crack your block. If you start to smell rubber, your tires are overheating, and you could have a blowout. Stop, in the shade if possible, to let them cool. If the car won't restart, often it's just a little vapor lock in the gas line. Try wrapping a wet rag around the line between the fuel pump and carburetor.

If you're exploring the back country, always inform a friend, park ranger, or highway patrol office where you're going and when you'll be back. (And don't forget to check in upon returning.) Carry double the amount of water you ordinarily would on such an outing, plus an extra five-gallon (19-liter) containerful in your vehicle. If your vehicle gets stuck in the sand, let some air out of the tires for traction. Stay with the vehicle. If you have to dig it out, do it in the evening after the sun has set.

Wear dark glasses. Cover up to avoid burning. Conserve body water: don't eat, avoid urinating, minimize conversation. Drink regularly, but not to excess. If outside help is required, send the strongest member of the party to the main road, but only after the sun is down. Most desert deaths occur from dehydration by walking too long in the sun.

Your life expectancy, in extreme heat, resting, in the shade, will be three days with no water; four days with one gallon (3.8 liters) of water; five days with two-and-a-half gallons (nine liters); and one week with five gallons (19 liters).

Try not to verify these statistics.

The ill-fated colony was plagued from the start with problems. A vast desert surrounded the Meadows; the summer heat and winter wind was unbearable; millable timber had to be hauled a great distance; and Las Vegas's isolation sapped what little morale existed among the new settlers. Still, with proverbial Mormon diligence, the missionaries dug irrigation ditches, cultivated farms, managed to befriend a few Paiute, and erected a fort. The mission might have succeeded, but the colonists's discovery of lead nearby prompted Brigham Young to dispatch a party of miners to Las Vegas. The already meager rations were soon stretched to the limit by the miners' demands. As was so often the case in early Nevada settlements, deep-seated tensions between miners and Mormons erupted into bitter disputes—even at Las Vegas where the miners *were* Mormons. Their disagreements, compounded by crop failures, morale problems, and constant theft, finally caused the mission, with Young's permission, to disband in 1858—leaving the second ghost town in Nevada.

Soon after, discovery of the Comstock Lode in western Nevada triggered the first backwash of miners and migrants from the gold fields of California. The Mormon lead mine, known as Potosi, was re-prospected and further developed, attracting hundreds of fortune seekers. Enterprising growers started gardens in Las Vegas Valley and sold produce to the new locals. Many prospectors fanned out from Potosi and discovered gold on the west bank of the Colorado River at Eldorado Canyon. Among these gold miners was Octavius Decatur (O.D.) Gass who, in 1865, settled near the Big Springs in Las Vegas Valley, building a ranch house and shop inside the decaying Mormon stockade. The Gass family irrigated 640 acres (260 hectares), raised produce, grain, fruit, and cattle. By the mid-1870s, Gass had bought up or taken most of the homesteaded land in the valley, and he owned the rights to most of the water.

Still, only a handful of whites lived in Las Vegas at that time. Violence by and against the Paiute occasionally flared. In 1860, three white travelers were killed by Indians, later thought to be encroaching Utes; a punitive expedition led by Major James H. Carleton resulted in the deaths of five Paiute. The Gass family experienced many scares—soldiers were stationed around his ranch from 1867 to 1869. By the 1870s, the Southeast Nevada Indian Agency had been established, and President Ulysses S. Grant had granted nearly 4,000 acres (1,600 hectares) near the Moapa and Virgin rivers, not far from Las Vegas, for a Southern Paiute reservation. Two years later he reduced this to 1,000 acres (400 hectares). But it proved difficult to "confine" even a small portion of Nevada's early settlers: as nomads, the Paiute were completely unaccustomed to living in a large, restrictive society governed by a central authority.

Even so, the Las Vegas Paiute fared slightly better than some of their neighbors. Many found work at the mines or on the ranches. The men harvested grain, hauled wood, cut hay, and ran cattle. The women cooked, cleaned, and laundered. The Gass ranch was taken over by Archibald Stewart in 1881. After he was murdered in 1884, his wife Helen Stewart continued to operate the prosperous spread. An enlightened and capable pioneer, Mrs. Stewart also championed the Paiute cause. Today, long after her death in 1926, she is still known as the First Lady of Las Vegas.

Throughout the last years of the nineteenth century, Las Vegas remained isolated enough for the Paiute to retain a certain modicum of their tradition. Occasional violence, though, evinced the uneasiness of this brief pause before the end. For example, in 1897 a renegade known as Mouse, half-Indian and half-Mexican, was connected to several murders in the Overton-Valley of Fire area east of Las Vegas.

■ TWENTIETH-CENTURY PAIUTE

The arrival of the San Pedro, Los Angeles and Salt Lake Railroad in 1905 ushered in decades of hardship for the Indians. As the white population exploded, the Paiute population was decimated, primarily through disease and despair. In 1912, Helen Stewart deeded 10 acres (4 hectares) of what remained of her Las Vegas Ranch to the Paiute, in the desolate desert north of town. The U.S. government paid her $500 for the land, but drew up the title in the name of the Paiute band. The "colony" was surveyed in 1919, but remained impoverished. Tourists in the 1920s created a market for Paiute baskets—but at wildly exploitive prices. Family heirlooms, or new authentic creations which took a year to make, sold for only $5-10. Paiute children were sent away to boarding school, first at Fort Mojave, Arizona, and then to the Stewart Indian School in Carson City, Nevada.

A final episode of rebellion occurred between 1910 and the early 1920s, when the killer Quejo terrorized remote areas of Clark County. The facts are sketchy. It's unclear whether he was a Paiute or Mohave Indian, and legends conflict as to whether he began his career as a bounty hunter, or by killing another Indian in an intra-tribal row. At least seven murders were attributed to him, including the shooting of a miner's wife near Eldorado Canyon. Quejo was never caught. His weapons and bones were discovered in a cave near Eldorado in 1940.

Improvements were planned for the Las Vegas Indian Colony in the early 1930s, but never implemented. By the late 1940s, the colony had been completely enclosed by the growing city. In the late 1950s, local officials tried to sell the land out from under the Indians, but Helen Stewart's foresight—giving title to the Paiute—prevented it. The colony finally received water and sewer services in 1962.

In 1968, an $8-million settlement was awarded the Southern Paiute from the Indians Claims Commission to compensate for lands taken. In 1975, legal access to their colony, surrounded by privately owned land, was finally granted.

(above) The only tree endemic to the Mojave is the Joshua. All palms have been either planted or imported.

(opposite) From here to eternity.

UNNATURAL HISTORY
BOOM TOWN, DOOM TOWN, ZOOM TOWN

RARELY HAVE UNLIKELIER CIRCUMSTANCES ENSURED the growth and greatness of a city. From its spontaneous generation as a railroad boomtown, its struggle for survival in a remote and parched land, and its salvation by Hoover Dam, World War II, and legalized casino gambling, Las Vegas seemed always possessed of some evolving equation for success. And rarely has an unlikelier cast of characters shared such an unflappable faith. From Helen Stewart's patient anticipation of the railroad to Charles "Pop" Squires's tireless campaigning for the dam, from Bugsy Siegel's grand vision of the glamour of vice to Howard Hughes's master plan for the ultimate Southwestern megalopolis, countless believers have invested their imaginations, fortunes, even lives to secure Las Vegas's place on the map. And today, the sum total of all the events, people, and destiny has made Las Vegas the undisputed gambling, entertainment, convention, neon, and cash capital of the known universe.

■ HELEN STEWART

The first important "boom" in Las Vegas Valley was the shooting of Archibald Stewart. At age 18, Stewart rushed from Scotland to the California gold fields, and by the time he turned 30, he owned a sizable freighting company. The taciturn and miserly Stewart relocated to Pioche, Nevada, 156 miles (250 km) north of Las Vegas, during its fleeting heyday as a silver-mining center. There, Stewart's ore hauling expanded into lumber milling which eventually financed cattle ranching. Even after *borrasca* (terminal decline of the mines) in 1874, Stewart remained prosperous enough, at 45, to own a house in Pioche and a large ranch just north of town. A few years later, O.D. Gass, perennially out of cash, used his 800-acre (324-hectare) Las Vegas Ranch and 400 head of cattle to secure a $5,000 loan from Stewart. It's an insight into Stewart's character, and Gass's desperation, that they agreed on a 30-percent interest rate, due in one year. When the year was up, Gass couldn't pay, and they rescheduled the loan for another nine months. When the grace period expired, Gass again couldn't pay, and Stewart foreclosed. The 800 acres and 400 cattle became his.

The only other ranch in the Big Springs area, just two miles (three km) north, was owned by Conrad Kiel, a close friend of Gass. Thus, when Stewart took possession of the Gass ranch and moved next door, the blood already ran bad between Kiel and him. In July 1884, Stewart and a ranch hand named Schuyler Henry got into a fight. Carrie Miller Townley, in the *Nevada Historical Society Quarterly* (Winter 1973), says that Schuyler Henry "badgered" Mrs. Helen Stewart and "spread rumors about her conduct during her husband's absences." Nothing more sensational has been hitherto conjectured concerning this incident. But, given the Las Vegas tradition, literary and otherwise, of extravagance, one might conjure the following scenario. Stewart, 48, had admonished Henry, 33, about the manner in which the latter looked at the former's wife Helen, 29. Yet despite Stewart's warnings, one hot evening while Stewart was away on business, the frustrated ranch hand propositioned Helen, who might or might not have held him off with a gun. Whichever, Henry bragged that his advances had been encouraged and accepted, and then left. When Helen told Stewart, he went after Henry to defend his wife's honor. Since Stewart emerged on the dead side, divine justice might absolve Henry of idle bragging. Human justice certainly did: the grand jury ruled that Henry acted in self-defense.

Helen Stewart (left) sharing the fine points of her Paiute basket collections with a friend.

(above) Neon might be neon without Las Vegas, but Las Vegas could never be Las Vegas without neon.
(opposite) Vegas Vic flicks his Bic.

SIGN LANGUAGE

In 1898, British chemist Sir William Ramsey took some air, liquefied it, boiled it, and fractionally distilled it into its separate components. In the process, he discovered monoatomic, or inert, gases: helium, argon, krypton, xenon. And neon. Of all the gases, neon best permitted the ready passage of an electric current. In 1910, a French inventor, Georges Claude, attached an electrode to a glass tube full of neon gas—*et voila!* A jewel-like, bright-red shimmering glow materialized. And an exciting new form of illumination had been invented.

Neon (and the different colors its neighbor gases produced) immediately captivated Parisian sign-makers. In 1923, a visiting automobile dealer from Los Angeles ordered a custom neon sign that spelled out "Packard" in bright blue letters with orange edging. Installed on Wilshire Boulevard, it caused a nationwide sensation. Six years later, a forward-looking lighting businessman from Ogden, Utah, Thomas Young, emplaced a neon sign in the Fremont Street window of the Oasis Club, thus establishing the inseparability of neon, Las Vegas, *and* the Young Electric Sign Company.

The 1940s and 1950s became the Golden Age of Neon in America. Thanks to its decorative and advertising values, neon invaded Las Vegas with a vengeance. Its artistic value benefited enormously by the famous local tradition of one-upmanship, inspired by the fierce competition between the major hotel-casinos. The old Boulder Club downtown featured YESCO's first major neon creation in Las Vegas: a free-standing 40-foot (12-meter) sign with vertical letters, topping a bright marquee. Almost immediately, the Frontier Club and Sal Sagev Hotel followed suit. The Pioneer Club then introduced the elaborate Vegas Vic, which has become the city's most enduring image. But the Golden Nugget took the early prize with a 100-foot-high (30-meter), blindingly bright sign that remained downtown's centerpiece for nearly 50 years.

When Bugsy Siegel opened his fabulous Flamingo in 1946, he abandoned the frontier motif in favor of two 80-foot (24-meter) neon highball glasses fizzing with pink champagne, which framed the non-descript boxes of the lowrise motor inn. This set the standard for the Las Vegas Strip, and helped introduce a new commercial vernacular along suburban "strips" across the country. The western-style false-front architecture of Fremont Street yielded to the modern false fronts of the desert highway: high, wide, and bright signs all delineating dark, recessed, and one-story buildings. Remove the signs and the hotels would disappear. The quintessential example was embodied by the Stardust, which opened in 1958. The huge colorless casino building supported the largest sign, at the time, in the world: more than 200 feet long (60 me-

(opposite) Signs of another time at YESCO's graveyard.

ters) and nearly 30 feet high (9 meters), with a gleaming Earth turning in a welter of planets, comets, and flaring meteors.

Since then, competition along the Strip has been as intense as the neon itself, promulgated by a number of commercial artists, set designers, and animators attracted by Las Vegas's liberal sign policies. The Dunes installed the tallest sign in the world, 180 feet high (55 meters), in 1962, only to be topped by the Frontier's sign in 1966, at 184 feet (56 meters). The present-day Stardust sign was built in 1967 at 188 feet (57 meters)—and 26,000 bulbs and 30 miles (48 km) of wiring! The Sahara claims today's tallest freestanding sign at 220 feet (67 meters), though Vegas World takes first prize for the world's tallest sign at 227 feet (69 meters).

Neon does not burn out. Undisturbed, a sign can last 30 years or more. Wind and rain, birds, short circuits, and vandalism, however, keep large sign-company spotter

and repair crews busy year round. But neon's popularity around the rest of the country has diminished since the 1960s. In Las Vegas, the new electronic billboards, or message marquees, have supplanted static neon with increased brightness, versatility, and animated effects; Caesars's 32,000-bulb readerboard was installed in 1984 for a cool million. Also in the mid-1980s, the famous Golden Nugget sign downtown was replaced by an elegant marble and brass facade. The designers of the new Mirage and Excalibur hotels consider neon the "old Las Vegas." And avant-garde artists, who've recently rediscovered the gas, seem to be trying to separate the art form from the gaudy glow of Las Vegas.

Nevertheless, Glitter Gulch and the Strip remain the undisputed brightest city blocks in the world, with a total of 15,000 miles (24,140 km) of tubing. Maybe neon could be neon without Las Vegas, but Las Vegas could never be Las Vegas without neon.

Helen Stewart, 10 years married with four kids, and three months pregnant with the fifth, buried her husband and ran the ranch. She took time off only to give birth to a son, Archibald. Her parents moved to Las Vegas, and she hired a Scot, James Megariggle, to tutor her brood. Helen and her father speculated in real estate along the imagined right-of-way of the rumored Salt Lake-Los Angeles railroad. She established a comfortable campground for travelers and miners, with water, good grub, and shade. She befriended the Paiutes and had a collection of their finest baskets. Finally, in 1902, at 47, she'd amassed 1,800 acres (728 hectares) to sell to William Clark's San Pedro, Los Angeles and Salt Lake Railroad for $55,000. Helen Stewart then married her longtime foreman, Frank Stewart (no relation to Archibald), and reigned as the first lady of Las Vegas till her death in 1926. That she married a second Stewart, 20 years after the death of the first, retained water rights to her family cemetery, deeded 10 acres of land to the few remaining Las Vegas Paiute, and was buried next to her original husband could confirm that she did indeed hold that gun on Schuyler Henry.

■ THE COMPANY TOWN

It took 35 years (starting in 1870) and a total of six different railroad companies to complete the track that connected Salt Lake City to Los Angeles, built along the old Mormon Trail. Toward the end, two determined companies competed for the single right-of-way. Scattered violence and expensive legal maneuvering finally shut down construction and propelled the parties to the bargaining table. Two years later, William Clark's San Pedro, Los Angeles and Salt Lake Railroad merged with E.H. Harriman's Oregon Short Line, and construction began anew.

During this time, Helen Stewart hired J.T. McWilliams to survey her property for sale to the railroad. McWilliams discovered and immediately claimed 80 untitled acres (32 hectares) just west of the big ranch. He platted a town site and began selling lots to a steadfast group of true Las Vegas "sooners." Thanks to its strategic location and plentiful water, Las Vegas had already been designated as a division point for crew changes, a service stop for through trains, and an eventual site for

Map of the San Pedro, Los Angeles and Salt Lake Railroad's town site, oriented to the tracks. Each of the 40 blocks was 300 by 400 feet, with 32 lots for sale.

repair shops. A year later, in fall 1904, tracks converged on Las Vegas Valley from the southwest and northeast. In January 1905, the golden spike was driven into a tie near Jean, Nevada, 23 miles south of town—in a brief, formal, one-cheer ceremony arranged by, and reflective of, the Company.

LAS VEGAS GLOSSARY

action—sum total of all wagers made

bankroll—amount of money an individual or a casino has to gamble with

basic strategy—computer-generated strategy for blackjack based on the best odds for player's hand against dealer's up card

book—among many meanings, the room where sports and race gambling take place

boxcars—rolling a 12 in craps

boxman—craps dealer who supervises the game

cage—main casino cashier

card counting—the ability to track cards already played at blackjack and to base play on the variable odds of the remaining deck or decks

carpet joint—casino catering to high rollers

checks—casino chips

comp—freebie; free rooms, meals, drinks, shows, escorts; also see *RFB*

compulsive gambler—a gambler who will gamble on anything and everything, anywhere, any time, has no control over the urge to gamble, and will not stop until all the money, credit, assets, and hope are gone

crossroader—casino cheat

degenerate gambler—a gambler who will play until his or her bankroll is gone—but can stop then

drop—total cash traded for chips at the gaming tables

"Easy Money"—Billy Joel song from the album *Innocent Man*, which could be Las Vegas's theme song

folding money—greenbacks

george—a gambler who tokes or places bets for the dealer

grind—low roller

grind joint—casino that caters to low rollers; also known as *sawdust joint*

hard count—counting the change from slot machines

high roller—any gambler able and willing to spend $5,000 or more in a weekend at Las Vegas; there are an estimated 35,000 bona fide high rollers (almost all of them men) in the world

(previous pages) The new Mirage, as seen from an upper balcony in the Sand's "periscope."

By the time the first train had traveled the length of the track, McWilliams's Las Vegas town site, better known as Ragtown, boasted 1,500 residents, brickyards, weekly newspapers, a bank, an ice plant, tent hotel, and mercantiles. Miners and freighters came from and went to the new booms north: Bullfrog, Rhyolite, Gold-

---

hold—house profit from all the wagers; what the casino wins

house advantage—mathematical winning edge that the casino gives itself by manipulating the rules of the games to ensure profitability; also known as the *percentage, P.C., vigorish, vig*

juice—power; influence; knowing the right people

junket—group of high rollers, usually flown in on a plane chartered by the casino, and accorded full RFB

ladderman—baccarat supervisor

Las Vegas total—typical Las Vegas experience of room, food, gambling, show, and commercial sex

low roller—typical tourist making $1 and $2 bets; also known as *grinds, suckers, tinhorns*

Marryin' Sam—wedding-chapel minister

percentage (or *P.C.*)—house advantage, measured in percentage points

pit—casino employee area behind the table games

plunger—gambler who chases his losses; also known as *screamer* or *pigeon*

points—percentage of ownership in a casino

The Pencil—having the juice to write comps

rfb—means room, food, and beverage: a full comp

Runnin' Rebels—University of Nevada-Las Vegas basketball team, which won the NCAA championship in 1990, and has been in trouble with authorities for the allegedly questionable recruiting practices of head coach Jerry Tarkanian

sawdust joint—casino catering to grinds

shnorrer—Yiddish for compulsive borrower

soft count—counting the folding money

stickman—craps dealer who handles the dice

stiff—winning gambler who doesn't toke the dealer

toke—gratuity; tip

turkey—gambler who's unpleasant to the dealer

vigorish (or *vig*)—house advantage; comes from the five-percent commission on all wagers charged by the original bank-craps operators, which brought in money with "vigor." Gamblers added a syllable of jargon to get vigorish.

field, Tonopah. In April 1905, with the start of regular through service, the San Pedro, Los Angeles, and Salt Lake Railroad organized the subsidiary Las Vegas Land and Water Company, platted its own town site, bulldozed all the desert scrub from the 40-block area, and scheduled the auctioning of lots for May 15. Each block was a regulation 300 by 400 feet (91 by 122 meters), consisted of 32 lots, each 25 by 140 feet (8 by 43 meters), fronted by an 80-foot-wide (24 meters) street and split by a 20-foot-wide (6 meters) alley. Block 20 was reserved for public purposes; liquor sales were assigned to blocks 16 and 17. The railroad advertised heavily in newspapers on both coasts, and transported speculators and investors to Las Vegas from Los Angeles ($16) and Salt Lake City ($20)—fares deducted from the deposit on a lot.

The auction was conducted at the north corner of Fremont and Main, site of today's Union Plaza Hotel. In the heat of the moment, choice corner lots listed at $150 to $750 sold for up to $1,750; well-located inside lots ($150 to $500) sold for up to $800. The literal heat (115°F, 46°C) became so oppressive that the auction concluded at 3 P.M., after 175 lots had earned the railroad $80,000, roughly $450 apiece. Ragtown locals grumbled about the railroad tactics of encouraging out-of-town speculators to bid up the prices. Stan Paher quotes an observer who commented, "The auction was a nice clever scheme—the simplest way of giving everybody a fair shake (down)." In response to complaints, the following day's auction was canceled and the remaining lots were sold for fixed prices within the listed range. In all, more than 700 lots were purchased, netting the company $265,000, an almost 500-percent profit over what they paid Helen Stewart for the whole property. And Las Vegas was on the map—one of the last railroad boomtowns on one of the last major lines across the United States.

This boom resonated for a mere month and a half. Initial euphoria gave way to the dismal demands of domesticating a desert. Service policies of the railroad management as implemented by Walter Bracken, the imperious manager of the Las Vegas Land and Water Company, were conservative and bureaucratic. Flash floods tore up track and interrupted service. And the usual fires, conflicts, and growing pains of a new company town dampened local optimism. Even so, frame houses replaced tent shelters, and the new Las Vegas boasted hotels, saloons, restaurants, warehouses, mercantiles, a school, and a two-story bank. Las Vegas Land and Water lived up to its pledge to grade and oil city streets, construct curbs, and lay water mains, pipes, and hydrants—but only within the boundaries of the railroad's own town site. Although a dozen 8-foot-deep (2.5-meter) wells had been drilled around McWilliams's "old town," west of the tracks, lack of access to company water sealed its fate: most of it burned to the ground in September 1905. It was then that after-hours revelry was transplanted to Block 16.

Bounded by First, Second, Ogden, and Stewart streets, this infamous block served as Wild West Central, surrounded by the buttoned-down company town. The Double O, Red Onion, Arcade and others served ten-cent shots, featured faro, roulette, and poker, and sported cribs out back for commercial copulators. Bibulous burros begged for beer from bearded bartenders, while bow-tied ivory ticklers pounded out ragtime tunes on honky-tonk uprights. The Arizona Club became the "Queen of Block 16," with its expensive glass front and $20,000 mahogany bar; a few years later a second story was added for the convenience of its ladies of the night and their gentlemen.

Distribution of water to the town site turned out to be secondary to railroad operations, and requests for water outside the railroad's half-sold town were consistently refused. Similarly, other railroad policies, handed down from Los Angeles and Salt Lake City, discouraged land speculation and subdivision of the surrounding desert. Still, Las Vegas slowly expanded in area and population for the next five years. Charles "Pop" Squires, publisher of the *Las Vegas Age* and indefatigable town booster, together with Walter Bracken, founded the Vegas Artesian Water Syndicate, which "mined" water around the valley. The first deep well was drilled in July 1907 to a depth of 301 feet (92 meters); by 1911, 100 artesian wells had been tapped. William Clark's new Las Vegas and Tonopah Railroad reached the boomtown of Beatty in late 1906, furthering Las Vegas's ambitions as a crossroads. To further its ambitions as an administrative seat, in 1909, supporters of slicing a new county off vast Lincoln County emerged victorious from a hotly contested election, and immediately pushed a bill through the state assembly. Clark County, named after the railroad magnate, became official in July 1909. When Las Vegas incorporated two years later, the town counted a population of 1,500 residents.

■ SLOW BUT STEADY

When completed in 1911, the locomotive repair shops created 175 new jobs, which stimulated additional residential subdivisions outside the original town site. The population doubled to 3,000 between 1911 and 1913, two years marked by growing prosperity and progress. A milestone was reached in 1915, when round-the-clock electricity was finally supplied to residents.

But the 10-year crescendo of the first boom had climaxed, and Las Vegas went into a slow but steady slide over the following decade. In 1917, the Las Vegas and Tonopah Railroad suspended operations; hundreds of workers were laid off and left. By 1920, the population had dropped to 2,300. An elderly William Clark sold his interest in the renamed Salt Lake and Los Angeles Railroad to Union Pacific in 1921. If the old management in Los Angeles had run Las Vegas like a company store, the new management in New York City barely knew Las Vegas existed. Its employees, immediately dissatisfied, joined a nationwide strike of 400,000 railroad workers in 1922. Locally, some violence erupted between strikers and scabs. When the strike was settled, Union Pacific punitively closed the Las Vegas repair shops, eliminating hundreds more jobs and residents.

In the early 1920s, though many urban improvements had been accomplished in the town's first 15 years, Las Vegas remained at its lowest and remotest. Long-distance telephone service was still nonexistent. Telegraph messages had to be sent along the railroad's private wires, and three-day delays for public use were not uncommon. To travel to the state's capital at Carson City or its urban center at Reno, one had to ride the train via Los Angeles and San Francisco, or Salt Lake City. A primitive auto road followed the old Las Vegas and Tonopah rail bed, but it was better suited for a desert safari than a joyride. Decisions and instructions from corporate headquarters concerning urgent situations faced by Las Vegas Land and Water, such as large leaks in water mains, often took two weeks to be made and dispatched.

But the key to Las Vegas's resurrection lay just 25 miles away in the Colorado River. By 1924, the Bureau of Reclamation had narrowed locations for a dam on the Colorado to Black and Boulder canyons, east of Las Vegas. Anticipation alone began to fuel noticeable growth. During the latter half of the 1920s, laws were passed, interstate details negotiated, and money allocated for "Boulder" Dam— named for the Boulder Canyon Project Act, even though the site chosen turned out to be Black Canyon. (The dam was eventually named to honor Herbert Hoover, Secretary of Commerce at the time.) By the end of the decade, Las Vegas had long-distance phone service, a federal highway from Salt Lake City to Los Angeles, regularly scheduled airmail and air-passenger services, over 5,000 residents, and one of the world's most colossal engineering projects about to begin just over the next rise.

■ THE BEST TOWN BY A DAM SITE

In October 1929, Hercules broke out of his chains and proceeded forthwith to force the New York Stock Exchange and the American economy to their knees. That accomplished, he boarded the Union Pacific Railroad, full fare, and rode to southern Nevada, to plug the Colorado River. As the nation's banks went down like dominoes, and the dam went up like building blocks, lawmakers in Carson City passed a typically Nevada version—front-running, nonconformist, and permissive—of the New Deal. Wide-open gambling was finally legalized in 1931, and the divorce residency requirement was reduced to a scandalous six weeks. Combined with unimpeded bootlegging, quasi-legal prostitution, prize fights, and no-wait marriages, Nevada become the only state in the union to spurn the moral backlash that followed the Roaring Twenties. Vice-starved visitors and hopeful dam workers flooded southern Nevada, thereby converting Las Vegas from a dusty railroad stopover into, in historian Florence Lee Cahlan's words, "a bright spot on the gloomy horizon of the Great Depression"—first step on the yellow-brick road to becoming the ultimate Oz.

The dam, when completed, was 60 stories tall, 600 feet (183 meters) thick at the base, and nearly a quarter mile long at the crest—the sum total of over three million cubic yards of concrete. At its peak, the dam employed 5,000 workers, with a monthly payroll of half a million dollars. Over 50 miles of new railroad track connected Las Vegas to the dam site and to Boulder City, the government's model employee town, and the dam site; Las Vegas's railhead warehouses and freight yards were expanded to handle the innumerable tons of building supplies transferred from the mainline. Almost overnight, Las Vegas's permanent population increased by 50 percent, to 7,500, with transients and visitors further swelling the ranks. The local infrastructure—power, phone, sewer, school, medical, fire, and police—underwent urgently needed improvement. Hotel and housing construction boomed. Business prospered. Congress appropriated millions of New Deal dollars for a new post office, federal building, and general relief. Urbanization accelerated.

"Dateline Las Vegas" became a staple of newsreel and newsprint, and tens of thousands of tourists arrived to enjoy the spectacle of dam construction and the Wild West excitement of the unique boomtown nearby. Grind joints, clubs, and hotels experienced the stress of success under the sheer volume of visitors. Down-

(top) Looking up at the Las Vegas Hilton; (bottom) Looking down at Hoover Dam

(top) The Big Six migrated from the carnival to the casino after Nevada legalized gambling in 1931. (bottom) World's largest gold nugget on display at the Golden Nugget.

town, the venerable Northern Club, the neon-lit Silver Club, and the low-roller Tango Club received the earliest gambling licenses—all within the red-lined confines of Fremont Street between First and Third. To escape the restrictive policies of the conservative officials of incorporated Las Vegas, Tony Cornero, a gambler from Southern California, opened the posh $31,000 Meadows Club just beyond city limits on the road to Boulder City. Las Vegas's first "luxury" hotel, the Apache, opened downtown. Five thousand Shriners from southern California inaugurated Las Vegas, in 1935, as a convention town.

Also from Southern California, on the heels of Tony Cornero, arrived Las Vegas's first wave of outside illegal gambling operators. Fletcher Brown, a crusading L.A. mayor elected in 1938, immediately began to enforce the city's previously ignored vice laws and close its brothels and casinos. (It has also been suggested that Benjamin "Bugsy" Siegel, dispatched in the late 1930s by East Coast Syndicate bosses to "organize" the California underworld, provided additional incentive for the freelance gamblers to flee Los Angeles.) Guy McAfee, commander of the L.A.

EXACTLY AS IT REMAINS TODAY

Las Vegas is seat of Clark County and distributing center for a very large but thinly populated mining and ranching country. It is also developing into one of the chief travel and recreation centers of the Southwest. In part this new role is a matter of accident, the result of a key position in an area with widely varying natural attractions plus the man-made wonder, Boulder Dam. A sound and far-sighted public policy, however, has taken advantage of national interest in the dam to make the city and the area around it attractive enough to bring visitors back repeatedly. Public buildings and houses are under construction all over town. The rows of catalpas and poplars planted during the early days are being protected and lengthened. Relatively little emphasis is placed on the gambling clubs and divorce facilities—though they are attractions to many visitors—and much effort is being made to build up cultural attractions. No cheap and easily parodied slogans have been adopted to publicize the city, no attempt has been made to introduce pseudo-romantic architectural themes, or to give artificial glamour and gaiety. Las Vegas is itself—natural and therefore very appealing to people with a wide variety of interests.

—*Nevada—A Guide to the Silver State,* 1940

vice squad *and* operator of gambling parlors, quickly moved to Las Vegas and purchased the Pair-o-Dice Club, three miles (five km) south of city limits on the Los Angeles Highway. Sam Boyd, a bingo mogul in L.A. and Honolulu, started with a roulette concession at the Eldorado Club. Tudor Scherer and partners opened the Pioneer Club. With their experience and expertise, these L.A. operators immediately gained respectability within the budding legal casino business, and helped improve not only its management, but its image as well.

An expected exodus of dam builders lightened Las Vegas's load in the late 1930s. Controversy continued between the Las Vegas Land and Water Company, still reluctant to service the growing city with new mains, sewers, and adequate water pressure, and the residents, whose optimism prompted them to waste enormous quantities of the precious commodity. Emergency ordinances banning water overuse, limiting lawn-sprinkling hours, and requiring recirculating pumps for the new "swamp-cooler" evaporation units were passed. But the continued uncontrolled mining of water, based on an assumption that Las Vegas rested atop an inexhaustible underground lake, finally led to a 10-year crisis that was alleviated, in 1948, only by tapping the water filling up behind Hoover Dam in new Lake Mead.

A second world war on the horizon fueled the renewal of federal spending in southern Nevada. In 1940, with the population at 8,500, city officials teamed up with the Civil Aeronautics Agency and the Army Air Corps to develop the old Western Air Express property into a million-acre (404,700-hectare) training facility for pilots and gunners. Over the next five years, the Las Vegas Aerial Gunnery School trained tens of thousands of military personnel; the facility expanded to three million acres (1,214,100 hectares). In 1942, a monster metal-processing plant, Basic Magnesium, Inc., was constructed halfway between Las Vegas and Boulder City—large enough to eventually process over 100 million tons of magnesium, vital to the war effort for flares, bomb housings, and airplane components. At its peak in 1944, BMI employed 10,000 factory workers, many of whom lived nearby in housing projects at the new town site of Henderson. Thus, all three of the cities in Las Vegas Valley had been laid out by "the company": Las Vegas by the San Pedro, Los Angeles and Salt Lake Railroad in 1905, Boulder City by the Bureau of Reclamation in 1931, and Henderson by the Defense Housing Corporation in 1942.

Now, with Hoover Dam on line, the gunnery school at full bore, and Basic Magnesium booming, the Las Vegas area clearly had the power to accommodate large-scale industrial payrolls, the "juice" to attract massive infusions of federal capital, and the magic to lure hundreds of thousands of vacationers with a year's savings in their pockets.

All it needed was a good hotel.

■ THE FOUNDING OF THE STRIP

Guy McAfee, Los Angeles cop and gambler who owned the Pair-o-Dice Club (named after a small subdivision, Paradise, and later renamed Club 91), drove the few miles between his roadhouse and downtown so often that he began referring to it as "the Strip," after the beloved Sunset Strip in his hometown. Though there's no record of any meeting, it seems likely that McAfee would've had a chat with another Southern Californian, Thomas Hull. A number of other civic leaders certainly did, convincing Hull, who owned a chain of El Rancho motor inns, to build a franchise in Las Vegas. The grand opening for El Rancho Vegas was held on April 3, 1941. The 65-room lowrise motor inn, on the corner of Highway 91 (now the Strip) and San Francisco Avenue (now Sahara), came complete with casino, steakhouse, showroom, shops, swimming pool, palm trees, and lawns. Just beyond the city line, Hull's El Rancho Vegas attracted the traffic coming in from Southern California, as well as locals escaping the claustrophobia of downtown's Glitter Gulch. Business boomed from the beginning, and Hull quickly expanded the hotel to 125 rooms. Management difficulties compelled Hull to sell the hotel, and a fire destroyed it in 1960. The site, across the Strip from the Sahara Hotel, to this day remains a vacant lot. The El Rancho Vegas experience, however, initiated a number of trends, all of which remain in place a full 50 years later: a hurricane of subsequent construction and competition, the desirability of building outside the city limits along Highway 91, and the high turnover of managers and owners.

Eugene Moehring, a resident historian in Las Vegas, has written that the El Rancho, in one bold and brilliant stroke, revolutionized Las Vegas development. By building in an unincorporated area of Clark County, Hull avoided the higher city taxes on property and gambling revenues, as well as the control of powerful

(previous pages) Vegas World—the final frontier.

city casino operators. Less stringent building codes reduced the cost of construction, and the wide-open spaces permitted ease of accessibility and parking for motorists unavailable in congested downtown. In fact, this "motel" triggered the transition from a town organized around and dependent on the railroad to one better served by cars and trucks. Hull's bold move coincided with an overall suburbanization of America in the 1940s, and specifically with Los Angeles's spreading urban sprawl. Indeed, by the grand opening of the El Rancho Vegas in April 1941, Las Vegas was a mere seven hours from Los Angeles by car.

Only a month after the El Rancho opened, two Southern California real estate dealers financed construction of the El Cortez Hotel on Fremont and Sixth Street; it took nine months and nearly $325,000 to complete downtown's first resort hotel. By then, R. E. Griffith, a movie-theater magnate, was already building the Strip's second "casino ranch," the Last Frontier, a mile south of the El Rancho on property purchased from Guy McAfee. Designed by Griffith's architect nephew, William Moore, like its predecessor Strip hotel, the casino, showroom, restaurants, and lounges were contained in the main building, while the 107-room motel stretched behind it. But the Last Frontier inaugurated a tradition of one-upmanship that has not changed over the course of 50 years and half as many major hotels. In *Playtown U.S.A.*, Best and Hillyer described it thus: "Its lobby was a rustic, big-beamed conglomeration of mounted buffalo heads, of huge sandstone fireplaces, of Pony Express lanterns hanging from old wagon wheels. Its sluicing parlor was a replica of an old forty-niner saloon, with Texas cattle horns mounted on panel walls, a mahogany bar with bullet holes in it, and leather bar stools in the shape of saddles. Its casino was plushly pioneerish with a ceiling of pony hide and ornately papered walls hung with paintings of nudes done in gold-rush gaudiness. A dip of the flag for the self-described Early West in Modern Splendor."

Eugene Moehring picks up the theme. "In addition, the hotel provided guests with horseback and stagecoach rides and pack trips. To reinforce the frontier ambience, Moore later added the Last Frontier Village, a small town site filled with 900 tons of Robert "Doby Doc" Caudill's Western artifacts. The collection was extensive, consisting not only of wagons, antique firearms, bar stools, barbers' chairs, and the like, but also big items, including a Chinese joss house, full-size mining trains, and actual jails from Nevada's smaller mining camps." Without a doubt, the Last Frontier was Las Vegas's first major tourist-attraction hotel.

This continuing influx to the Strip of Southern California capital and expertise effected major changes downtown, which felt the competition acutely. Guy McAfee expanded his operations by purchasing the Frontier Club, then acquiring enough property along Fremont between Second and Third to open the Golden Nugget, at that time the largest casino in Las Vegas. This club set a standard for extravagance that obliged the reconditioning of many Fremont Street sawdust joints. Tony Cornero, whose Meadows Club on Boulder Highway had failed 10 years earlier, returned from L.A. to open the Rex Club. Wilbur Clark, a gambler from San Diego, set up shop with the Monte Carlo Club. Benny Binion, a well-known Texas gambler, arrived, invested in the Las Vegas Club, then bought the Western Club. By the end of the war, Fremont Street was already one of the most glittering stretches of downtown in the entire country.

The war years had fueled the growth of Las Vegas to an unprecedented degree. By the time the Last Frontier had settled into a profitable routine, classes of 4,000 aerial gunners were arriving and departing Las Vegas every six weeks. Basic Magnesium was shipping five million pounds of magnesium ingots to airplane and

Downtown Las Vegas was already a glittering gulch in the early 1950s; the Golden Nugget boasted the largest casino and sign.

(opposite) Wilbur Clark and Moe Dalitz opened the Desert Inn in 1950, fifth hotel on the Strip.

ordnance factories in Los Angeles every day. Subdivisions were mushrooming to accommodate an exploding Las Vegas population of 35,000, which doubled between 1940 and 1943. The War Department in 1942 pressured Las Vegas to finally shut down Block 16 (which heralded a shadowy, volatile, and extremely ambivalent era of commercial copulation that continues today). Owners of a hotel chain and a movie-theater chain, real estate investors, Southern California gamblers, and influential long-term locals at that time encompassed the civilian power elite, the early 1940s' Las Vegas Establishment.

■ GANGSTER ANGST

Las Vegas and Benjamin Siegel, better known (though only behind his back) as "Bugsy," were born in the same year, 1905—Las Vegas in southern Nevada and Benny in Brooklyn, New York. In 1923, when Las Vegas was graduating from high school, Siegel had already committed every heinous crime in the book: assault, burglary, bookmaking, bootlegging, extortion, hijacking, murder, mayhem, narcotics, numbers, rape, white slavery. In the early 1930s, Las Vegas was married to a construction worker, with two kids and one on the way. Siegel was also working—for a demolition company, known as Murder Inc. In the late 1930s, big boss Meyer Lansky sent Benny to Los Angeles to consolidate the disparate elements of the California mob, where he quickly eliminated the competition (including Guy McAfee, who beat a hasty retreat to Las Vegas), bankrolled offshore gambling ships (including the *Rex*, run by Tony Cornero), established a smuggling ring for Mexican narcotics, and grabbed control of the bookmakers' national "wire." At the same time he hobnobbed with the nabobs of Hollywood, befriending movie stars such as Cary Grant and Clark Gable, seducing starlets and countesses, and initiating his love affair from hell with Virginia Hill, ultimate "Mistress of the Mob." As Carl Sifakis writes in *Mafia Encyclopedia,* "Just because Siegel was a bit of a psychopath doesn't mean he wasn't a charmer."

In the early 1940s, Lansky ordered Bugsy to muscle in on the Las Vegas racebook wires, and soon he had his grubby paws in several casino counting rooms. But with his new Hollywood sensibilities, he envisioned a resort hotel straight out of Xanadu (or maybe Miami)—the highest-class casino for the highest-class clientele. Over the next several years, Siegel managed to raise a million dollars for his

POOL WARS

Gaming industrialists generally did not rival one another in the practical matters, but in areas in which they did compete, encompassing the more superficial aspects of the vacation experience, resort hotels went to extremes to differentiate themselves...When Wilbur Clark opened the Desert Inn in 1950 with a fancy pool, the Last Frontier across the highway promptly filled in its old pool and built a heated one of AAU dimensions with a subsurface observation room at the deep end and a deck-side bar. Whereupon the Desert Inn tore up its brand new pool and dug a bigger one. Then the Sands created a thing of free-flow design large enough to float a cruiser. A few years later the Tropicana made its bid in the rivalry by equipping its shell-like, semicircular pool with canned music that could be heard underwater. Pool wars had supplanted price wars among Las Vegas competitors.

—John M. Findlay,
People of Chance—Gambling in American Society from Jamestown to Las Vegas

Flamingo Hotel (Flamingo was his nickname for redhead Virginia Hill, after the "lucky" birds that lived at a pond inside the Hialeah Racetrack in Florida, in which he had a part interest). Construction began in 1946.

Bugsy hired the Del Webb Company of Phoenix to put up the Flamingo. But building materials were scarce after the war, and Siegel's extravagance was limitless, matched only by his greed; he dispatched Virginia Hill to Switzerland on occasion to deposit cash skimmed from construction costs. Overruns, fronted by his old pal Lansky, finally reached a healthy (or unhealthy, as it turned out) five million bucks, and the project began to exact a heavy toll on Siegel's already questionable nerves, not to mention his silent partners' notorious impatience. At a meeting of the bosses in Havana on Christmas Day 1946, a vote was taken. If the Flamingo was a success, Siegel would be reprieved, and given a chance to pay back the huge loan. If it failed . . . *muerta*.

The hotel opened the next day. Movie stars attended, headliners performed, but the half-finished hotel, miles out of town, on a rainy and cold day after Christmas, flopped. Worse, the casino suffered heavy losses, which the bosses suspected to be further skim. In a prophetic and now-famous statement, Bugsy reassured a nervous Del Webb, "We only kill each other." In early January 1947, the Flamingo closed. It reopened in March, and started showing a profit in May, but Siegel's fate

Palms and flamingos entered the Nevada neon scene by way of Los Angeles and Miami.

had been sealed. In Virginia Hill's Beverly Hills mansion in June, Benny Siegel was hit. Before his body was cold, Phoenix boss gambler Gus Greenbaum had already taken over the Flamingo.

So began 20 years of the Italian-Jewish crime-syndicate's presence in Las Vegas. And 10 years of the biggest hotel-building boom that the country had ever seen. It also triggered an increasing uneasiness among state officials who quickly moved to assume further regulatory responsibilities from the counties, which had overseen the casinos since gambling was legalized in 1931. Back in 1945, the Nevada Tax Commission had been authorized to collect one percent of gross gambling revenues over $3,000, and to have a hand in approving licenses for operators. After two years of tax collecting, with a better idea of revenues, the state increased the tax to two percent. And in 1949, with Las Vegas gaining a reputation as a haven for the underworld and its money, Tax Commission agents were deputized, and given broad powers of investigating license applicants.

Meanwhile, the threat of mob muscle from one side and state heat from another began closing in on established casino operators. In addition, the number of tourists was reaching toward a million. These factors compelled owners to begin cooperating by adopting industry-wide standards. One immediate result was the end of a ferocious price war which had been waged by downtown clubs for several years. By regularizing the gaming rules, club owners stabilized the house percentages; this "price-fixing," according to John Findlay in *People of Chance,* "was a crucial step ensuring uniformity of gambling that Las Vegas was destined to mass produce for the United States."

■ TWO BOMBS DROP ON SOUTHERN NEVADA

Then a new type of heat was felt in Las Vegas.

The feds.

In November 1950, the Committee to Investigate Organized Crime, led by Tennessee Senator Estes Kefauver, came to town. Questioned were Wilbur Clark and Moe Dalitz of the Desert Inn, Bugsy's advance man Moe Sedway, Nevada Tax Commissioner William Moore (of the Last Frontier), Lieutenant Governor Clifford Jones, and others. In two days of hearings, many new Las Vegas trends were clarified: there *was* indeed a connection between the casino industry and the national crime syndicate; gangsters from California, New York, Cleveland, and Chicago *were* running the big hotels and gambling dens, having been licensed by the county and state officials, who overlooked their convictions for gambling offenses in other states; millions in mob money were already invested, and millions more were redistributed as profit; and the out-of-state operators were quickly gaining a measure of respectability as bona fide Nevada businessmen.

The Kefauver Commission revealed beyond any shadow of a doubt that Las Vegas had completed its transition from a railroad company town to a gambling company town. The biggest gamblers were in charge. On the twentieth anniversary of legalized gambling in 1951, the state, the feds—everyone—publicly woke up to the questionable histories of the people waist deep in counting-room gambling revenues. After Kefauver departed for Los Angeles, the spotlight turned to the Tax Commission, the state's licensing board. Best and Hillyer write that, "The tax commissioners were businessmen of unassailable reputation chosen from the fields of real estate, mining, ranching, and other unsullied-by-gambling endeavors —in other words, the least likely to know about muscle men. Their traffic with underworld characters had been, up to the Bugsy Siegel affair, negligible, and newspapermen who attended license-application meetings after that reported that often commission members would ask such unsophisticated questions as 'Who is this Frank Costello?' and 'What does the witness mean when he refers to snake eyes?' These ingenuous gentlemen were suddenly called upon to control an almost uncontrollable situation."

The Kefauver hearings triggered two additional, unexpected, though typical events. First, it created a media hysteria which flooded the rackets divisions of police departments around the country with funds and guns to wipe out the illegal gambling operations within their jurisdictions. This, of course, engendered a large migration to Las Vegas of expert casino owners, managers, and workers, all sticking a thumb into the perfectly legal, largely profitable, and barely policed pie. It was the Comstock's second coming, the Wild West reenacted—and not just for tourists. Black money from the top dons of the Syndicate and their fronts and pawns poured in from the underworld power centers of New York, Chicago, and Havana. Illegal casino operators, with their bankrolls, dealers, enforcers, and tricks, made a beeline for the promised land from the big-time games of Boston, Miami, New Orleans, St. Louis, Cleveland, Dallas, Phoenix, and Los Angeles.

Hustlers, scam artists, small-time hoods, prostitutes, thieves, degenerate and compulsive gamblers, boomtowners, tradesmen, and tourists flooded the place. But a strange reversal occurred at the state line: the crooks became businessmen and the tourists turned into bad boys and girls. The more money one had, the less money one had to use. Juice, sex, comps—all "free." Money assumed paramount importance, yet most people lost all sense of value. Every winner was eventually a loser. All to feed the great god Greed, His Eternal in Perpetual Need.

But who could resist? Certainly not the legions of gamblers, dreamers of jackpots, the millions hoping beyond hope to be struck by the lightning bolt of sudden and eternal fortune. Besides, this was true glamour: drinking and shooting craps with mobsters, movie stars, and millionaires. The publicity was priceless, even if it was of an infamous sort. The Chamber of Commerce, of course, did its bit to focus on the "good" aspects of the town, with their "Howdy Pardner," "Fun in the Sun," and "Come As You Are" ad campaigns. And the Desert Sea (later Las Vegas) News Bureau was established to keep the national media supplied with uncritical and non-sensational local PR.

The second bomb to hit Las Vegas was, in fact, The Bomb. Two months after Kefauver blew through town, the Atomic Energy Commission conducted its first above-ground nuclear test explosion in the vast uninhabited reaches of the old gunnery range, which now encompassed the Nellis Air Force Base and the Nuclear Test Site. For the next 10 years, nearly a bomb a month was detonated into the atmosphere 70 miles (112 km) northwest of Las Vegas. For most blasts, the AEC erected realistic "Doom Town" sets to measure destruction, and thousands of soldiers were posted within a tight radius to be purposefully exposed to the tests. Hundreds of news and camera men who covered the tests began to be referred to as "Men of Extinction." Moe Dalitz and Wilbur Clark planned the opening of the Desert Inn to coincide with a detonation; the former garnered more coverage than the latter. Locals worried which way the wind blew, and seemed to contract a strange "atom fever"—marketing everything from atomburgers to cheesecake frames of a mushroom-cloud bathing-suit-clad Miss Atomic Blast. But mostly, Las Vegans reveled in the AEC and military payrolls, massive attention from the media, notoriety approaching cosmic dimensions, and the neon-thermonuclear aspects of the whole extravaganza.

■ "I Just Met a Man Who Isn't Building a Hotel"—Joe E. Lewis

In 1948, the Thunderbird Hotel was built, and in 1950 the Desert Inn. Two years later, the Sahara and the Sands opened. Then the Showboat, afloat out on Boulder Highway. Within three years, the Riviera, Dunes, Royal Nevada, Moulin Rouge, New Frontier, Hacienda, Fremont, and Mint held grand openings. By 1958, the $7-million Stardust and $10-million Tropicana had joined the ranks. Since conventional sources were stingy with the capital necessary to build casinos and resorts, mobsters from all over the country financed construction, and installed their own front men, managers, and workers. Lansky and his New York gang controlled the Flamingo and had an interest in the Thunderbird, Sands, and others. Cleveland's Moe Dalitz controlled the Desert Inn, with Wilbur Clark out front. Chicago's Sam Giancanna, Tony Accardo, and the Fischetti brothers were connected to the Riviera and Stardust casinos. New England's Raymond Patriarcha was suspected of being behind the Dunes. When don Frank Costello was shot in an attempted assassination in New York, a slip of paper found by detectives in his pocket contained the exact number of the Tropicana's first-month profits; the connection was quickly traced to Phil Kastel, of the New Orleans syndicate. Clearly, Las Vegas had been declared "open territory" by the Mafia, meaning that any family with the inclination could operate there, without fear of territorial reprisals. If it hadn't, Carl Safakis writes, "Las Vegas would doubtlessly look today like Dresden after World War II."

Instead, Highway 91 was becoming the ultimate Fifties American suburban strip. From the service stations, diners, bars, restaurants, casinos, motels, and highrises to the row-house subdivisions housing literal nuclear families, from the hardest-bitten 20-year scammer on the road to respectability to the most tender-footed cocktail waitress on the road to moral compromise, Las Vegas shared in the innocence and optimism (if not the Victorian morals) of 1950s' America.

However, all was not, in Oz, what the publicists claimed. By 1955 the town was spectacularly overbuilt, and an epidemic of hotel-casino failures, mergers, buy-outs, buy-backs, shuffling owners, and musical-chair managers kept the two state investigators for the Tax Commission fairly busy. That year the state finally created the Gaming Control Board, separate from the Tax Commission, specifically for licensing and policing duties. In one of its first actions, the new board suspended the gambling license of the Thunderbird Hotel, after discovering that Jake Lansky, Meyer's brother, held a hidden interest. But by 1959, when the legislature tightened its grip on the gambling industry with the formation of the policy-making State Gaming Commission, the 10 major Strip hotels were veritable fiscal monoliths. Hundreds of constantly changing names and faces held points in the operations. In addition, the regulators faced a mosaic of corporations: some owned the casinos and others ran the casinos, some owned and others operated the hotels, some held the real estate and others held the holding companies. Furthermore, the state found itself walking a tightrope between hindering casino operations and helping them, since gambling taxes provided a major share of its own revenues. Even so, gone were the freewheeling days of the $5-million hotel; it now took 15 million sanitized dollars to open a viable resort.

Still, after a smooth 15-year run and high profits, some not taxed, the big bosses were entrenched. The local heat conscientiously protected the action and got its cut. The state heat was lukewarm, safeguarding its own cut and holding its own against only the most notorious "undesirables." The federal heat was just begin-

Vegas Vic waiting for Vegas Vickie on Fremont Street in the mid-1950s.

ning to refuel in Washington, D.C., as the new Attorney General, Robert F. Kennedy, planned to pick up where Estes Kefauver left off. But the most heat came from the media. Crime reporters, investigative journalists, magazine staff writers, scholarly essayists, and pulp novelists all descended on this Wild West set of a tough town that refused, as late as the 1960s, to be tamed. Their collective characterization of Las Vegas has come to be called the Diatribe. Books such as *The Great Las Vegas Fraud, Las Vegas—City of Sin, Las Vegas—Playtown U.S.A.*, and *Las Vegas—City Without Clocks* combined a wide-eyed view of the glittery surface with a peek at its slimy underbelly. Diatribe journalism culminated with *Green Felt Jungle*, a savage indictment of the corrupt, immoral, mob-controlled, whore-ridden, crime-infested den of iniquity that was Las Vegas. Though highly sensational, this book was lively and authoritative, and it became a veritable desk reference for many exposé writers to come.

■ STALEMATE

Regardless of the titillating power plays among the top owners, politicians, tax collectors, law enforcers, and whistle-blowers, everybody else was *partying*. Las Vegas sucked up gamblers, tourists, migrators, movie stars, soldiers, prostitutes, petty crooks, musicians, preachers, and artists like a vacuum cleaner. Between 1955 and 1960, the city's population mushroomed from 45,000 to 65,000 (a 44-percent jump), with another 20,000 people living in Henderson and Boulder City. A dozen major hotels on the Strip, and several downtown, accounted for nearly 10,000 rooms, along with the pools, shops, restaurants, and chuck-wagon buffets. A score of showrooms and lounges featured topless floor shows, Hollywood's and television's biggest stars, and up-and-coming acts. In the casinos, one of W. C. Fields's suckers was born every *second*—eleven million visitors lost a record $375 million to the house in 1963, up from $50 million in 1953. Juice flowed as freely as champagne: a lowly pit boss could comp rooms, food, tickets, and hookers. The Rat Pack—Frank Sinatra, Milton Berle, Sammy Davis, Jr., Joey Bishop, Don Rickles, Henny Youngman, Jerry Lewis—appeared everywhere nightly, all earning $25,000 a week, and during the day filmed *Oceans 11*, a prototype celluloid "Great Las Vegas Heist." Thirty-thousand weddings and ten-thousand divorces were performed yearly. A convention center and meeting facility opened in 1959,

providing potential visitors with a reason other than gambling to come to Las Vegas. Atom bombs went off like clockwork up the road.

No new hotels were built between 1958 (Stardust) and 1966 (Aladdin). This allowed the Gaming Commission to consolidate and pontificate, and the Control Board to investigate and repudiate. They tightened licensing procedures and took stricter account of revenue reporting. Tax collections spiraled. State investigators even circulated the infamous "black book" of absolute undesirables, whose very presence could cost a casino its gaming license. Journalists continued asking nosy questions and publishing unflattering answers. Just as Las Vegas had a somewhat naughty image in the public consciousness, the image of the casino industry throughout conventional financial institutions remained anathema. Publicly traded corporations were ineligible for licensing since each "stockholder" in a casino had to be approved individually and personally. On the other hand, the industry's high profitability continued to attract non-mainstream capital—the Teamster Union's Central States Pension Fund, for example, with its ties to the Chicago-Midwest syndicate. Teamster money, which had dribbled into Las Vegas since the mid-1950s, arrived in a big way in 1963, financing major expansions of the Desert Inn, Dunes, and Stardust.

By then, Las Vegas found itself the biggest battleground in the intensifying federal war on organized crime. Robert Kennedy embarked on an intense crusade to rid Las Vegas of the underworld which he strongly believed controlled it. A planned full-scale invasion by 65 Justice Department agents was barely headed off at the pass by Nevada's Governor Grant Sawyer and Senator Pat McCarran. But the FBI moved in wholesale, wire-tapping, bugging, photographing, and harassing. The IRS was simultaneously dispatched to investigate suspected large-scale cash-skimming operations. The Department of Labor, the Bureau of Narcotics, and several task forces all came calling. The Diatribe reached a feverish pitch. In 1963, just as the Nuclear Test Ban Treaty forced the explosions underground, so federal heat sent the questionable investors deeper under cover. Even legitimate owners were besieged. The situation stagnated in a tense stalemate.

Rare photo of Howard Hughes in all his sartorial splendor, probably taken at the Los Angeles County Courthouse in the mid-1950s.

■ HOWARD ROBARD HUGHES

Enter Howard Hughes, from an ambulance, through the back door, at midnight, incognito, trailing a truckload of Kleenex and a retinue of Mormon advisers, most of whom had never laid eyes on the man himself. Like Las Vegas and

Bugsy Siegel, Howard Hughes was born in 1905. At age 21, he'd inherited the multi-million-dollar Hughes Tool Company, and made a beeline for Hollywood, where he launched an eclectic career as film producer, airplane designer, pioneer pilot, airline mogul, and sex investor—"probably no other person in history invested as much money in his sex life as did Howard Hughes," according to *The Intimate Sex Lives of Important People*. He had just sold TWA for a half billion dollars, *cash*, giving him a larger bankroll than anyone else in the world, and he felt like spending some, seeing how much a money-crazy city, or even a whole state, might cost.

The story of his official entry into the scene is pure Las Vegas, and combines all the divergent elements of the Hughes myth. Apparently, Howard wore out his welcome at the Desert Inn; he and his non-gambling assistants occupied all the high-roller suites of the ninth floor. But he'd grown so "comfortable" (with armed guards stationed at the entrances, an air-purifying system working round the clock, blackout draperies, and a special phone system), that he didn't feel like moving out. So in March 1967, he paid Moe Dalitz, by now 68 years old and sweating under the unrelenting federal spotlight, $13.2 million for the whole hotel.

Hughes didn't move again for over three years. But he moved his cash in a big way, embarking on the most robust buying spree in Nevada history. When the dust settled, Hughes owned the DI, the Sands, Castaways, and Frontier, and was ready to buy the Stardust when anti-trust laws were invoked. That sale failed, but he did later buy the Silver Slipper, the Landmark, and large lots on the Strip and around the city, the North Las Vegas Airport, the Alamo Airways facility next to McCarran Airport, a TV station, a small airline, casinos in Reno, and other property around Nevada. He already owned, since the early 1950s, 27,000 acres of prime desert real estate west of the city, known as Husite. And he finally unveiled, in a personal statement that broke 15 years of official silence, his master plan to build a space-age airport to accommodate the giant supersonic (SST) jets of the future. This would turn Las Vegas into the air gateway to the western states. In all he dropped $300 million.

And suddenly, according to conventional chronology, Las Vegas was swept clean of its entire undesirable element by the huge broom of corporate respectability. Although Hughes ultimately contributed nothing to the Las Vegas skyline or industrial sector, the presence alone of the billionaire master financier added an enormous degree of long-needed legitimacy to the city's tarnished image. And

though his ex-FBI, ex-IRS and MBA managers managed to alienate high-rollers and entertainers, and send his hotels into a major decline, Hughes's investments stimulated an unprecedented speculation boom. The Aladdin, Caesars Palace, Four Queens, Circus Circus, Landmark, and the International had all joined the ranks by 1970. In addition, the Fremont, Mint, Riviera, Sands, Sahara, and others all expanded with higher rises.

In the final analysis, the Hughes era was a rousing success for everyone but Hughes himself. In 1970, he divorced his wife, Jean Peters, lost a $150-million lawsuit to TWA and fled Las Vegas the way he came, on a stretcher. Yet the special dispensations Hughes received from the Control Board and Gaming Commission paved the way for the Nevada Corporate Gaming Acts of 1967 and 1969, which allowed publicly traded corporations to acquire gambling licenses without the need for every stockholder to be individually licensed. MGM, Hilton, and Holiday Inn quickly secured financing from legitimate sources to build their own hotels. Best of all for Las Vegas, the Diatribe ended, and the mob story passed into history.

■ "MOB ON THE RUN"

The mob story might have passed out of the *media* spotlight, but some original connections continued to play themselves out. In 1973, for example, past owners of the Flamingo pleaded guilty to a hidden interest by Meyer Lansky from 1960 to 1967. In 1976, the audit division of the Gaming Control Board uncovered a major skimming operation that amounted to a full 20 percent of slot revenues at the Stardust. Along with the Fremont, Marina, and Hacienda hotels, the Stardust had been purchased by Allen Glick of Argent Corporation with nearly $70 million in loans from the Teamsters Pension Fund arranged by Allen Dorfman, long known to maintain connections to the Chicago mob. This group of hotels made Glick, a thirty-something whiz-kid lawyer from Los Angeles, the second biggest owner in town, behind Hughes's Summa Corporation. His partner, Frank "Lefty" Rosenthal, was accepted and admired by Las Vegans as an influential and charitable civic leader, who hosted his own weekly TV talk show, and was honored as Las Vegas Man of the Year in 1975. When the dust settled from the skimming revelations, however, the Stardust slot manager disappeared. Glick and Rosenthal, found to be front men for the Midwest crime syndicate, lost their hotels. A Las Vegas de-

(opposite) A roof with a view—looking north at the Strip from the Tropicana.

tective, newspaper manager, and insurance executive were implicated in the skim. Suspicions even reached the governor, Robert List, and the four-term senator, Howard Cannon, costing them both their jobs in the next election.

According to Ned Day, in his 1987 two-hour special report for Las Vegas Channel 8 Eyewitness News, the Argent scandal coincided with the Organized Crime Treaty of 1977, in which the New York-East Coast families assumed control of the new gambling cash cow, Atlantic City. In return, the Chicago-Midwest families were guaranteed control of Las Vegas.

Meanwhile, in 1979, four men were convicted in Detroit of concealing hidden mob ownership in the Aladdin Hotel, which had been funded with $37 million of Teamsters' money. Also in 1979, casino and hotel executives of the Tropicana were recorded meeting with Nick Civella, reputed Kansas City don, who also turned out to be connected to St. Louis attorney Morris Shenker, part owner of the Dunes Hotel, from which Tony "The Ant" Spilotro, cold-blooded enforcer for the Chicago interests in Las Vegas, had recently been banned. By 1983, Allen Dorfman, the Pension-Fund fixer, had been assassinated, the Stardust's Frank Rosenthal barely escaped with his life (his Cadillac exploded), and Allen Glick, along with Carl Thomas and Joe Agosto of the Tropicana, had turned state's evidence. Their testimonies helped convict the *capos* of the Chicago, Kansas City, and Milwaukee organizations—leaving them, in the words of Ned Day, "monsters without heads." Subsequently, Tony Spilotro made a bid to fill the void left by the dons' imprisonment; he and his brother Michael were later found buried in a cornfield in Indiana. Ned Day concludes that for the first time since Benny Siegel muscled into town over 40 years previously, Las Vegas is finally free of mob involvement. The Metro police, state gaming officials and attorney general, FBI, federal organized-crime strike forces, among other law-enforcement agencies, intend to keep it that way.

■ VIVA VEGAS!

As the feds were cleaning out the last (known) mobster interests in Las Vegas, the corporate sanitization begun by Howard Hughes had rendered the city's image, in a word, kosher. But not without its own costs. The 1930s' innocence, the 1940s' Wild West period, the 1950s' freewheeling days, the 1960s' saber-rattling, and the

1970s' consolidation had all metamorphosed into the 1980s' bottom line. That line, however, did hit bottom in the late 1970s and early 1980s. The early days of Atlantic City as the East Coast's casino center, along with the deep recession of the early Reagan years, considerably reduced visitor volume and gambling revenues. The terrible fire at the MGM Grand left 84 dead and nearly 700 injured; the Grand closed from November 1980 to July 1981. A fire at the Las Vegas Hilton in February 1981 took another eight lives. But the recovery of the economy in the mid-1980s, along with Atlantic City's stabilization (and gradual decline) triggered what might be Las Vegas's biggest boom yet.

Twenty million people are expected to visit Las Vegas in 1990. They'll lose close to five *billion* dollars inside the casinos, and spend *another* five billion outside. Two million of them will attend conventions. Roughly 200,000 will get married. Another 60,000 people—more than 1,000 a week—will relocate to Las Vegas in 1990. The population will swell to nearly the three-quarter-million mark by 1991, making Las Vegas the fastest growing city in the country, and by far the largest city in the country to have been founded in the twentieth century.

The 3,000-room Mirage, which opened in November 1989, and the 4,000-room Excalibur, which opened in June 1990, have increased the Las Vegas hotel-room count to nearly 75,000. The 5,000-room MGM Grand, due to open in early 1992, will accord the city nine of the top ten largest hotels in the world. Some people might be worried that the city is, as in 1955, overbuilding and heading for another crash. But most insiders consider that Las Vegas is just a bit overgilded, and heading for more cash.

C I T Y S C A P E
A TALE OF FIFTY HOTELS

TRAVELERS ALONG THE OLD SPANISH (MORMON) Trail paused at well-watered, shady, and bountiful Las Vegas Ranch while the Gass family tended it (1865-1883), and the tradition continued throughout Helen Stewart's stewardship (1883-1904). Rough lodging was available at McWilliams's original Las Vegas townsite (1904-1905) in a large tent, euphemistically signposted Ladd's Hotel, where two strangers were assigned one double bed for eight hours at a cost of a dollar apiece—but only after both had passed the "body-bug test."

As the Las Vegas Land and Water Company auction neared, in spring 1905, a long tent-cabin was constructed a block north of the auction site to accommodate investors. The Hotel Las Vegas boasted 30 rooms with canvas walls, a modern kitchen and dining room, cold beer and a large stock of cigars, and an interior temperature of over 120 degrees. Two blocks from there, at Fremont and Main, Miller's Hotel was one of the first downtown establishments to receive water service from the company.

Prominent Las Vegans began hankering for a major hotel as early as 1911, when Charles "Pop" Squires, publisher of the *Las Vegas Age* and the man who invented Las Vegas boosterism, wrote, "An up-to-date, not too expensive, winter resort hotel in Las Vegas will prove a bonanza, without a doubt." In the mid-1920s, the Chamber of Commerce, promoting the town's "healthful climate, year-round sunshine, and lure of the desert," predicted that Las Vegas could become "an international attraction, if we can only get a hotel built to accommodate wealthy travelers."

But it wasn't until the early 1930s, with Hoover Dam under construction and wide-open gambling legalized, that Las Vegas experienced the first of its many and ongoing tourist-hotel building booms. The Nevada Hotel, which replaced the early Miller's Hotel, added a third story. Across the street, the venerable Las Vegas Club opened. The MacDonald Hotel on North Fifth added 16 rooms. Hotel Virginia was built on South Main. The Miller-turned-Nevada turned into the Sal Sagev (Las Vegas spelled backwards). But Las Vegas's first "luxury" hotel, the Apache, finally opened in March 1932, at the corner of Fremont and Second (where the Horseshoe now stands), complete with elegant furnishings, a large banquet room, and the town's first elevator and air-conditioned lobby.

(previous pages) Caesars's famous fountains front the pink portico and soft-blue neon building border.

Still, throughout the 1930s, Las Vegas retained its "Western-frontier" flavor. The newly legalized "casinos" remained saloons and sawdust joints—where railroaders, miners, construction workers, and gamblers drank cheap whiskey and played faro and poker. The Kiel Ranch, renamed Boulderado, became a dude ranch in the Reno tradition, where wealthy guests waited out the six-week residency requirement for divorce. And the first two truly luxurious resort hotels built beyond downtown on what is now the Strip were the hacienda-style El Rancho Vegas and Last Frontier.

■ THE FABULOUS FLAMINGO

None of this Wild West theme-park hokum for Benjamin "Bugsy" Siegel. Bugsy had a dream. He would become the greatest guardian of legal gambling and private prostitution in the country. His hotel would provide the best resort facilities in the world. His casino would feel the most luxurious and offer the finest service. His employees, down to the lowliest janitor, would wear tuxedos. His guests

The original Flamingo Hotel, muscled into place on Highway 91 in the desert far south of town by Benjamin "The Bug" Siegel.

(top) 7-Eleven is lucky in Las Vegas.
(bottom) The gilded arches brand the night sky.

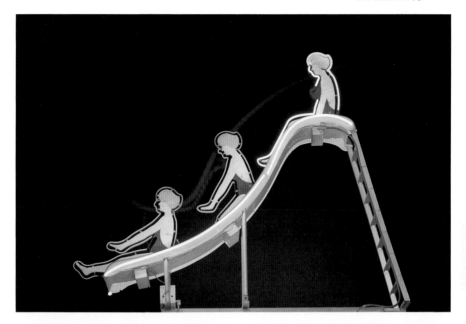

(top) Even the swimming pool companies get into the act.
(bottom) The Fremont Hotel fronts Fremont Street.

would be the famous, the glamorous, the beautiful, big-moneyed and smartly dressed. He spent $6 million to bedeck his dream palace and pop out the eyes of his mobster financiers, movie-star friends, competition past and future, and the battalions of suckers who'd come, play, and deposit their bankrolls in his vault. And the best part? It was all legit! He didn't even have to buy off, scare off, or run from the cops. It was poifect.

The Flamingo transcended any mere tourist attraction. Las Vegans took the long drive out Highway 91, 12 miles roundtrip, just to stare. The incomparable Tom Wolfe, in *The Kandy-Kolored Tangerine-Flake Streamline Baby*, explains, "Siegel put up a hotel-casino such as Las Vegas had never seen—all Miami Modern. Such shapes! Boomerang Modern supports, Palette Curvilinear bars, Hot

LIGHT SHOWS

Las Vegas and light shows are synonymous. Glitter Gulch downtown is so bright that you can't tell day from night. The five-mile-long (eight-km) stretch of neon art against the black desert sky along the Strip is, of course, the famous cliché. Long neon tubing, in brilliant reds, whites, blues, and pinks, borders the edges of shopping centers, car washes, apartments, and restaurants. And it's not just their designs and colors and size and intensity. In addition, they're all *moving*—flickering, twitching, blinking; turning on and off; running up and down and across; shooting across space and back again; starting at the bottom, speeding to the top, and exploding there. The latest and brightest rage is electronic message displays—programmable colors, graphics, dissolves and splashes, and animation. Topping it all off are the huge, square, black-on-white marquees, advertising everything from buffets to burlesque, from baccarat lessons to Bloody Marys. And all the exterior glass reflects the effects in a cosmic double exposure.

Outside, at least, you have some perspective against which to measure this massive ion icon. Once inside the casinos, however, the light show closes in on top of you, and there's no escaping the border neon, million-bulb chandeliers, flickering ceiling and wall "fireflies," slot spots, alternately flashing floor, stairs, and railing beacons, and facing mirrors stereoscoping it all into infinity.

Of course, the realistic undercoat of the place is sun-scorched, bleached-out, drab-desert beige. But the ultimate hue, one that's lacking from both the natural and man-made palette, but that underlies every visible color in the Las Vegas spectrum, is green.

Shoppe Cantilever roofs, and a scalloped swimming pool. Such colors! All the new electrochemical pastels of the Florida littoral: tangerine, broiling magenta, livid pink, incarnadine, fuchsia, demure, Congo ruby, methyl green, viridian, aquamarine, phenosafranine, incandescent orange, scarlet-fever purple, cyanic blue, tesselated bronze, hospital-fruit-basket orange. And such signs! Two cylinders rose at either end of the Flamingo—eight stories high and covered from top to bottom with neon rings in the shape of bubbles that fizzed eight stories up into the desert sky all night long like an illuminated whisky-soda tumbler filled to the brim with pink champagne."

Wolfe makes the point that throughout the history of art, the aristocracy had been solely responsible for *style*—for the simple reason that aristocrats alone had the time and money to cultivate it. World War II, however, changed all that forever. "The war created money. It made massive infusions of money into every level of society. Suddenly, classes of people whose lives had been practically invisible had the money to build monuments to their own styles. Las Vegas was created after the war, with war money, by gangsters."

But all that—the signs, colors, shapes, architecture—was just the exterior, the false front, designed to grab your eye as you cruised by at 30 miles an hour, and then your steering wheel as you turned in and parked. Then you were drawn inside. There you were presented with another false front: the promise. Of the indulgence. Of the three oldest, most primal, irresistible, and taboo pastimes of human nature: drinking, gambling, and sex. All this electric glamour in the desert, all this style, seduction, and cushioned comfort—all to debar the barrier to your bankroll. And then! From the backstage special-effects control booth appeared the wizard, controlling this Oz, wielding the Percentage. The Edge That Must Be Obeyed. A legal game, an honest game, but by no means a fair game. All designed to pass the cash over to the secured side of the pit. Never to return. It *was* perfect.

Except that Bugsy, like most empire builders and some lifestyle creators, either suffered from delusions of immortality or clearly recognized the imminence of his own death. Whichever, along the way, he forgot to cover his ass. He literally gave his life to the vision, but not before initiating the Golden Age of Las Vegas.

In early January 1947, 14 days after it opened, the Flamingo financially flopped. The doors closed. When they reopened in May, the hotel and casino were managed by Gus Greenbaum, boss gambler from Phoenix, and Davie Berman, boss gambler from Minneapolis. Both had arrived a few years earlier in Bugsy's

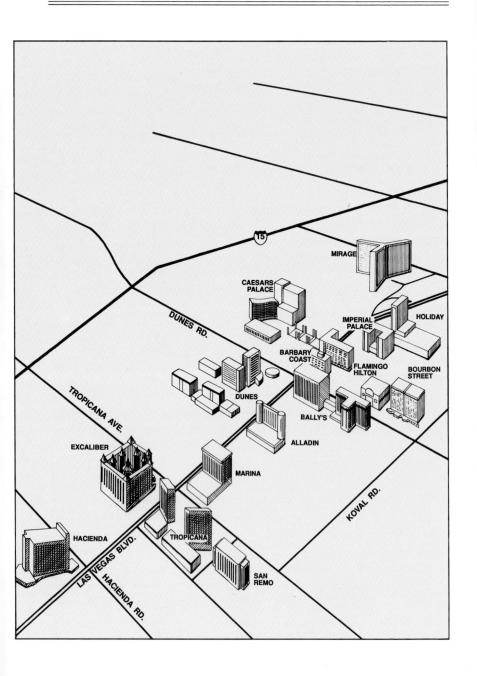

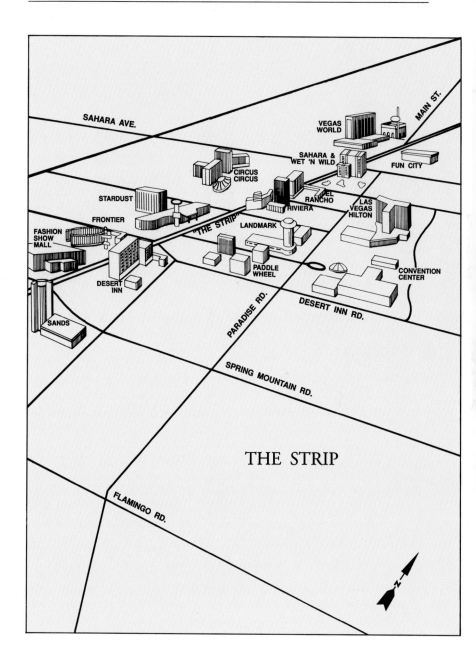

THE STRIP

EL CORTEZ HOTEL

The El Cortez Hotel opened in November 1941, and occupied half a city block a little beyond congested downtown on Fremont Street between Sixth and Seventh, just outside Clark's original Las Vegas town site. It boasted 71 rooms and eight two-bedroom suites, cost $325,000, and sported a Wild West resort motif to compete head-to head with the new El Rancho Vegas out on Highway 91. In 1945, the El Cortez was bought by Benny Siegel, along with Davie and Chickie Berman, Gus Greenbaum, Willie Alderman, and Meyer Lansky's money. But when they all moved over to the Flamingo in 1947, the downtown resort was sold to a group of 19 investors, which included such luminaries as J. Kell Houssels, Bill Moore, Sam Boyd, and Joe Kelley. By 1954, attrition had reduced the group to Houssels and Kelley; they sold it back to Marion Hicks, who'd built the place, in 1961. Eventually, Jackie Gaughan acquired the property, and he owns it today.

A $12-million, 14-story, 200-room tower was added in 1983 at the corner of Sixth and Ogden, giving the El Cortez a whole city block. Fortunately, part of the 50-year-old hotel, at the southeast corner of Fremont and Sixth, has been left undisturbed all these decades, and remains today exactly as it appears in this historical black-and-white photograph from the early 1950s, even then unchanged from the day it opened in 1941. Thus this small wing of the El Cortez is by far the oldest original casino in Las Vegas.

wake, purchased the El Cortez downtown, and fronted the Flamingo for hidden owner Meyer Lansky. In 1955, after Greenbaum and Berman moved over to the Riviera, the hotel was sold to Thomas Hull, who'd built the El Rancho Vegas, and Al Parvin, who was to buy and sell a number of hotels over the next 20 years. In 1960, the Flamingo was again sold, to a large group of investors headed by Miami hotel magnates Morris Lansburgh and Sam Cohen. Lansky received a hefty "finder's fee" for both sales. It was later determined that he'd held an interest all the way up to 1967. That year, entrepreneur Kirk Kerkorian bought the Flamingo for $13 million during the Hughes whirlwind, to use as a "hotel school" for the core staff of the huge International that Kerkorian was then planning. He immediately sank another $2.5 million into improvements: the casino and theater were expanded, and the champagne towers were torn down.

Hilton Corporation bought the Flamingo in 1970, becoming the first major hotel chain to enter the Nevada market. Hilton embarked on a colossal expansion program which added a 500-room tower in 1977, a second 500-room tower in 1980, a third in 1982, a fourth in 1986, and a final 728-room tower in 1990, for a total of 3,530 rooms (largest in the world till the arrival of the Excalibur three months later, with 4,000 rooms). Poolside at the Flamingo, though the towering walls loom above, the original lowrise buildings are strictly old Las Vegas. Bugsy himself lived on the fourth floor of the Oregon Building. His elaborate security precautions involved extra-thick walls, four exits, plus a trap door from which a ladder descended to the basement, where a tunnel led under the New Mexico Building to a door at the driveway for a quick getaway. It's even rumored that Bugsy built a secret vault where he stashed cash from the skim. But don't let Geraldo Rivera hear of it!

■ THE THUNDERBIRD

Next came the $3-million Thunderbird, named for a mythological Navajo creature. Built in 1948 by Marion Hicks (a local contractor who also constructed the El Cortez) and Clifford Jones (then lieutenant governor of Nevada—at age 35), the Thunderbird catered to local families with great food and an informal setting. Since Lt. Governor Jones had the juice, the Thunderbird became the hangout of many prominent politicians. But the Nevada Tax Commission exercised its au-

All that glitters.

thority upon the hotel in 1955, when a sting operation conducted by local newspapermen uncovered a loan to the owners by Jake Lansky, Meyer's brother. Its license was revoked, and though it was later restored by the courts, the Thunderbird's aura faded.

Del Webb purchased the hotel in 1964 for $10 million. Eight years later, Caesars World bought it for $13 million, but management quickly realized they didn't want it, and turned it over to E. Thomas Parry of Valley Bank for $9 million. He sold it to the Dunes's Major Riddle in 1977, who changed its name to Silverbird. Riddle sold it in 1981 to Ed Torres, a longtime Las Vegas hotel manager, who changed its name to El Rancho, after the original hotel on the Strip, which once stood across the street.

■ THE DESERT INN

In 1950, the $4.5-million Desert Inn opened. Possibly no other Las Vegas hotel has generated more ink than the DI—about Wilbur Clark on the bright side, and about Moe Dalitz on the shady side. Clark started out in Southern California as a bartender, luggage handler, and craps dealer, and later owned a string of taverns. After selling out in California, he set up in Las Vegas in the late 1930s, and speculated in casino stocks. In 1946 he sold his share in the El Rancho for $1.5 million, and began construction of his dream hotel, Wilbur Clark's Desert Inn, modeled after its posh Palm Springs namesake. Like Bugsy, he immediately ran out of money, and work ground to a halt. A full three years later, in 1949, Clark finally obtained three million dollars from the boss gambler of Cleveland, Morris Dalitz, and his three partners, who retained an equivalent 75 percent ownership in the Desert Inn. Immedi-

Moe Dalitz, the ultimate Las Vegas survivor, looking dapper and happy at age 82.

ately, Clark reverted to front-man status, and he initially played his role as media manipulator with gusto and a touch of brilliance. He fondly displayed a veritable Strip-sized billboard of articles, clips, and ads about the hotel and himself, and even was proclaimed Ambassador of Las Vegas, the ultimate shill. But Dalitz held all the juice.

Moe Dalitz was 50 when he moved to Las Vegas to run the DI. He'd grown up on the streets of Detroit, and was already a big-time bootlegger, having run booze between Canada and Cleveland in his mid-twenties. He branched out into racketeering and eventually operated a string of illegal casinos from Cleveland to Kentucky. He also had extensive interests in legitimate business and industry: steel, real estate, race tracks, and his family laundry operation in Detroit (which is how he came to know Jimmy Hoffa). In *Green Felt Jungle*, Dalitz is described as having "the big fix in half a dozen city halls, organizational ability which he used for corruption, and legitimate enterprises which simplified the fix—stock deals and percentages are the modern ways to pay off graft." This is supported by Carl Sifakis in *Mafia Encyclopedia:* Dalitz was expert at "the deft use of the bribe rather than the bullet," and even so great an organizational genius as Meyer Lansky "derived inspiration from him."

In *Gambler's Money*, Wallace Turner delves deeply into the skills and qualities that eventually earned Dalitz the most juice of all the bosses in Las Vegas. These young illegal gamblers learned many unusual and useful lessons. They learned, for instance, how to conduct business without the benefit of legally binding contracts or legal recourse—by paying off police and political officials. They developed their own code of trust in a world where a man's word was his deed: enemies and possible betrayers were cultivated and respected but never trusted, while a solid reputation for honoring the pledged word among allies held the highest value. They considered their fellow men as suckers to be plucked, dishonest authorities to be bribed, thieves to be caught, usurpers to be foiled. They learned the mechanics of the games: how to analyze percentages, how to spot cheaters, how to cheat the players without being spotted. They learned the psychology of the compulsive gambler, and perfected the means of taking *all* his money. They were well versed in all the tricks that the underworld used to protect its illegal investments. "They could soon learn the tricks the legitimate world had devised to protect its investments through courts, contracts, and franchises," Turner concludes.

Gus Greenbaum, Davie Berman, and Moe Dalitz absorbed Bugsy's vision and proceeded to make it work. They mustered all their knowledge and experience to accent the old tricks, and invent new ones. They immediately revealed the weaknesses, gaping loopholes, and naiveté of the state's regulatory apparatus. They celebrated their own styles—perfecting the seduction and worshipping the great god Percentage. They made enviable profits look easy. And best of all, they became respected elders of the local community—influential, charitable, religious. Ultimately, they opened the door for a veritable flood of gamblers from around the country to invest their hot cash in legalized gambling and personal legitimacy. They built the Strip, fine-tuned the system, and laid the foundation for modern Las Vegas.

Dalitz (and Clark) also inaugurated a number of other trends. For opening night, timed to coincide with an atomic test blast, they spent $13,000 to fly in a hundred high rollers. They opened the first resort golf course, and sponsored the Tournament of Champions (1953). They hired a famous sheriff, Don Borax, to be Chief of Security.

In 1963, the DI added its first nine-story tower. In 1964, Wilbur Clark finally sold his minority interest in the DI to Dalitz (Clark died of a heart attack a year later). In March 1967, Dalitz sold the "whole schmear" to Howard Hughes for $13.2 million. Though licenses often took months to process, Hughes's application was approved post haste, *sans* fingerprints, photographs, interview, or investigation. The 14-story Augusta Tower was built in 1978, and shortly thereafter the seven-story Wimbledon Tower, fronting the golf course, was added. Kirk Kerkorian bought the DI (along with the Sands) from Summa Corporation in February 1988 for $161 million; perhaps he intends to use it as a training facility for his new, 5,000-room MGM Grand (opening in 1992). Celebrating its 40th anniversary in 1990, the Desert Inn remains a small, 821-room resort, catering to a select clientele. It's still, as it's always been, one of the three classiest joints in town, and secure in that knowledge.

■ THE HORSESHOE

Meanwhile, downtown, Benny Binion opened his Horseshoe Club in August 1951. Binion was born in 1904 in Pilot Grove, Texas. Like Moe Dalitz, Binion started out as a rough kid on the rough streets, then became the boss bootlegger of

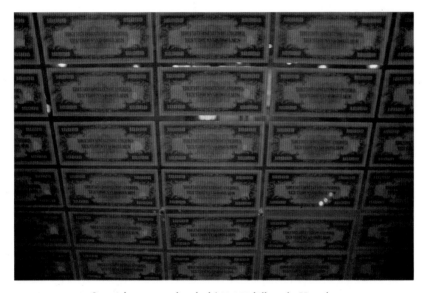

Step right up to one hundred $10,000 bills at the Horseshoe

Dallas before he was 25, and the boss gambler before he was 30. Reid and De-maris quote "a retired Dallas police captain who had been active during the gang wars of the Binion era," whose story included a litany of bloodletting and gore that would make a Sam Peckinpah movie look like *Mary Poppins,* and that was be-fore Binion's alleged gangland feud with Herbert "The Cat" Noble, the body count of which would make an Arnold Schwarzenegger movie look like Disney. (It's all there in *Green Felt Jungle* for anyone who's interested.)

On the other hand, in an interview with Binion recorded in 1973 for the Uni-versity of Nevada's *Oral History Project,* he claims, "The Texas Rangers, the FBI, and the whole works know that I didn't have nothin' to do with the Noble killin'. It would've took me a half hour to kill Noble if I'd wanted to kill him. There's no way in the world I'd harm anybody for any amount of money. But if anybody goes to talkin' about doin' me or my family any bodily harm, I'm very capable for easily takin' care of 'em in a *most* artistic way."

Binion fled the Texas heat in 1946 for downtown Las Vegas, where he quickly bought into and sold out of two downtown casinos. He then purchased the old Apache Hotel and the Eldorado Casino next door, and rebuilt the properties into

Benny Binion posing in front of his cool mil.

the Horseshoe, which opened in the same month that Herb Noble was finally laid to rest. Binion paid some dues by serving four years at Leavenworth in the mid-1950s for that old workhorse, federal income-tax evasion. He had to "sell" the Horseshoe before he went away to Joe Brown, a multimillionaire friend who, in Benny's words, "held it together" in a "kind of a deal" until he regained his freedom and "bought back" the hotel.

Above all, Benny Binion was a survivor—the Dallas gang wars of the 1930s, the Las Vegas cutthroat competition of the 1940s, the federal confinement of the 1950s. He didn't only survive, he prospered. And ultimately Benny reached a status not unlike Dalitz's: beloved elder statesman. In *Las Vegas— Behind the Tables, Part Two*, Barney Vinson shares a folksy tale of Binion as gunfighter, boss gambler, Las Vegas founding father and gambler emeritus, and describes an open-house, half-million-dollar, 83rd-birthday party at Thomas and Mack Arena for Benny in 1988, attended by 19,000 people. Moe Dalitz was there, 90 years old and stone deaf. Binion died in early 1990 at the age of 85; he had acquired the famous Mint Hotel next door in 1988, giving the Horseshoe, still owned wholly by the Binion family, its own city block.

■ THE SAHARA

In December 1952, the $5.5-million Sahara Hotel opened across the Strip from the El Rancho, replacing the popular Club Bingo (which is well remembered after almost 40 years). Milton Prell, a Los Angeles jewelry mogul, lined up a grubstake from Portland boss gamblers, Desert Inn owners, Sam Boyd (a clever West Coast bingo operator who'd worked his way up through a decade of Las Vegas ranks to be a juiceman), and Del Webb, whose construction company built the Flamingo, and then the Sahara in return for 20 points in the property. The hotel's sign was 100 feet tall, free-standing, with a letter design that hasn't changed in almost four decades. The Sahara added an African style to the desert theme of the Las Vegas

---

T-MEN IN LAS VEGAS

In the spring of 1955, U.S. Treasury agents walked into the Horseshoe Club and asked to see owner Joe W. Brown, a Texas multimillionaire, and his right-hand man Robert "Doby Doc" Caudill, former Texas gambler and collector of Western Americana. This is not a moment especially savored by casino owners, but the T-men weren't up to anything more sinister than enforcing an obscure federal statute that forbids the reproduction of paper currency.

The Horseshoe has on display in its casino one million dollars, one hundred $10,000 bills in actual currency. The hundred $10,000 bills are pasted in rows of twenty length-wise and five across on heavy paper and framed in two layers of plate glass in the shape of a horseshoe. It's what Las Vegas calls its "most authentic" display and costs a small fortune in lost interest. But it is a customer attraction beyond the dreams of a promotional genius and is goggled at by thousands of tourists every day, all of whom then drop a dollar or two in the slots, and is by far the most popular backdrop in Las Vegas for snapshots to send the folks back home who have never seen a $10,000 bill, much less a hundred of them.

The T-men didn't mind the display, no matter how lurid it may have seemed to them. What they minded was the photographs. They confiscated 150,000 souvenir post cards of the display from the club, and combed the town for prints and negatives of all photographs ever taken. Misters Brown and Caudill weren't exactly amused, but they weren't unamused, either. They foresaw a lifetime's work for the government agents. Some 8,000 photographs had been taken in front of the million dollars and mailed all over the country; souvenir post cards had gone out by the hundreds of thousands; the display had been photographed in scores of newsreels and had appeared in several television shows including Ed Murrow's "See It Now" program. "I never did see a T-man's job," said Doby Doc. "Now I really don't."

—Katherine Best and Katherine Hillyer, *Las Vegas: Playtown, U.S.A.*

Strip, with big plaster camels out front, and the Caravan coffeeshop, Casbah Lounge, and Congo Showroom inside. (Clydie the camel remains, and the original names haven't changed.)

In *Playtown, U.S.A.*, Best and Hillyer described the Sahara, the fifth hotel on the Strip. "Its casino was larger than anybody else's—up to that time. Its swimming pool was the biggest in Las Vegas—so far. Its theater-restaurant had greater seating capacity than any other in town—as of that date. Its stage was the most spacious on the Strip—right then." Two weeks later the Sands opened, prompting

---

HOTEL-ROOM ART

Martin Lowitz, a jolly German-born art collector and one-time Latin scholar, sells some 20,000 original pictures a year that he has mass-produced for him by a string of assembly-line artists who are able with fair aim to imitate their peers at the rate of a dozen a day. Anyone wanting 50 Vermeers, 25 Roualts, a dozen Eakinses, may have same at prices as low as $17.50 each, with frame.

The Lowitz operation is strictly a cut-rate, noncreative performance that has caused art connoisseurs to recoil as though stabbed with a poisoned paintbrush. But his boys' pictures are bright and effective and, on the whole, much appreciated by the inhabitants of hotel bedrooms who have been whimpering in silence through the years at the seemingly limitless sight of mordant ducks and dying swans. Strip hotels have bought thousands of Lowitz originals.

In 1947, Martin Lowitz sold 83 of these originals to Marion Hicks, who was then building his Thunderbird Hotel. The Thunderbird opened in September 1948, and two days later it was discovered that three paintings had disappeared from a room. Mr. Hicks wasn't particularly disturbed. "Wait," he said to the distraught housekeeper. "The guest who was in that room plays roulette in our casino. Besides, he has a reservation to return."

The Thunderbird evidently had made the absconder feel so at home that he now wanted home to seem more like the Thunderbird. He returned shortly, stayed one night, played roulette and departed next morning laden with oversized luggage. Mr. Hicks again was not only unperturbed, he was pleased. His casino books showed that the visitor had lost $6,000 his first visit and $8,000 his second. The pictures he had stolen cost less than $200. In a happy haze of appreciation of art, Mr. Hicks wired Mr. Lowitz an order for 200 more paintings.

—Best and Hillyer, *Las Vegas: Playtown, U.S.A.*

the authors to add, "Periodically, Las Vegas sits back, takes a deep breath, and asks itself: When will the saturation point in all this prosperity come? When will the one-too-many swank caravansary go up on the Strip? When will all these millions of tourists stop streaming into town?" They were writing in 1954.

The Sahara's owners built the Mint Hotel downtown in 1956. Del Webb purchased controlling interest in both properties in 1961. In 1964, the Sahara's entertainment director, Stan Irwin, booked the Beatles for two shows at the Convention Center. Performing for 8,500 Las Vegans at $4 a ticket, the shows have been called "Las Vegas's biggest entertainment event of all time." A 14-story, 200-room tower was added to the Sahara in 1966, less than a year after the Mint Hotel downtown rose to 26 stories, tallest building in Nevada, with its skydeck pool. In 1968, a 24-story, 400-room tower was added to the Sahara.

The Sahara's owner today, Paul Lowden, came to Las Vegas as a musician in 1965. He was promoted to music director first at the Flamingo and then at the Hacienda in which he purchased points. Lowden wound up owning the Hacienda in 1977 (after the Allen Glick scandal), and parlayed it into purchasing the Sahara from Del Webb in 1982 for $50 million. He installed a third tower (26 stories, 575 rooms) and a convention center in 1988, and put up a 600-room tower in 1990. Lowden is now building a new hotel, the Santa Fe, which will have an ice arena and bowling alley, out on Rancho Drive in the fastest-growing residential section of Las Vegas.

■ THE SANDS

When the Sands opened in December 1952, two weeks after the Sahara, nearly three million visitors were passing through Las Vegas annually. The hotel's original 200 rooms, contained by five two-story Bermuda-modern buildings named after race tracks and set in a semi-circle around the pool, provided accommodation even more luxurious than the Flamingo next door, and remained filled, continuously, for the rest of the decade. According to the (admittedly sensational) *Green Felt Jungle*, the Sands was controlled when it opened by more different mobs than any other casino in Nevada. Sid Wyman, a gambler from St. Louis, Ed Levinson, a Kentucky bookie, Hymie Abrams, a Boston restaurateur, Jack Entratter, a club owner from New York all fronted for interests that, in 1952, were not too deeply hidden. But Joseph Stacher, a New Jersey mafioso, allegedly held the ultimate juice. (Stacher merited his own chapter in *Green Felt Jungle*.) Of course, all of them, including Stacher, survived the bumpy transition to Las Vegas's liberalized legitimacy, and indeed became big-time bosses and pillars of the community.

In a shrewd maneuver, Frank Sinatra and Dean Martin were sold nine points each in the Sands, to provide incentive for the superstars to perform there, in the famous Copa Room. Their friends Milton Berle, Sammy Davis Jr., Danny Thomas, Lena Horne, and others hung out at the Sands; together, these Hollywood glitterati came to be called the Clan, and later the Rat Pack. The Sands's $40,000 steam room was famous for 15 years as a gathering place of the Clan and its functionaries. Jack Entratter, a big, savvy manager of New York's Copacabana Club before coming to the Sands, reigned as the juiciest entertainment director in Las Vegas for long years; he had the golden touch for handling superstars, especially when it came to massaging and assuaging the famous ego of Frank Sinatra. In fact, Entratter was revered as a celebrities' celebrity, to whom everyone, from up-and-comers to superstars, flocked for bookings. Red Skelton, Carol Burnett, Nat King Cole, Judy Garland, Paul Anka, and Van Johnson, among others, all per-

In 1952, Sinatra was sold nine points in the Sands Hotel, where he held court for the next fifteen years.

formed in the showroom, bracketed by the *crème-de-la-crème* Copa Girls (Entratter's standards were legendary). Ezio Pinza sang opera and Tallulah Bankhead did a club act, at Entratter's insistence. The Sands itself reigned as *the* in place for glamour and style throughout the 1950s. Its motto, "Where the Fun Never Sets," was true.

In 1962, the U-shaped, three-story, $1.2-million Aqueduct Building was opened at the rear of the property, adding 83 rooms and suites. In 1965, a $9-million expansion doubled the size of the casino and Copa Room. In July 1967, Howard Hughes purchased the Sands for $14.6 million. A few months later, Sinatra threw what is perhaps his most famous public tantrum in the Sands casino, when Howard cut off Frankie's credit. Sinatra defected to Caesars Palace, taking some of his friends and any number of high rollers with him. Jack Entratter, however, survived the transition, remaining as entertainment director until his death in 1971.

A year after Hughes's purchase, the familiar 16-story Sands "periscope" was completed; its upper-floor rooms remain some of the classiest in Las Vegas, with rich wood appointments, sliding glass doors onto balconies, and incomparable views. The Summa Corporation sold the Sands (and the Desert Inn) to Kirk Kerkorian in 1988 for $161 million. Kerkorian turned around and sold the Sands in April 1989 for $110 million to the Interface Group, the world's leader in trade conferences and exhibitions (it sponsors the gargantuan Consumer Electronics Show that invades Las Vegas every January). Interface is constructing a 1,300-room tower and 650,000-square-foot (60,380-square-meter) convention center at the rear of the historic property, costing a cool $150 mil.

■ THE RIVIERA

The Riviera, in April 1955 the seventh hotel to open on the Strip, provided a major departure from the distinctively dry styles of the Desert Inn, Sahara, and Sands. Built by Miami hotelmen and reminiscent of the princely palaces along the Mediterranean, the T-shaped Riv rose nine stories from the desert floor, and cost nearly $10 million—about $4 million more than the investors were able to pay. The New Frontier, Dunes, Royal Nevada, and Mint opened right on the Riv's heels, and Liberace was paid an unheard-of $50,000 a week to headline; within three months, the hotel was bankrupt.

Gus Greenbaum (right) and Moe Sedway (middle)—major elders in the Fifties' Las Vegas Jewish community.

The Chicago mob immediately moved in and came away with the pie, then blackmailed Gus Greenbaum of Phoenix out of retirement into running it. Reluctantly taking over the unchecked casino, Greenbaum, along with his old cronies Davie Berman and Willie Alderman, managed to strong-arm the operation into submission and began to turn a profit—for Chicago don Sam Giancana's "front seat in the counting room." But Gus again couldn't stay away from his old bad habits—the gambling, drugs, and showgirls. He owed a million dollars in markers to Chicago loan sharks. And his old bosses at the Flamingo were irritated that he'd gone to work for the competition, taking with him all the Flamingo's secrets. (On a visit home to Phoenix for Thanksgiving in 1958, Gus and his wife Bess had their throats slashed in a hit ordered from on high.)

The Riviera, which has had one of the most upwardly mobile histories—with an occasional crash—was taken over by a group including local millionaire Jerome Mack and Broadway producer David Merrick. In 1967 they added a $10-million,

11-story wing during the great expansion race of the late 1960s, then sold the hotel, in 1973, to Meshulam Riklis of Boston's American International Travel Services, one of the largest travel companies in the world. Riklis built a $20-million, 12-story tower in 1975, added 200 more rooms ($6 million) in 1977, paid Dolly Parton a jaw-dropping $350,000 *a week* in 1981, and was bankrupt within two years, first of a series of major hotel failures in the ruinous recession of 1983-84.

The Riviera recovered by 1985, and in 1988, a $28-million, 24-story tower was completed. In April 1990, a major addition gave the casino, at 125,000 square feet (11,600 square meters), the undisputed claim to largest in the world (Donald Trump's Atlantic City Taj Mahal included). It's also perhaps the brightest and airiest casino on the Strip. In addition, a 43-story, 1,600-room tower, which will be the tallest in Nevada, is scheduled for completion in 1992.

Wait—there's more. Riklis is also planning an amusement park behind the hotel, which will stretch nearly all the way to Paradise Road across from the Hilton. The rides, including a ferris wheel, will be enclosed in a dome for year-round recreation. Total cost of the casino, new tower, and amusement-park expansion?

Three hundred million.

The Riviera—under construction almost continually during its 35 years.

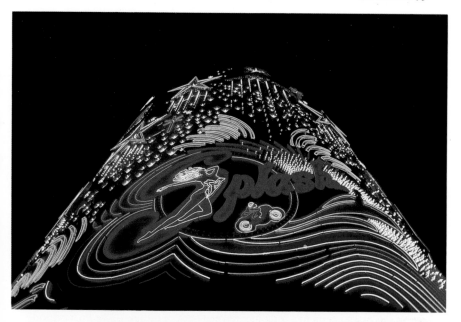

The "Splash" revue is electrifying inside and out.

■ THE SHOWBOAT

The $2-million, 200-room Showboat opened in 1954, owned by William Moore of the Last Frontier, and J. Kell Housells, a longtime downtown casino juiceman. The casino was managed by Moe Dalitz and the DI gang. The Showboat was quite an anomaly—a Mississippi riverboat, complete with paddlewheel and smoke-stacks, out in the boondocks of Boulder Highway just down from the venerable Green Shack restaurant. The day before the grand opening, an enormous storm dumped torrential rains, which almost washed the Boat away! But the hotel float-ed along with the Las Vegas current, steering around snags, pausing in port for re-pairs, but rarely foundering, all under the able captainship of Joe Kelley, appropri-ately a one-time Southern California offshore gambling-boat manager.

In 1959, Kelley built bowling lanes at the hotel and sponsored tournaments, which attracted low rollers from around the country. He also introduced the 49-cent breakfast, which brought the locals running. And later, he was first to hook all his slot machines up to a computer to keep track of earnings. The Boat expand-ed in 1963, got a facelift in 1968, added nine stories and 250 rooms in 1973, and again in 1975. Today, only a small vestige of the Showboat facade (and some orig-inal rooms around the pool) remain, but the bowling alley, large bingo parlor, and low rollers keep it steaming full speed ahead.

■ THE DUNES

The Dunes, across the Strip from the nearly 10-year-old, still-fabulous Flamingo, was next to open—and close. Third major hotel-casino to enter the fearful fray in that fateful spring of 1955, the $4-million, 200-rooms Dunes, built on an 85-acre (34-hectare) site, was the project of Joe Sullivan, a Rhode Island restaurant mogul, and Al Gottesman, a Connecticut movie-chain owner, whom the *Green Felt Jungle* authors believed to be fronting for Raymond Patriarca's New England mob. The group of owners, whose horror story is detailed in Ed Reid's *Las Vegas—City With-out Clocks*, had no casino experience among them, and were picked clean by the earliest patrons. By the fall of 1955, the Sands casino managers tried to apply a tourniquet to the bankroll bleeding, but that, too, failed. In January 1956, the casino closed, leaving the Dunes the toniest motel on the Strip, with its 200 rooms, 150-foot-long (46-meter) lagoon with a 90-foot (27-meter), V-shaped

In the driest part of the country, there is always an Oasis at the Dunes.

swimming pool (longest in the country at the time), and a 40-foot (12-meter) Sheik of Baghdad statue smiling down on the Strip.

Six months later, new investors resurrected the casino corpse; one of them, Major Riddle, owned a large Indiana trucking company, and had close ties to Jimmy Hoffa and his limitless Teamsters Pension Fund stash. With proper financing, Riddle took decisive action, raising the eyebrows of the big boys on the block. He immediately pioneered the topless floor show, "Minsky's Burlesque," which packed the house, which fed the percentage, which turned the profits, which injected Riddle full of juice. Within three years, the Dunes offered 450 rooms and an 18-hole golf course.

In 1961 Riddle sold major shares in the Dunes to Charlie Rich (lately of the Riviera) and Sid Wyman (lately of the Sands), and opened the Sultan's Table gourmet room (which remains today one of the oldest and best restaurants in Las Vegas). He also added the 250-room Olympic Wing. But within a few years, business slumped again. Big Julius Weintraub to the rescue! This New York jewelry dealer and hustler got in with the Dunes's juicemen, and was hired to collect markers from New York gamblers. He became friendly with these high rollers, began steering them toward the Dunes, and making their travel arrangements.

This put him in a position to begin managing regular junkets from New York, an idea which was just gaining steam in Las Vegas. "The Dunes was transformed instantly from a tottering operation to a highly profitable one," writes Edward Limm, in *Big Julie of Las Vegas*. And Big Julie Weintraub remained the Junket King of Las Vegas for more than a decade.

In 1965, at the beginning of the Hughes-era expansion boom, Riddle opened his 24-story "Diamond of the Dunes" addition, breaking the 1,000-room plateau. He also installed a new sign which, at 180 feet tall (55 meters) and largest in the world, triggered a decade of sign one-upmanship. In 1969, the Dunes entered one

---

OWNER–GAMBLERS

All departments in the Dunes Hotel that fateful first month had been geared to lose, with the exception of the casino, which had been expected to come through with a handsome profit that would wipe out the red ink. Instead, the management found, "silver dollar" players had taken up the spaces around the tables. However, there was a bunch of high rollers at the Dunes one night. At one time they were behind $70,000. Then a dollar player came along and rolled 28 numbers in a row, and the group quit with $18,000 of house money. The dollar roller also quit—$200 ahead, part of which was a tip given him by the exultant gambling group.

Gottesman learned the hard way. He learned, for instance, that the house can't count on its percentage with any reality unless it keeps expenses within the limits of the anticipated income based on that percentage. Also, that you can pick your high-priced star but you have no power over the selection of your customers, and cannot choose between 700 paupers and 700 millionaires. Another fact is that the player who wins cashes in his chips at the handy casino cage any time he wishes. When the casino wins it has to carry much of the load in the shape of checks, markers, IOUs, etc. In six weeks the Dunes had a huge backlog of such uncollected debts. Of little help was a list of 15,000 names of persons who are considered bad risks in the gambling capital.

In the three months after the hotel opened, Gottesman and his partners added an additional $600,000 to the casino bankroll. This happens frequently when a hotel suddenly finds itself short of cash. Though gaming officials screen the initial bankroll carefully, there can be no proper record of money dropped into the casino cage later on. This is one method by which "silent partners," meaning anybody, can get into a casino operation at any time and take over.

—Ed Reid, *Las Vegas—City Without Clocks*

of the most tortuous ownership periods of any hotel in town, when Continental Connector Corporation bought in for $59 million. ConCon later got into big trouble with the SEC for defrauding stockholders. In 1975, Kansas City (and Teamster) attorney Morris Shenker bought in; he got into trouble with the Gaming Control Board for alleged underworld connections. Several additional investor-suckers and convoluted corporate consignees came and went over the next decade, and a 17-story tower was added in 1980. But the Dunes finally went bankrupt in 1985. It was once again revived in 1988 by a Japanese investor, Masao Nangaku, who has reinvested the property with some of its former glory.

Today the Dunes is one of the more good-natured and somewhat tranquil oases in the Las Vegas desert, with the venerable Sultan's Table and Dome of the Sea restaurants, arrowhead pool and original lowrise rooms, and country club and golf course extending from the back of the property all the way to the freeway.

■ THE NEW FRONTIER

If ever the transformation of a hotel symbolized the transformation of Las Vegas—in time and space—it was on the day, April 4, in the critical year, 1955, that the Last Frontier rode off into the sunset and the New Frontier dropped whole from high orbit in its place. The old hotel, which opened in 1942, had been sold in 1951 to Bernie Katleman and Jake Kozloff, who also owned the El Rancho Vegas. By 1955, the Last Frontier, second hotel to be built on the Strip and 13 years old, was one of 10 competing properties, and long due for a complete modernization. Luckily, Best and Hillyer were there to describe it. "The Frontier, New, had a lobby of black and white Italian marble, and a casino carpeted in French lilac weaving so deep that sparks flew when the mauve-tinted slot machines were touched. Some said even the sparks were mauve. Chandeliers in the shape of men from outer space, flying saucers and spinning planets hung from raspberry *glacé* and daphne-pink ceilings. Walls of diadem violet and Ruby Lake magenta displayed three-dimensional amethyst murals depicting the twelve signs of the zodiac. The cocktail lounge was named Cloud 9, the dining room was called Planet, and the theater was known as Venus. On this particular afternoon, the doors closed on the dear old homespun grandeur of the Last and opened, a few hundred feet up the corridors, on the Out-of-this-World-ly phantasmagoria of the New."

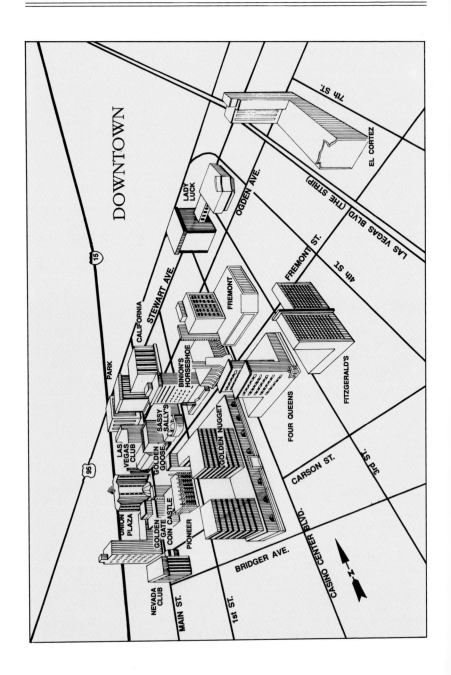

Immediately after the renovation, Kozloff and Katleman sold the hotel to a group of L.A. investors, which leased it to other operators, who ran it into the ground. The casino closed and stayed shut throughout most of 1957, until it was leased to Warren Bayley, who owned the Hacienda. He ran the New Frontier profitably until his death in 1964, at which time his rights reverted to the estate executors. The casino again closed through most of 1965; a year later the entire old New Frontier was razed to raise the new Frontier. Just before it opened, in July 1967, Howard Hughes bought it—all 650 rooms, along with the million-dollar sign, 200 feet (60 meters) tall, largest in the world. In 1982, Hughes's Summa Corporation expanded the casino to the tune of $7 million, and finally sold the hotel in 1988. A 15-story, 396-room tower was opened in 1990.

■ THE FREMONT

Next came the $6-million, 155-room Fremont Hotel. Ed Levinson, a partner in the Sands, and Lou Lurie, a San Francisco investor, got together and built the first Strip-type carpet joint and highrise in downtown: its 15 stories made it the tallest building in Nevada when it opened in May 1956. The Fremont used all the Strip tricks—tony casino, gourmet restaurants, and a showroom with big-name entertainers (including a teenage Wayne Newton, who had to be escorted through the casino). At the same time, it addressed downtown sensibilities by incorporating a large parking garage, a local television studio, the telephone company and Las Vegas Press Club business offices.

The Fremont had two unusual characteristics: it sparkled in the sun, thanks to quartz aggregate chips in the outer walls, and employed a cantilevered design in which the rooms were staggered, instead of on top of each other, for support, saving millions in construction costs. The hotel expanded in 1963, using nearly $5 million in Teamsters Pension Fund loans, secured, in *Gambler's Money* terms, "by a traditionally shaky second mortgage in a highly speculative enterprise with questionable backers." The 14-story Ogden Tower had another unusual feature for downtown: an above-ground swimming pool. The Parvin-Dohrman group bought the Fremont in 1966, which led to wunderkind-turned-bad-boy Allen Glick's ownership in 1973. Glick gave the Fremont its famous face-lift, adding the block-long neon marquee for $750,000. After Glick, the Fremont changed hands several times, until the Boyd Group added the hotel to its holdings in 1985.

■ THE HACIENDA

The $6-million, 266-room Hacienda Hotel, at the far southern end of the Strip across from McCarran Airport, opened in June 1956. Like the El Rancho Vegas, the Hacienda was one of a chain of California lowrise motor hotels, owned by Warren ("Doc") and Judy Bayley. Like the Showboat, the Hacienda was and still is located just far enough off the beaten track to pursue its own course along the rocky road of hotel competition. It catered to low rollers and families, mostly from Southern California. Its "Hacienda Holiday" billboards were prominently placed along West Coast highways. A fleet of DC-4 airplanes shuttled customers in high style. A rebate of $10 in play money greeted arrivals. The adult entertainment budget was miniscule, while a go-kart track entertained the kids.

Reid and Demaris, who saw spooks in every shadow, claimed that Bayley was "one of the few owners along the Strip not connected with the underworld. The fact that it (the Hacienda) is known as 'Hayseed Heaven' may have discouraged the boys." Still, the casino itself didn't open for business for nearly a year after the hotel did, while the Gaming Control Board steadfastly refused to license Jake Kozloff, who'd recently sold his share of the New Frontier Hotel—and got into trouble for not immediately reporting it to the Nevada Tax Commission. When Bayley abandoned his quest to get Kozloff licensed in early 1957, the casino finally joined the exploding number of Las Vegas gambling houses.

Bayley was quite successful in Las Vegas for the next eight years, until his death in 1964. The Hacienda, at its peak, owned and operated more than 30 airplanes, running junkets from half a dozen major cities. It boasted the Strip's first heliport. It also chartered a veritable fleet of buses. After Doc Bayley died, Judy Bayley turned into the Strip's female counterpart of Wilbur Clark, attracting continuous media coverage with equal measures of flamboyance, philanthropy, and self-promotion. When Judy died in 1971, the Bayley estate sold the Hacienda to Argent Corporation's Allen Glick, who reigned supreme on the Strip until his decline and fall behind Stardust skimming and Chicago mob revelations in 1976. In 1974, though, Glick sunk $7 million into an expansion of the casino, restaurants (including the exquisite Charcoal Room), and pool area (which remains today one of the most luxuriously landscaped, on a comfortable scale, in town).

Organist-investor Paul Lowden became entertainment director in 1972 and bought 15 points. He assumed total ownership in 1977 at a bargain-basement price ($21 million) from motivated seller Allen Glick. In 1980 Lowden spent $25 million on the Hacienda's 11-story, 300-room tower. In 1983, he sold 25 percent of his stock (800,000 shares) in the hotel for another $25 million. The first Las Vegas casino to go public in many years, the stock sold out in one hour. In 1990, the Hacienda embarked on another major expansion: a 400-room tower addition, and a renovation of the casino, rooms, and restaurants.

■ THE TROPICANA

Here it was, a full 25 years since wide-open gambling was legalized in Nevada, and more than 10 years since the Nevada Tax Commission had been granted policy and procedure powers over the casino industry. Fifteen major resorts amounted to a total investment in Las Vegas of more than $100 million, and already accounted for more than half of the entire state's gaming revenues. Yet, the state Gaming Control Board had been in existence a mere two years. Mob money, and the jungle law of gamblers and hoods, ruled the day. Nowhere was this more evident than in the situation of the last two hotels to be built on the Strip in the grifty Fifties: the Tropicana and the Stardust.

The Trop was the brainchild of "Dandy" Phil Kastel, who'd spent 25 years managing the entire Louisiana gambling scene for Frank Costello, a boss of bosses for the national Organization. Kastel enlisted Ben Jaffe, of the Miami Fontainebleau Hotel, to invest and front for him in the Tropicana. Jaffe held an interest in the recently completed Riviera, and hired the same Miami construction company to build the Trop. On opening night in April 1957, Jaffe had infused more than $7 million, plus another $7 million of other investors' capital (to Kastel's $300,000); licensing had been held up for a year, until Kastel's name was dropped from the application.

The $15-million, 300-room, Y-shaped Tropicana Hotel quickly earned the nickname, "Tiffany of the Strip." Designed as the ultimate resort hotel, like the Riviera, the Trop oozed elegance in a Havana Modern style. Its 60-foot (18-meter) tulip-shaped fountain in the center of a 110-foot-diameter (33-meter) pool stood as a landmark at the south end of the Strip for 20 years. The mahogany-paneled casino was tastefully screened from the lobby by ornamental horticulture, and "Peacock Alleys" from the front desk to the rooms actually bypassed the gaming

tables! The Celebrity Gourmet Room was enclosed by a 150-foot (45-meter) curved glass wall, highlighted by colorful dancing fountains and massive Czech chandeliers.

The genteel calm, however, was shattered a month later, when Frank Costello was wounded in an attempted hit in New York, and detectives found a slip of paper in his pocket with a tidy sum of figures, which turned out to be the gross profits from the Trop's first three and a half weeks of operation. Out went Kastel as *persona non grata* and in came J. Kell Houssels, a powerful downtown juiceman. Housells had earned his stake at a blackjack table in Ely, Nevada, in the 1920s. He then moved to Las Vegas just after gambling was legalized, and had spent 25 years as an owner of the Las Vegas Club, El Cortez, and Showboat before taking on the Trop. He managed the hotel for 10 years, adding 300 rooms, an 18-hole golf course and country club across Tropicana Avenue, and the famous Parisian floor show "Folies Bergere."

The Trop changed hands several times in the 1970s, until heiress Mitzi Stauffer Briggs bought it. She expanded the theater, brought back the "Folies," and built the $25-million, 600-room Tiffany (now Paradise) Tower, which finally doubled the size of the hotel (removing the landmark fountain in the process). However, organized-crime trouble returned a year later, when a conversation among entertainment director Joe Agosto, casino executive Carl Thomas, and Kansas City don Nick Civella was recorded, in which the three discussed duping Briggs and skimming casino cash. (Later, Thomas and Agosto turned state's evidence; their testimony helped convict many Midwestern *capos*, which finally broke the grip of the Chicago mob on Las Vegas.)

Ramada Corporation acquired the Trop in 1979, and immediately redesigned the casino in art nouveau-style, adding the breathtaking $1-million, 4,000-square-foot (370-square-meter) leaded-glass dome and 28-color carpeting. They built a stunning five-acre water park, and the 22-story, 806-room Island Tower. Today, the Tropicana has been returned to its original glory, and once again claims its rightful place among the top three or four hotels in Las Vegas.

(opposite) Famous 4,000-square-foot leaded stained-glass dome ceiling at the Tropicana.

■ THE STARDUST

Eighth, last, and largest hotel to go up on the Strip in the 1950s, the Stardust also possesses perhaps the most outrageous and scandal-scarred history of them all. It all began in the mind of Tony Cornero as a Bugsy Siegel-like vision: to build the biggest resort hotel in the world. Cornero had already survived an incredibly checkered career as a bootlegger, hijacker, rum-runner, freelance spy, gambling-boat and freighter operator, smuggler, and legitimate Las Vegas businessman. In 1955, he launched his hotel company with $10,000 cash and two million shares of stock that he neglected to mention to the Securities and Exchange Commission. He personally sold his stock to speculators and gamblers, mostly in L.A., and bought 36 acres of land right next door to the Royal Nevada (which opened and closed in 1955). He drew up grandiose blueprints, and arranged for contractors, labor, and building supplies. The Stardust began to rise from the desert in that boom-and-bust spring of 1955 across the Strip from the Desert Inn.

But by this time, Cornero was so notorious for his unusual business practices that the governor of Nevada himself, Charles Russell, intervened to prevent him

The Stardust in the late 1950s, after swallowing whole the Royal Nevada next door.

from receiving a gaming license. The SEC, too, began insisting that he subscribe to standard stock-registration procedures. As these and other pressures mounted, Tony Cornero, like Bugsy, began to unravel. By summer 1955, 3,000 investors had contributed $6 million—some of which was quickly dropping into the abyss behind the Desert Inn craps tables. The DI's Moe Dalitz and his Cleveland boys, too, were holding a grudge against Cornero, for building his monstrosity directly across from them. Ironically, Cornero suffered a massive coronary the night of July 31, 1955, shooting dice at the DI! But even death didn't end his troubles.

SEC auditors pieced together the financial puzzle of Stardust, Inc., and found $4 million owed to contractors and suppliers, and no cash. The hotel was half finished. The investors were all finished. To the rescue rode John "Jake the Barber" Factor, cosmetic magnate Max Factor's brother and, according to *Green Felt Jungle*, an L.A. realtor, self-proclaimed philanthropist, stock-swindler par excellence, and Al Capone crony. Factor promised to pay off the 3,000 investors at 34 cents on the dollar, wrote checks for over $4 million to cover construction debts, and poured another $6 million into completing the behemoth.

When it finally opened, in July 1958, the Stardust claimed 1,032 hotel rooms (largest in the world), a 16,500-square-foot (1,530-square-meter) casino (largest in Nevada), 105-foot (32-meter) swimming pool and 20,000-square-foot (1,850-square-meter) casino (both largest in Nevada), and a landmark electric sign (largest in the world). The sprawling Stardust also boasted "Horseman's Park," a rodeo arena with stables and bleachers, the first casino dealer school, and the "Lido de Paris," appearing in the town's largest dinner theater on one of the biggest and most high-tech stages in the world. Donn Arden, the Desert Inn's entertainment director, was hired to import the famous French nude floor show, which necessitated McCarran Airport to set up a special customs facility to process the performers, wardrobes, and equipment. The show opened the same day as the hotel, and has been playing there ever since; more than 25 million people have seen the "Lido." In 1959, the Stardust absorbed the rusting Royal Nevada next door, adding 300 rooms and a convention center.

Factor was widely suspected to be a mere front for the Chicago organization, bossed by the notorious Sam Giancanna. Moe Dalitz's group leased and operated the gigantic casino for 10 years, then sold it to Parvin-Dohrmann Corporation which also had a bad rep with the SEC for stock manipulation. In 1968, when Howard Hughes cast his wanton gaze toward the Stardust, he already owned five

(top) The Landmark has more than one cross to bear. (bottom) Fantasy, climax, neon—the Stardust sign says it all.

(top) The Golden Nugget—downtown's original carpet joint. (bottom) Julius Caesar, hailing a cab.

casinos, and the Stardust's sale to Hughes was enjoined by the Justice Department as monopolistic. That same year, Ad Art of L.A. installed the brilliant Stardust sign: 188 feet (57 meters) high, with each letter between 18 and 22 feet (5 to 7 meters) tall and the name nearly 100 feet (30 meters) across, 286 multicolored stars, and 27 different lighting sequences. The Stardust sign is to the Strip what Vegas Vic is to downtown: Las Vegas's most enduring and representative images.

Allen Glick's Argent Corp. purchased the Stardust in 1974 from Recrion, an offspring of Parvin-Dohrmann, as part of a four-hotel deal using $70 million in Teamsters Pension Fund loans arranged by fixer Allen Dorfman. Glick, a Vietnam vet, graduated from Ohio State and went on to law school, and was a member of the Pennsylvania and California bars. He was all of 34 years old when he fronted the Recrion-Argent deal, which made him the second largest casino owner in Las Vegas. But a massive skimming operation on his properties was uncovered by the audit division of the Gaming Control Board. This revealed the Chicago-Midwest underworld's continuing interest in Argent's hotels, and insured that Glick's "era" in Las Vegas was short-lived. His license was suspended in 1979, and he later turned state's evidence to avoid prosecution.

The Stardust (and Fremont) were soon sold to Al Sachs of Trans-Sterling Corporation. Sachs had managed the Sundance Hotel (now Fitzgerald's) downtown, which was owned by Moe Dalitz. But the Stardust's troubles still were not over. In 1983, another raid exposed a phony fill-slip skim scheme perpetrated by four executives. Finally, in 1985, the Stardust was sold to the highly reputable Boyd Group, where it remains, along with two Sam's Town hotels, the Fremont and California hotels downtown, and the Eldorado in Henderson. Through the years, the Stardust only expanded once, when it added a nine-story, 176-room tower in 1965. But it is currently erecting a new 32-story, 1,500-room addition, which will give the now-respectable hotel a respectable 2,300 rooms.

■ THE ALADDIN

The Aladdin started out as the Tally-ho in 1963, a large motel which billed itself as the first non-gaming resort on the Strip. It was an idea whose time had not yet arrived, and it folded after eight months. When the Tally-ho reopened in 1964, it was called the King's Crown, which lasted six months. Finally, Milton Prell, the congenial L.A. investor who sold the Sahara to Del Webb a few years before, bought the property for $16 million in the fall of 1965. He added a casino, 500-seat showroom, lounge, and gourmet restaurant, and completely refurbished the rooms. Prell succeeded in completing the new Aladdin in a miraculous three months, in order to open on New Year's Day, 1966. Aladdin's Magic Lamp—15 stories high, 40,000 lightbulbs, $750,000—fronted the new Strip resort. Elvis and Priscilla were married in Prell's private suite in 1967.

Prell suffered a stroke not long after the famous wedding, and the glamour times of the Aladdin started to fade. It was bought in 1968 by the Parvin-Dohrmann group, which also owned the Stardust and Fremont. Continuing to decline, the Aladdin was sold to St. Louis investors in 1972 for a fire-sale $5 million. In 1974, the Aladdin was investigated by both the state and feds for its alleged role as an "R&R center for the underworld." And though a major expansion in 1976 added the 10,000-seat Theater for the Performing Arts (now the Aladdin Theater) and a 20-story highrise, two years later hotel executives were convicted of conspiring to allow hidden interests to profit from the property. In March 1979, the Gaming Control Board closed the Aladdin.

A year later, Wayne Newton and Ed Torres reopened it; the partnership failed, and Newton sold out quickly. Further legal and financial troubles plagued the hotel, which finally went bankrupt in 1984. In October 1985, Ginja Yasudi bought the Aladdin for $51.5 million in cash, and it has been in recovery ever since.

■ CAESARS PALACE

Of all the hotels in the world, Las Vegas's Caesars Palace is one of, if not *the*, most famous. And rightly so. Simply put, the fact that Caesars has so much to recommend it as an international tourist attraction and destination might explain why Steve Wynn felt he had to spend $650 million to put a hotel next door.

(top) Three of Caesars's huge "hairem." (bottom) Centurion! Which way to Cleopatra's Barge?

Start from the 20-foot (6-meter) statue of Caesar, hailing a cab, at the driveway to the main entrance. Beyond, 18 fountains spew 35-foot-high (10-meter) columns of water, and 50-foot-tall (17-meter) Italian cypresses guard the long approach to the front doors. Pause at the four-faced and eight-armed Brahma nearby to light some incense and kneel in meditation on the prayer cushions. This is a replica of one of Thailand's most popular shrines. The original was cast in 1958 to ward off bad luck after various disasters had befallen the Erawan Hotel in Bangkok during construction. Las Vegas's four-ton Brahma—cast in bronze, plated in gold—was presented as a gift to Caesars Palace in 1984 by a Thai tycoon to promote good fortune and prosperity for the hotel and its guests.

A statue of Apollo fronts the $2.5-million, domed World of Caesar, which houses a miniature Roman city presented in "simulated holography" (a three-dimensional video projection) and laser-powered sound. The central people mover, one of three from the sidewalk to the casino, carries you to your every fantasy. Once inside, wander through the new Roman Forum casino with its $100 slot machines, fed by specially minted tokens of 10-karat gold and pure silver plate. Stroll past Cleopatra's Barge dance lounge, and a replica of Michelangelo's "David": 18 feet (5 meters) high, 9 tons, 10 months to carve, and uncircumcised—one of the greatest artistic misrepresentations in history! In the boutiques along the Appian Way you can fantasize about how you might spend a Quartermania jackpot. Definitely make it a point to peak into the Bacchanal, Empress Court, Palace Court, and Primavera restaurants, and check out the Garden of the Gods pool area, modeled after the Pompeii baths with 8,000 inlaid tiles imported from Carrara, Italy, and all 243,000 gallons (920 kiloliters) of water filtered through the cleansing system every four hours.

Conventional history gives the credit for Caesars Palace to Jay Sarno, hotel builder and owner of the Cabana Motor Inn chain (though Ed Reid, in *Grim Reapers*, reports it a little differently). The $25-million hotel received Teamsters Pension Fund financing, and opened in August 1966, with 680 rooms in a crescent-shaped, 14-story tower, the Bacchanal restaurant, and the 1,200-seat Circus Maximus Showroom. In September 1969, the hotel was bought by Lum's Corporation, which owned a chain of 440 restaurants around the country. In 1970 the 14-story, 222-room Centurion Tower was added, along with Cleo's Barge and the Ah So Japanese restaurant. An expansion in 1974 incorporated the 16-story, 361-room, $16 million Roman Tower, and another in 1979 added the 600-room, $47-million

SPEEDY CHECK-OUT
DEPOSIT HERE

Olympic Tower. Behind the big two-story windows of the Olympic Tower are 10 two-story, two- to four-bedroom suites, complete with sunken tub, round beds, and giant wet bar, as enjoyed by Tom Cruise and Dustin Hoffman in *Rainman*.

Another $20-million expansion in 1985 opened the spectacular Race and Sports Book, with 21 video screens, one of them 19 by 26 feet (6 by 8 meters). In 1989, to compete for street trade with the new Mirage next door, another people mover was added on the north end of the property, a hop and skip from where the Mirage's people mover moves people back from the hotel to the sidewalk. A large parking structure was also built in the rear. A new mall, the Forum at Caesars, is scheduled to open in 1991: 90 stores, 875,000 square feet (81,300 square meters), with gondolas plying artificial lakes, at a total cost of $100 million.

One final note: the hotel's name was the object of one of the great all-time editorial decisions over the use of an apostrophe. After critical consideration and long deliberation, the possessive apostrophe in "Caesar's" was purged because, instead of implying that the hotel belonged to a single Caesar, Jay Sarno "wanted to create the feeling that everybody in the hotel is a Caesar." Whether the punctuation is correct or the gender inclusive is academic. The main thing at Caesars is to feel like a Roman emperor.

■ CIRCUS CIRCUS

The success of Caesars apparently went to Jay Sarno's head. Two years after his Palace coup, in 1968 Sarno opened Circus Circus across from the Riviera. Unlike the Tally-ho, the hotel without a casino, Circus Circus was a casino without a hotel. It *did* have elephants, acrobats, clowns, trapeze and high-wire performers, popcorn and peanuts—and an admissions charge! No lie. Unless you had a local ID, *you had to pay to get in to gamble.* Needless to say, Circus Circus struggled for several years. And though Sarno did manage to build a 15-story, 400-room tower in 1972, in 1974 he finally sold out to William Bennett, an Arizona furniture mogul and Del Webb casino executive. Bennett's arrival triggered Circus's meteoric rise to the top of Las Vegas's profitable properties.

One year after Bennett took charge, a 15-story, 395-room tower was added. In 1979, Circus acquired Slots-A-Fun next door and added its 421-space RV park in back. In 1980 it added five three-story motel buildings and a year later acquired

(previous pages) The front desk at Vegas World.

BLACKJACK UNDER THE BIG TOP

The Circus Circus is what the whole hep world would be doing on Saturday night if the Nazis had won the war. This is the Sixth Reich. The ground floor is full of gambling tables, like all the other casinos . . . but the place is about four stories high, in the style of a circus tent, and all manner of strange County Fair/Polish Carnival madness is going on up in this space. Right above the gambling tables the Forty Flying Carazito Brothers are doing a high-wire trapeze act, along with four muzzled Wolverines and the Six Nymphet Sisters from San Diego. . . . So you're down on the main floor playing blackjack, and the stakes are getting high, when suddenly you chance to look up, and there, right smack above your head is a half-naked fourteen-year-old girl being chased through the air by a snarling wolverine, which is suddenly locked in a death battle with two silver-painted Polacks who come swinging down from opposite balconies and meet in mid-air on the wolverine's neck. Both Polacks seize the animal as they fall straight down toward the crap tables—but they bounce off the net; they separate and spring back up toward the roof in three different directions, and just as they're about to fall again they are grabbed out of the air by three Korean Kittens and trapezed off to one of the balconies.

This madness goes on and on, but nobody seems to notice.

—Hunter S. Thompson, *Fear and Loathing in Las Vegas*

the Silver City across the Strip. In 1983, Bennett took the company public. Three years later the 29-story Skyrise Tower was added. From $189 million in sales in 1984, Circus jumped to nearly $600 million in 1989, with more than $100 million in gross profits. These have helped Circus's empire expand: a sister hotel in Reno, two properties in Laughlin, and the 4,000-room Excalibur, now the largest hotel in the world.

Today, Las Vegas's Circus Circus runs at nearly 100 percent occupancy year-round, and *over* 100 percent during high seasons (by reselling rooms cancelled past refunding time). It has been called the K-mart of casinos. Or, in the words of reporter Tom Dunkel, Circus Circus Enterprises has come up with a "kind of corporate twist on the Frankenstein fable—putting the brain of a McDonald's franchise owner into the body of a casino comptroller." Circus features low table limits, nearly 3,000 slot machines, one of the cheapest buffets in town (the hotel claims to lose 50 cents on every buffet meal served), and a midway for the kids, with every dime-tossing, quarter-pitching, ball-rolling, hoop-ringing, clown-drenching, camel-chasing, milkcan-drowning, and rubber-chicken-propelling carnie come-on known to man. The circus acts are presented continually throughout the day and evening—all of which make the place less a circus and more a zoo!

■ THE LANDMARK

The Landmark's original plan was a 14-story circular tower, its top three floors a wide dome suspended in space. With a $3.3-million loan from Whirlpool Corporation's finance company, builder Frank Carroll, originally from Kansas City, broke ground for the Landmark Hotel on a corner of Paradise Road across from the new Convention Center in 1961. But by early 1963, Carroll, who wanted to erect the tallest building in Nevada, had entered into a skyscraper war with the Mint tower downtown, and Whirlpool cut off his credit. The Landmark sat, a half-finished shell, for the next three years. The bottomless Teamsters Pension Fund fronted another $5.5 million in summer 1966 to finish the hotel. Completed, it stood 31 stories, a full 7 feet (2.3 meters) taller than the Mint. By then, however, Carroll and his partners had long since run out of cash and credit, and again the Landmark was reduced to white-elephant status. To add insult to injury, the Gaming Commission rejected Frank Carroll's application for a license in late 1967. The hotel immediately went up for sale.

More than three dozen creditors were owed nearly $6 million. Principal and interest from the Teamsters' loans had reached nearly $9 million. And Carroll and his partners had to be paid $2 million. Luckily, Howard Hughes was still on a spending spree, and he saw the opportunity to acquire his sixth gaming establishment. Hughes made an offer of $17.3 million cash, so generous that the federal antitrust regulators, who recently nixed the sale to Hughes of the Stardust, could scarcely refuse. In January 1969, they approved the sale.

The opening date was set for July 2, 1969. The whole hotel had to be finished and refurnished, hundreds of employees hired, gaming and liquor licenses approved, vendors contracted, acts booked, even escrow closed. Hughes reportedly dropped another $3.5 million preparing the hotel for its grand opening. To further increase the urgency, Hughes's arch-rival Kirk Kerkorian planned to open his 1,500-room, $60-million International Hotel, across Paradise Road, a day later.

Both hotels opened over July 4th weekend. Danny Thomas headlined in the 31st-floor Top o' the Landmark, with a panoramic view of the city. Thomas attracted a good crowd, though Hughes could easily have saved a lot of money, and rounded up half of Nevada, by simply showing up himself! For all the grand-opening excitement, however, the Landmark immediately went back into decline, losing an estimated $5 million in the first week of operation. Summa adopted a policy of benign neglect, and finally sold it in 1978 to three small-time operators.

Since then, the hotel has not expanded, it's changed hands several times, and has rarely been profitable. The latest saga began in 1983 when the Landmark was bought by Bill "Wildman" Morris for $20 million. In early 1990, the hotel filed Chapter 7 bankruptcy liquidation, with debts totaling $35 million. At press time, the Landmark was about to be sold to an undisclosed buyer for $35.5 million.

■ THE INTERNATIONAL

Kirk Kerkorian was born in 1917 in California's San Joaquin Valley, the fourth of four children of an Armenian farmer and landowner. But when Kirk was five years old, his father went broke and moved the family to teeming Los Angeles. Kirk grew up by his wits, selling newspapers, caddying, amateur boxing, and doing a stint in the Civilian Conserva-

(below) Hughes's Landmark and Kerkorian's International opened during the same weekend in 1969.

tion Corps. His first entrepreneurial venture was steam-cleaning engines for used-car dealers. Though the steam-cleaning failed, he succeeded in used-car dealing, which revealed the keen talent that would eventually elevate Kerkorian's bankroll to nine digits: horse trading. At another job, working for an oil-burner company, a fellow employee who was a private pilot introduced him to what would become his second great skill: flying. Kerkorian quickly earned his private pilot's wings, became a flight instructor in the early 1940s, and then went to work for the British Royal Air Force, ferrying airplanes from their North American manufacturers to England for the war effort.

After the war, he went into business buying and selling military surplus airplanes. In 1947, he bought the Los Angeles Air Service, one of a number of charter flying companies that offered non-scheduled flights around the country for a fraction of the fares charged by the major airlines. It was then he began flying charters to Las Vegas, and behaving like a high roller at the blackjack and craps tables. In *Kirk Kerkorian, An American Success Story*, Dial Torgenson describes the fierce competition and hand-to-mouth existence of the 150 post-war "non-sked" airlines as "part jungle and part comic-strip adventure." Kerkorian's was one of only a few that were successful, thanks to supplementing his uncertain income from the air-charter business with his shrewd used-airplane dealings. In 1962, Los Angeles Air Service became the first non-sked to put a jet, a DC-8, into operation. By then, the company had been renamed Trans-International Airlines.

In the mid-1960s, Kerkorian sold TIA to Studebaker, and later bought it back at a profit. He then sponsored a public stock offering in the company, which he merged with TransAmerica Corporation. He leveraged that to become the major stockholder in Western Airlines. By then Kerkorian was worth hundreds of millions. In one deal, for example, he bought property on the Las Vegas Strip for less than a million dollars, and leased it to Jay Sarno for his Caesars Palace. After collecting $4 million in rent in Caesars' first two years, Kerkorian sold it to the owners for another $5 million.

In 1967, he bought 82 acres (34 hectares) on Paradise Road, a few blocks east of the Strip, next to the Convention Center, for a new pet project: building the International, largest hotel in Las Vegas. That same year, he also bought the Flamingo, which he used as a "hotel school" to train the International's staff. The sale finally eliminated the 20-year, behind-the-scenes involvement of the eastern underworld in the Flamingo.

The International was big news in Las Vegas. It was several hundred rooms larger than the Stardust, which had been the biggest for 12 years. It was designed as a single unit, as opposed to the "tacked-on towers and leap-frogging cubes of rooms" of the other Strip properties. All $60 million of the construction costs were borne by Kerkorian himself. The hotel opened on July 3, 1969, with Barbra Streisand appearing in the 2,000-seat theater, a packed 30,000-square-foot (2,780-square-meter) casino (largest in Las Vegas), a Benihana of Tokyo hibachi restaurant, and a $25 million yearly payroll for 3,000 employees.

Elvis Presley made his great Las Vegas comeback at the International during opening month (and performed there exclusively until his death in 1978). But Kerkorian quickly left all the hotel ballyhoo behind. As soon as it was up and running, the financier was off on a new venture: buying Metro-Goldwyn-Mayer Studios. While distracted by Hollywood, however, Kerkorian's emerging Las Vegas empire was caught short by unforeseen events. The recession of the early 1970s was gaining steam, and the SEC, due to the controversy surrounding the Flamingo, disallowed a public offering of stock in the International, which would have paid off the hotel's debt in full. Kerkorian was unable to produce old financial records, which the feds needed to bolster its skimming case against past owners. Thus deprived of expected revenues, in 1970 Kerkorian was forced to sell part of the International to Hilton for $21.4 million, less than half of what the stock was worth. One year later, he received another $31 million for the Flamingo and the rest of the International, renamed Las Vegas Hilton. In 1973, a new 1,500-room wing was added, giving the Hilton more than 3,000 rooms, and making it one of the largest hotels in the world. It remained the largest in Las Vegas for 16 years, until the Flamingo Hilton surpassed it, with 3,500 rooms, in March 1990.

■ THE MGM GRAND

But Kirk Kerkorian wasn't through with Las Vegas. Not by a long shot. As controlling stockholder of MGM Studios, only a year after selling his two hotels he unveiled company plans to build a hotel even larger than the Hilton. The Grand Hotel was named after the 1932 movie of the same name, and designed to spotlight great movie events, personalities, and legends. The property, on the corner of Flamingo Avenue and the Strip, was originally occupied by the Bonanza Hotel, a

$2.5-million, 160-room sawdust joint that, facing the Dunes, the Flamingo, and Caesars Palace, lasted a surprisingly long three months. Closed for a year, it was bought, reopened to marginal success, then closed again. Through a series of complicated legal, corporate, real estate, and financial maneuvers involving MGM stock, Kerkorian's personal portfolio, and even the money of the still-ubiquitous Moe Dalitz, the studio acquired the Bonanza and some adjacent property in 1971. They closed the casino, managed the hotel as a training facility, and began construction in June 1972 on the mammoth, L-shaped, 2,100-room, 26-story, 4,500-employee, $120-million Grand Hotel. Eighteen months later, in December 1973, it opened—with the world's largest casino, a 2,200-seat jai alai *fronton*, and the third-largest shopping mall in the state.

To finance hotel construction, Kerkorian's MGM Board of Directors had divested itself of almost all the studio's production facilities and employees, to the vociferous objections of some stockholders. Once again, Kerkorian's gamble paid off: in 1974, MGM earned a record $29 million in profits, $22 million of which were from the Grand.

In September 1980, the Grand added a second, 800-room wing, at the south end of its parking lot. On November 21, 1980, the worst disaster ever to strike a Las Vegas hotel occurred at the Grand, when fire erupted in one of the kitchens. Before it was brought under control, the whole main wing had been engulfed by flames or smoke. Seven hundred people were injured. Eighty-four died. Refurbished, the Grand opened again nine months later, in July 1981.

In 1985, Bally Corporation bought the hotel for $550 million, $110 million of which was earmarked for settling the unresolved lawsuits from the fire. But Kerkorian isn't through with Las Vegas. Not by a long shot. In 1988, he bought the Sands and the Desert Inn, then sold the Sands. In 1990 he bought the Marina Hotel, in back of which the *new* MGM Grand, all 5,000 rooms of it, is scheduled for completion in 1992.

■ AND THE HOTELS JUST KEEP ON COMING

In 1970, the 238-room Royal Las Vegas (now the **Best Western Royal**), opened on Convention Center Drive near the corner of the Strip with 238 rooms, same as it has today. A year later, Sam Boyd built downtown's largest (at that time) hotel,

(previous pages) Circus Circus's Excalibur Hotel under construction in March 1990.

the $20-million, 500-room, 22-story **Union Plaza**, at 1 Main Street, site of the 1905 railroad auction where modern Las Vegas was born. Appropriately, the back of the building overlooks the Union Pacific yards, while the front stares right down the throat of Glitter Gulch. A 26-story, 526-room tower was added to the Union Plaza in June 1983. The swimming pool from the original construction was replaced by the Centerstage Restaurant, in a glass dome which commands a front-row view of the "garden of neon."

In 1972, Holiday Inn came to town, in the form of the 1,000-room **Holiday Hotel**, next door to the Flamingo. A 35-story, 734-room tower was completed in December 1989, making it the largest Holiday Inn in the world. In 1990, a major facelift transformed the Holiday into a 450-foot-long (37-meter) Mississippi riverboat. Its 80-foot-diameter (24-meter) paddlewheel, 85-foot-tall (26-meter) stacks, and gangways, crow's nest, and pilot room have earned the hotel the nickname, "Ship on the Strip."

In 1975, the **Continental Hotel** opened, on the corner of Flamingo Avenue and Paradise Road. It has expanded once, to its present 400 rooms. Also that year, the Boyd Group opened the $10 million, 12-story, 325-room **California Hotel** downtown on Ogden Street. Like Benny Binion, Jackie Gaughan, Moe Dalitz, and J. Kell Houssels, Sam Boyd is a beloved pioneer of the Las Vegas gambling industry. He started out as a carnie, then worked at bingo clubs in Southern California in the 1930s. He dealt cards and craps on the offshore gambling boats, then moved to Hawaii as a bingo-parlor operator from 1934-40. He relocated again to Las Vegas and, starting with bingo parlors downtown, worked his way up to an executive position at the Sahara, and later the Mint. He went on to build the Union Plaza in 1971, and formed the Boyd Group, chaired by his son Bill, in 1975. The Boyd Group is a "large family business," whose 60 stockholders were handpicked from among friends and associates, mostly Las Vegans, and has a reputation for its enlightened employee policy. The California started out with a So.-Cal. theme— Long Beach Lounge, Balboa Bay Bar, and Santa Barbara Buffeteria—and now attracts a large Hawaiian clientele. The Boyd Group subsequently opened Sam's Town in 1979, Sam's Town Laughlin in 1984, and acquired the Fremont and Stardust in 1985.

Also in 1975, the **Marina Hotel** held its grand opening on the Strip just north of Tropicana Avenue. It began with 870 rooms, 165 of them in a motel building already occupying the property. The lowrise was subsequently knocked down for a parking lot, leaving the Marina with 705 rooms in the 14-story tower—one of the few hotels in Las Vegas to have actually shrunk in size. Kirk Kerkorian bought the property in early 1990, and renamed it the **MGM Marina**.

The **Maxim Hotel** opened in 1977 with 400 rooms; another 400 were added in 1980. Also in 1977, the **Golden Nugget** finally became a hotel. After nearly 30 years as one of downtown's major casinos, the Nugget, under the direction of Steve Wynn, opened an $18-million, 579-room tower. Steve Wynn first visited Las Vegas in 1952, at the age of 10, with his father, an East Coast bingo operator and compulsive gambler. The younger Wynn graduated from University of Pennsylvania in 1963 a few months after his father's death, and took over the Baltimore bingo parlor. In 1967, he moved to Las Vegas and was quickly taken under wing by E. Parry Thomas, juiciest banker in town. Wynn bought and sold Strip real estate and a liquor distributorship, then acquired 100,000 shares of Golden Nugget stock in 1972. Within a year, at the age of 31, he controlled the Golden Nugget. In 1978, he built the Golden Nugget in Atlantic City, which he sold in 1987. Two

highrise extensions in the 1980s gave the Las Vegas Nugget nearly 2,000 rooms, largest in downtown, with an amazing two full blocks of rooms, plus a quarter-block-long parking structure. Today, Wynn is possibly Las Vegas's top celebrity owner, especially after opening the monumental Mirage on the Strip in 1989.

The ranks of Las Vegas hotels were greatly increased in 1979. **Sam's Town** opened out on Boulder Highway, and the **Barbary Coast** grafted itself onto the famous corner of Flamingo and the Strip, between the Flamingo and the MGM Grand. It opened with a classy casino and 150

Powder room sign at the classy Barbary Coast.

rooms; another 50 rooms were added in 1983, when the fourth floor of the parking garage was turned into the first floor of hotel rooms. On the other side of the Flamingo, the Flamingo Capri Hotel became the **Imperial Palace**. Over the years, the IP has undergone typically major expansions; the latest, a $50 million, 19-story, 547-room tower completed in December 1988, raised the count to over 2,000 rooms, and filled all the available space on the 12-acre (5-hectare) site. The IP boasts Las Vegas's only antique car collection. Finally, Bob Stupak's **Vegas World** came on line in 1979, with 100 rooms, at the very northern tip of the Strip. Two additions have added nearly 900 rooms to Vegas World, which pursues one of the most dynamic and energetic advertising campaigns in Las Vegas, and has one of the most unusual casinos. Stupak plans to erect a 1,012-foot (308-meter) space-needle tower, with an outside double-decker elevator and a restaurant on top, to be completed in 1992. That's approaching 100 stories!

Golden Nugget phone.

In 1980, the 33-story, 655-room Sundance Hotel opened downtown. It was built by Moe Dalitz, still wheeling and dealing at 84 years young! The hotel was managed by Al Sachs for a few years, and then Jackie Gaughan for another few, until the Gaming Commission finally forced Moe out of the Nevada gaming business for good. In late 1986, a group of investors who'd purchased Reno's Fitzgerald's Hotel in 1984 assumed the court-appointed supervisorship of the Sundance. They purchased the hotel in November 1987, and changed the name to **Fitzgerald's**. This 400-foot-high (122-meter) hotel is Nevada's highest skyscraper, finally overtaking the Landmark. The Fitzgerald's group purchased Harold's Club in Reno from Summa Corporation in 1988, thereby ending the Hughes era in Nevada, as it had ended the Dalitz era in Las Vegas a year before.

Also in 1980, like the Golden Nugget before it, the **Las Vegas Club** went from a venerable casino, dating back to the earliest days of legalized gambling, to a downtown hotel, by adding its 224-room tower. The **Lady Luck** also became a hotel, with 112 rooms, three years later in 1983. It had started out as a tiny slot joint in 1964, with 18 machines and a hot-dog stand. The east tower, completed in December 1986, and the west tower in July 1989, have given the Lady another 700 rooms. Also in 1983, the **Four Queens** expanded into a major downtown presence. It opened in 1965, and was named for the owner's four daughters. Eighteen years later, the 18-story, 400-room tower was added.

In 1984, the 500-room **Alexis Park** opened, and this casino-less hotel, near the corner of Harmon and Paradise, seems to be an idea whose time has finally come. The 500 suites range in size from 475 to 1,250 square feet (44 to 116 square meters), the smallest a one-bedroom, the largest a two-story, two-bedroom suite with a loft. The hotel's Pegasus Room is one of the top two or three gourmet restaurants in the state. Also in 1984, the 350-room Royal Americana, on Convention Center Drive next to the Royal Las Vegas, removed 140 rooms and became the 193-room **Paddlewheel**, owned by Horn and Hardart, of New York City "automat" coffeeshop fame.

In 1986, Michael Gaughan, son of Las Vegas pioneer Jackie, opened his second "Coast" hotel, the **Gold Coast**, just west of his Barbary Coast on Flamingo across Interstate 15. Starting with 150 rooms, the Gold Coast expanded in late 1987 with another 150 rooms, and again in 1990, with a 10-story, 400-room tower.

In 1988, the 166-room Shenandoah Hotel, on East Flamingo between the Barbary Coast and the Maxim, was purchased by Hotel Investors of Nevada, Inc., and renamed **Bourbon Street**. The Holiday Inn South, across from the Aladdin, was also sold and renamed the **Boardwalk**. And **Arizona Charlie's**, on the west side at Decatur and Charleston, opened with 100 rooms, and is already planning an additional 500.

In July 1989, the 322-room **San Remo Hotel** opened where the Polynesian Hotel had been, next to the Trop on East Tropicana. Already the San Remo is planning another 400 rooms to be completed in early 1991.

In January 1990, the **Rio Hotel** opened on West Flamingo next door to the Gold Coast, with 400 suites, a sandy beach by the pool, and a neon sign that finally, after eight years, beat out the Stardust for first place in the "The Best of Las Vegas" local competition in the *Las Vegas Review-Journal.* The Rio also took first place in cocktail-waitress uniforms. See for yourself.

■ THE MIRAGE

The Mirage picks up, 16 years and roughly 20 hotels later, where the MGM Grand left off. This $650-million, three-wing, 29-story, 3,049-room mega-resort is the first to be built from scratch since 1973, and officially inaugurates a $3-billion construction boom heard round the world. All of Las Vegas's roaring history combined perhaps hasn't made a noise louder than the one now butting up against the sound barrier. But leave it to Las Vegas to kick it off with a Mirage.

Has anybody not heard about the erupting volcano in front of the hotel? This show-stopping spectacle, with just a sidewalk between it and the Strip, takes place atop a 54-foot (16.5-meter) man-made mountain, for three minutes every half hour after dark, in which "steam escapes on cue with a serpentine hiss, flames lick at the night, water in the reflecting pool begins to roil, 'lava' magically flows—and pedestrian traffic grinds to a halt." The waterfalls and pools in the surrounding lagoon are fed by 15 20-inch (50-centimeter) pipes, through which 5,000 gallons (19 kiloliters) of water are pumped every minute. A thousand palm trees, grown, uprooted, shipped, and transplanted, shade the scene. Some people even walk inside the hotel after the eruption.

The three-million-square-foot building is fronted by an atrium with a 100-foot-high (30-meter) glass dome sheltering a tropical rain forest. A 57-foot-long (17-meter) aquarium backs the front desk: 200,000 gallons (757 kiloliters) of water, seven-inch (18-centimeter) acrylic walls, $1.2 million. Pygmy sharks warn credit customers against welshing on markers. So do the white Bengali tigers, stars of Siegfried and Roy's "Beyond Belief" show, displayed in a show-biz habitat on the Caesars' side. The hotel can accommodate 10,000 guests, including hundreds of high rollers in 260 penthouse suites. Nearly 6,000 employees make the staff larger than many towns in Nevada. And the electricity used could power a city twice the size of Carson City, the state capital.

Amazing what can be done in Las Vegas with $650 million.

■ THE EXCALIBUR

On the other hand, it's just as amazing what can be done with $290 million. The Excalibur has 1,000 more rooms than the Mirage, at less than half the cost. This

medieval monster, on the corner of Tropicana Avenue and the Strip where the Tropicana has sat in lonely splendor for more than 30 years, is listed in Guinness as the world's largest hotel. Turrets, spires, and a 265-foot-tall (81-meter) bell tower front four 1,000-room tower walls. Two dinner shows in the "arena" feature banquets where you must specially request knives and forks. The King Arthur theme includes music, dance, jousting, magic, even fire-eating. In the Renaissance village, employees dress in medieval uniforms. One anomaly is the Dynamic Motion Simulator, an ultra high-tech film experience, in which hydraulically actuated seats are synchronized to on-screen action. White-water rafts, bobsleds, racing cars, and runaway trains are shot in 70mm at 60 frames per second (twice the normal speed) for the simulated thrill of your life. The other anomaly to this carefully constructed old-world fantasy, of course, is the casino.

■ THE *New* MGM GRAND

Coming soon (1992) to the third corner of Tropicana and the Strip is Kirk Kerkorian's new 5,000-room, $1-billion Grand Hotel and Hollywood theme park. The 115-acre (47-hectare) facility will occupy what's now the Tropicana Golf Course and Country Club, and though it will undoubtedly hold the coveted world's-largest-hotel record for years, it will still add a mere five percent to Las Vegas's total number of rooms.

(previous pages) The volcano explodes regularly outside the Mirage, if the wind cooperates.

GAMBLING—VICE IS NICE

AT THE VERY CORE OF THE GREAT WESTERN PHILOSOPHIES, religions, paradigms, and laws is a crack, a jagged fault line between fate and free will. The tug of war over the two sides accounts for the continually shifting line between right and wrong, good and bad, virtue and sin.

At one extreme is superdeterminism, the belief that *everything*, from whom you marry to reading this . . . next . . . word . . . has already been scripted by the Great Casino Manager in the Sky. A lesser variation on the fate side of the fault line holds that the One True God strictly observes and sternly judges your every move, and rewards or punishes you accordingly. A more interactive interpretation rests with the many goddesses of fortune, cavorting among the deities atop the mythical mountains, all of whom can be influenced by the proper prayers and rites and behavior.

At the other extreme is pure atheism, in which nothing that occurs is influenced by anything other than chance, luck, or choice. Lesser variations on the free-will side involve a God whose critical notice only reflects one's personal morality, or libertine deities whose anything-goes-on-Earth policies are devised simply to promote their amoral entertainment.

The crack separating the two extremes is sometimes thought to be an insurmountable abyss, trapping attitudes on this side or that. Other times, the fault is believed to divide closely parallel lines, like narrow-gauge railroad tracks, which attitudes can follow singly, or switch, or straddle. But the one-point perspective, where the two lines converge, where fate and free will achieve a perfect balance, where V marks the spot, is destiny.

That balance point can be illustrated with the simple sticks-and-bones game played by the Las Vegas Paiute Indians for hundreds of years. Two players faced each other, each with five sticks. One player held a plain bleached bone and a black-banded bone in one or the other fist. The second player guessed in which hand or hands the bones hid. Sticks were exchanged over each right or wrong play. Then the guesser became the holder. This "handgame" combined all the elements on both sides of the crack. Choice, of course, was the name of the game. Intellectual exercise was provided by the endless opportunity to psych out the opponent. The gods and goddesses certainly watched and chose sides, tried to send signals to

THE GREATEST GAMBLER

Gronevelt gambled better than any man he had ever seen. At the crap table he made all the bets that cut down the percentage of the house. He seemed to divine the ebb and flow of luck. When the dice ran cold, he switched sides. When the dice got hot, he pressed every bet to the limit. At baccarat he could smell out when the shoe would turn Banker and when the shoe would turn Player and ride the waves. At blackjack he dropped his bets to five dollars when the dealer hit a lucky streak and brought it up to the limit when the dealer was cold.

In the middle of the week Gronevelt was five hundred thousand dollars ahead. By the end of the week he was six hundred thousand dollars ahead. He kept going, Cully by his side. They would eat dinner together and gamble only until midnight. Gronevelt said you had to be in good shape to gamble. You couldn't push, you had to get a good night's sleep. You had to watch your diet and you should only get laid once every three or four nights.

By the middle of the second week Gronevelt, despite all his skill, was sliding downhill. The percentages were grinding him into dust. And at the end of two weeks he had lost his million dollars. When he bet his last stack of chips and lost, Gronevelt turned to Cully and smiled. He seemed to be delighted, which struck Cully as ominous. "It's the only way to live," Gronevelt said. "You have to live going with the percentage. Otherwise, life is not worthwhile. Always remember that," he told Cully. "Everything you do in life, use percentage as your god."

—Mario Puzo, *Fool's Die*

players, and gambled among themselves. In turn, one's deities were beseeched by chants; the opponent (and his deities) were distracted by insults and jokes and nonsense. Often, the contest developed an intensity, in which the players seemed inspired by a supernatural force, possessed of a powerful magic (probably determined by the size of the stakes). Finally, side bettors had no opportunity to influence the outcome. Somehow these "primitive" desert Paiute hit upon and preferred to play a completely honest and fair game.

A variation of the handgame with teams, however, lent itself to the free-will side of the track. Five players faced each other, two to hold the bones, the other three to guard the stakes. The choices, the psyching out, the distractions, and the magic intensified. Side bets gained a power of their own, and introduced the possibility

(opposite) Sam's Town, Laughlin.

of tampering with the game. Bettors and players could now appropriate the role of the gods by manipulating the outcome. This required a trivializing of divine influence, or a rationalization that the gods would find the cheating acceptable. A secretly rigged game always indicates ungodliness.

A publicly rigged game, on the other hand, always points to providence. Nevada casino gambling, for example, is by all accounts a mostly *honest* game, but it's not a *fair* game. The house makes the rules, and the rules are made so that the advantage remains, eternally, with the house. The odds against the player vary according to the game, but that One True God, that all-powerful, all-knowing, all-controlling Boss Gambler in the Heavens possesses the ultimate instrument: the Percentage. Slavish mortals can pray, curse, apply every superstition on Earth, try to cheat, play with the highest skill, and even enjoy a favorable short-term fluctuation. But in the long run, nothing can overcome the Edge. Because the omnipotent Percentage takes the whole wager when you lose, *and* some spare change when you win. And ultimately, the spare change adds up to the whole wager.

But *all* doesn't have to be lost. What's gained is a matter of choice. For one thing, the odds of the games are well-known and therefore dependable. Since the danger of the Edge is built in, it adds to the challenge of playing and the excitement of winning. So the choice is in favor of the magic over the money. For another thing, losing is actually a very pure and appropriate payment to a God that fulfills, in return, many human desires: arousal, exhilaration, transcendence, color, pageantry, flesh, to say nothing of the potential for unearned income—the joy of a small profit or the ecstasy of a celestial jackpot! Finally, only the weakest can't control how much to sacrifice to this God. The vast majority of players successfully withstand divine determinism with the shield of free will. So whether they're ahead or behind, these millions of minions always walk away winners.

■ GAMBLING THROUGH THE AGES

"Human mortality renders life itself a game of chance," writes Jerome Skolnick. The notion of free will—the risk-taking and unpredictability inherent in existence—has always suited the gambler's instinct better than fate. "In our womb-to-tomb progress we never stop gambling, for we cannot know the outcome of many small decisions we must make every day," according to Alan Wykes. And Mario

Puzo claims, "Gambling is a primitive religious instinct, peculiar to our species, that has existed since the beginning of recorded history in every society, from the most primitive to the most complex."

Exactly when gambling began is impossible to establish. It's known that lotteries—using lots to choose a person for a position, task, or even human sacrifice—were practiced by earliest cultures, as were trials by ordeal, wherein chance outcome decided innocence or guilt. Adam won the apple, but lost the game. Hieroglyphs at Cheops Pyramid at Giza report that Thoth, the god of night, gambled with the moon and won five new days that were added to the Egyptian calendar, marking the transition from a lunar to a solar year. A checkerboard was found in the sarcophagus of Egyptian Queen Hatasu, dating from 1600 B.C.; square ivory dice found at Thebes turned out to be only 25 years younger. God instructed Moses to divvy up the Promised Land with a lottery.

Chinese records indicate that an ancestor of chess was invented by an emperor in 2300 B.C. to simulate war games for young military students. When the Chinese invented paper in 200 B.C., one of the first applications was to make playing cards. The Indian Vedic hymns from 2000 B.C. contain numerous references to the people's chief amusements—chariot racing and dice throwing. Their dice were made of *astragal,* or sheep anklebones, and cheating with loaded dice or sleight of hand was commonplace. In fact, the Vedas include the first-recorded mention of a crooked craps marathon in which the victim, after losing everything else, wagered his wife and lost her, too. The Greek gods shot dice for the universe: Poseidon won the oceans, Hades the afterlife, and Zeus the heavens (they were Zeus's dice).

Chasing the gamblers down through time, of course, were the moralists—religious leaders, lawmakers, social reformers, politicians, behaviorists, sore losers. Egyptians convicted of gambling were sentenced to hard labor. The Greeks had strict sanctions against gaming, which they believed to be detrimental to the integrity of the state. The Jewish courts excluded gamblers, assumed to be automatically susceptible to corruption, from the entire legal system. The Koran specifically forbids all types of game playing (except chess). But successful gamblers in all ages have possessed the qualities—action oriented, risk taking, portable, mobile, ingenious, pioneering—to consistently remain a step ahead of the civilizers and crusaders, one of whom summed it up succinctly: "The urge to gamble is so universal and its practice so pleasurable that I can only assume it must be evil."

ALONE IN THE CASINO,
JUST ME AND MY MACHINE-O

Gaming and Wagering magazine estimates that 110 million Americans gamble, nearly 45 percent of the population. The gross revenue of legalized gambling nationwide in 1988 was $210 billion. (Mario Puzo has calculated the illegal handle at $300 billion a year.) Upwards of 105 million of these people gamble for entertainment, recreation, excitement—to satisfy the basic, primal urge of financial risk-taking for fun and profit. For them, losing is a sensation they can live with. If they walk away from the casino with house money in their pockets, they had a great time. If they left some of their money with the house, they had a good time. But three to four million Americans (65 percent men, 35 percent women) are unable to simply walk away having had a good time. For them, gambling becomes compulsive, an addiction, a dangerous and deadly psychiatric disorder.

Gambling is no longer the vice it once was. Nevada-style casinos have been exported, in the last 15 years, to Atlantic City; Deadwood, South Dakota; Indian reservations; and now several Midwestern states introducing Mississippi riverboat gambling. Thirty-two states have turned to bookmaking with lotteries to generate tax revenues. Sports and race wagering has recently become a mega-business, with 35 race and sports books in Las Vegas alone. Bingo, financial markets, and office pools help make gambling more accessible and accepted than ever. However, public perception of compulsive gambling is 20 to 30 years behind that of alcoholism, for example. Though the ranks of addicted gamblers have swelled in the last few years, serious treatment remains hard to come by, and is often a case of too little, too late.

What makes a group of people turn to gambling for an escape, as opposed to alcohol, drugs, sex, or food, is a matter of endless conjecture. A gambling disorder starts out as a euphoria derived from the excitement of the activity—a more satisfying sensation than anything else these people have experienced. Whether it's the surging adrenaline of a craps game, the hypnotic trance of a video poker slot, or the fast pace and high stakes of a securities market, as long as these people gamble, they're riding the high; stopping means coming down, and they need to gamble again to get back up. The dependence is particularly insidious, since the various house advantages ensure that the longer they play, the more they lose. And the more they lose, the more they start chasing losses. Herein lies the danger signal. Nearly all compulsive gamblers spend their own, and their families', savings. Three out of four sell or hock valuables, and write bad checks. Almost half descend to theft or embezzlement. Finally, in the terminal stages of ruin, despair, fear, and shame, an estimated 20 percent of compulsive gamblers attempt suicide. And only then, if unsuccessful, do most addicts reach a point of seeking treatment.

There are 600 Gamblers Anonymous chapters nationwide, but only a handful of primary treatment facilities (one in Las Vegas). Dr. Robert Custer, considered the father of compulsive-gambling treatment, says that compulsive gambling is the "most under-researched" psychiatric disorder, and the most deadly. "No other psychiatric disorder even approaches" a 20-percent rate of attempted suicide, he points out. Of the 32 states with lotteries, only Iowa earmarks a portion (one-half percent— $762,000 in 1988) of lottery revenues for a Gamblers' Assistance Fund. Ironically, by the time a compulsive gambler is ready for recovery, expensive treatment programs are often beyond his shattered resources. Governmental assistance, so far, hasn't been forthcoming.

In Las Vegas, Gamblers Anonymous meetings are frequent and heavily attended. When asked how she could stay in a city in which she's surrounded by every form of gambling, one reformed addict replied, "I've tried leaving, but elsewhere in the country there's maybe one meeting a week, if that. Here there's two a day, every day. I had to come back to Las Vegas because I couldn't survive without my meetings."

A fool and his money are soon parted.

By the Renaissance, gambling had developed into a highly organized, stratified, somewhat degenerate, and morally ambiguous element of society. Pre-colonial Britain, for example, became gripped by gambling fever as it was transformed from an agricultural to an industrial state, and thus more affluent and leisurely. The English played for dangerously high stakes, which only noblemen and upper classes could sustain over the long run. Besides, gambling was a sensual pleasure—one, therefore, to deny the lower classes. Public displays of enormous wagers in exclusive London clubs were considered *de rigueur* for high society. Men won and lost and lost and won thousands of pounds sterling in single sittings. Bust-out women reportedly paid gambling debts with their honor; the higher the debt, the more deviant the payment. These gambling "infernos" proved to be the downfall of thousands of aristocrats and their family fortunes.

Even the British government turned bookmaker by sponsoring large public lotteries. Smaller private lotteries also raised funds for business, industry, and especially wild, harebrained, entrepreneurial schemes—such as financing the colonizing of the New World. In fact, from 1612 to 1621 the Virginia Company of England relied almost exclusively on continuous lotteries to supply and resupply the Chesapeake colonists—adventurers and gamblers every last one. But then King James outlawed private lotteries, the Virginia Company immediately went bankrupt, and the American settlers had to curtail their idle handgames with the Indians and start thinking about making a living.

■ GAMBLING COMES TO AMERICA

Meanwhile, the moralist Puritans in England were making little headway in their efforts to stem the tide of gambling lust, so they boarded boats, sailed the bounding main, and instilled New England with their morals. Gradually, the colonies divided along lines determined by attitudes toward gambling. Yankees considered all forms of betting to be sinful, while Southerners objected only when wagering was taken to extremes. In his epic survey of the evolution of American gambling, John Findlay explains that to Puritans, gambling was "akin to taking the Lord's name in vain; both were appeals to God to pass judgments on insignificant events." But the Virginians mildly counseled against "offending God by blaming Him for losses, while not crediting Him for gains."

Of course, gambling flourished in many forms from Boston to Savannah throughout colonial times. Horse racing and cock fighting occupied the landed gentry of the South, while card playing and dice games were favored by the common classes of the North. The lottery craze carried over from England barely subsided. Small, personal lotteries, such as the one sponsored by Benjamin Franklin to finance the defense of Philadelphia, proved more successful than large-scale lotteries, such as the one sponsored by the Continental Congress to raise its own funds for the upcoming confrontation with the British. Indeed, the Crown's attempts to regulate colonial lotteries provided a major spark for the Revolutionary conflagration.

Within one generation of the end of the War of Independence, civilization had emphatically replaced the colonial permissiveness of the Eastern Seaboard, and only "genteel" gaming had a place in the states. The Louisiana Purchase from France in 1803 added the enormous "Old Southwest" to American continental territory, and within a dozen years, this western frontier had been penetrated from Louisville (on the Ohio) and St. Louis (on the Mississippi) down to the notorious

OLD GAMBLERS DON'T DIE

Right now, finally, I have "aged out" as the dope addicts are said to do. I no longer really enjoy gambling, but the infantile lust can return. When I am too old for sex, when age withers my appetite for pizza and Peking duck, when my paranoia reaches the point that no human being arouses my trust or love, when my mind dries up so that I will no longer be interested in reading books, I will settle in Las Vegas. I will watch the ivory roulette ball spin, place my tiny bets on red and black numbers and some sort of magic will return again. I will throw the square red dice and hold my breath as they roll and roll along the green felt. I will sit down at the blackjack table and baccarat and wait for my magical Ace of Spades to appear and I will be a lucky child again.

Should I go to heaven, give me no haloed angels riding snow-white clouds, no, not even the sultry houris of the Moslems. Give me rather a vaulting red-walled casino with bright lights, bring on horned devils as dealers. Let there be a Pit Boss in the Sky who will give me unlimited credit. And if there is a merciful God in our Universe, he will decree that the Player have, for *all* eternity, an Edge against the House.

—Mario Puzo, *Inside Las Vegas*

DEGENERATE GAMBLING

The care, feeding, and stroking of the big player extends across the board...By the same token, when a man goes bust, they don't want him to dirty up their carpet. Like little Frankie Polovsky . . . .

Little Frankie was married to a wealthy woman who gave him a white Rolls Royce as a birthday present, and with that kind of a start they decided to drive across the country. When they got to Vegas he lost all their money, sold the Rolls, and came right back and blew that money, too.

It went on like that for two years. Frankie went through his wife's money and, when he sold their house, she left him. He lost that money too, of course, and then went into such debt that his business was taken away from him. "And now," Julie said, "he's in such serious trouble down here that he's like a bum."

"He's worse than a bum," Stan said. "A bum knows he's a bum."

"He has nothing. All his self-respect and everything else is gone. And everybody looks at him like he was a nothing human being."

"And now he's a mooch," Barbara said. "When he had money he was everybody's buddy. Now that he owes all over town, when he shows up at Caesars, they say what's that bum doing here again."

They beat little Frankie for maybe a million dollars and he was around the other day asking to borrow a couple of hundred. "I gave him fifty," Julie says, "and if you want to call it conscience money, how could I argue with you? I don't want to see him around, either. I admit it. I don't want to have to look at the guy when he sinks to where he's asking for ten."

—Edward Linn, *Big Julie of Las Vegas*

gamblers' stronghold of Natchez, up river from New Orleans. A colorful polyglot of cultures—Spanish and Mexican, New England and Dixie, French and English, Caribbean and African—all converged on the recently opened waterways, and contributed various influences to novel styles of gambling on the new edge of civilization: roulette, faro, *vingt-et-un* (twenty-one), three-card monte, poker. The rigged wheels and the fast card games lent themselves to the genesis of a large class of professional, mostly dishonest, gamblers who came to be called "blacklegs." Often working in teams, and thereby advancing a new concept of organized crime, the blacklegs suckered and fleeced all comers. At the same time, gambling operations in saloons and storefronts introduced the concept of public gaming houses to America; their licensing and taxing endowed a certain legitimacy both to

the enterprises and the proprietors. The New World's first prominent and elegant "casino" opened in 1827 in New Orleans.

But within one generation, a substantial migration of settlers to the Mississippi River valley had imported civilization, that time-honored enemy of the frontier fringe elements. Citizens cleaned up the port towns with laws and vigilantism. The famous lynching of five blacklegs in Vicksburg in 1835 triggered a wave of reform up and down the river valleys, forcing the gamblers into motion. The increasingly prevalent and luxurious passenger riverboats provided the perfect new setting for the gamblers' operations. Railroads and the Civil War curtailed steamboat travel after the 1850s, but not before the "riverboat gambler" had spread the new games and practices far and wide along the frontier, and had achieved the near-mythical reputation up till then reserved for the riverboat pilot or the mountain man.

The gold rush to California toward the end of the Mississippi steamboat era immediately attracted, in John Findlay's words, "hordes of sojourners whose restless and acquisitive

Whether on a hotel marquee or in the sign graveyard, luck is always a lady.

spirit came to typify the entire society." The new styles of gambling developed by the blacklegs accompanied the hordes, and were quickly emplaced and refined according to the requirements of the far western frontier. Public gambling houses were prevalent in the heart of San Francisco throughout the 1850s. Clubs were licensed and taxed, the operators and gamblers were known as "dealers," and the games and rituals evolved into a high-volume business dependent as much on favorable percentages for the house as on outright cheating and stealing. But casino betting was only one manifestation of the deeply ingrained high-risk instincts of the new westerners. The wide-open frontier presented many opportunities to gamble and hit a jackpot: mining gold, contesting claims, manipulating stocks, trading property, cornering commodities. Prospectors, miners, speculators, traders, and card players fanned out from the Mother Lode throughout the West, from British Columbia to Colorado, from Montana to Arizona, installing California's trend-setting styles of work, play, law and order, and inherent risk taking. But nowhere was the influence stronger, the connection more direct, than at the Comstock Lode, below Virginia City, in the new state next door.

■ NEVADA—THE GAMBLE STATE

Civilization caught up to San Francisco surprisingly early, at least in terms of cracking down on wide-open gaming. But a new form of public gambling began sweeping through the young city in the early 1860s, which appealed to all classes, ages, and sexes of residents. Over the Sierra Nevada, just east of the California state line, prospectors had located what would, in a very short time, turn out to be the richest place on Earth—the Comstock Lode. The vast silver strike immediately attracted a throng of gamblers—con men, highway robbers, murderers, fugitives, idlers, drunkards, prostitutes, speculators, and lawyers—as well as miners, freighters, traders, merchants, and journeymen. The thousands of claims staked, badly recorded according to vague laws enforced by Darwin's Theory, overlapped to the extent that the Comstock was "owned" in its entirety three or four times over. By 1863, at the height of the initial wildcat boom in Virginia City, why, you could stroll up Mt. Davidson, dig in the ground for an hour or so, post a claim notice with a high-falutin name, print up stock certificates, and be in the silver business! Speculation fever, heavy and sweaty, gripped Virginia City. Deeds were

(top) This lady is waiting—for a jackpot winner at Harrah's Del Rio in Laughlin, or a photographer. (bottom) At Fitzgerald's, Ho Tei, Chinese god of luck, likes his belly rubbed.

discussed, titles examined, claims traded, stocks bought and sold, one vast gamble, all dependent on the fluctuating value of the famed "feet" of Comstock pay dirt. A parade of lawsuits to determine ultimate possession of hundreds of millions of dollars was up for grabs: testimonies were bought cheaply; juries freely admitted to taking bribes; opponents were routinely threatened, slandered, and occasionally eliminated; the distinction between judge and auctioneer was rhetorical.

In order to handle the mining companies' stocks with some semblance of order and law, the San Francisco Mining and Stock Exchange Board was created in 1863. Speculation ran as rampant in the City by the Bay as it did in Virginia Town, especially since the enormous capital required to mine and mill the Comstock metals was supplied mostly by California money markets. Thousands of investors, big and small, clogged the Exchange and even the streets outside, gambling their savings on mining stock rumored or manipulated to be representative of valuable ore rising from the depths of the Lode. Thousands were enriched or ruined daily, depending on the outcomes of explorations, lawsuits, swindles, mergers, bankruptcies, and the like. Indeed, the Stock Exchange provided a similar excitement on the silvery streets themselves, where gamblers invested more according to the market situation in San Francisco than the mining situation in Virginia City.

Nevada became a state in 1864, and the five-year-old legal gridlock was unsnarled by a battery of new and unimpeachable federal appointees—just in time for the first *borrasca* (major bust) on the Comstock Lode. Most of the wildcat operations succumbed, the stock market crashed, and mining in even the largest, most California-capitalized claims was suspended. The small-time quick-buck scammers and lawyers left town, to be replaced by the big-time, big-stakes swindlers and bankers. William Ralston, president of the Bank of California, dispatched William Sharon to Virginia City to gain control of the desperate situation. Both had been born in Ohio in the 1820s; both had started out in the riverboat business; both were gamblers and empire builders. Sharon immediately began consolidating the bank's interests: buying out claim-holders for pennies on the dollar; approving loans liberally and accumulating collateral; exploring the shafts, tunnels and drifts; and conducting numerous and systematic assays. He studied geology, mineralogy, and ore bodies; the hoisting, pumping, and communications mechanisms of the mines and mills; timbering and teaming and transportation; the town's water and gas systems. Driven by determination, plus a natural greed and streak of ruthlessness, William Sharon, by spring of 1865, had emerged as the ultimate expert on the Comstock, the possessor of the big picture, the maestro of the maelstrom.

For the next seven years, "Ralston's Ring" ruled the Lode. Sharon accumulated a huge monopoly of mines, mills, transportation, utilities, and stock. He unearthed bonanzas from the deepening mines, and became quite adept at squeezing the stock market to fleece the gamblers, little or large. Even the swindlers had never imagined such a grand scale. All Sharon had to do, for example, was quietly buy up the stock of an unproductive mine at $10 a share, then plant a rumor of a possible bonanza at that mine. This would drive the price up to exalted heights, when he'd sell it off and fill the vault. Then the vault itself was no longer large enough. In June, 1867, the Bank of California moved into its new palatial headquarters at the corner of California and Sansome streets in San Francisco. The building immediately earned the subtitle, "The Wonder of the Silver Age."

This new style of public gaming gripped the country, west and east. Americans went mad for Comstock stock. The game, of course, was as rigged as a stacked deck, controlled from the inside. Ordinary players in the hundreds of thousands were humbled by the house advantage. The rich got richer. Even genteel society, as it caught up to *this* new frontier, embraced the vast shell game as legitimate. Ultimately, McKay, Fair, Flood, and O'Brien, the "Silver Kings" of the Big Bonanza—gamblers even larger, shrewder, and more poker-faced than Sharon and Ralston—beat them at their own game, and manipulated perhaps the largest stock market boom and bust of all time. In the end, the great gamble of the Comstock Lode left the state of Nevada with such a large and long-lasting legacy that civilization itself, with all its powers, pressures, and practices, could not and has not overcome it.

■ THE GAMBLE OF LEGALIZED GAMBLING

The first territorial governor of Nevada, James Nye, was an ex-police chief of New York City. In one of his first speeches to the new territorial assembly, he proclaimed, "I particularly recommend that you pass stringent laws to prevent gambling. Of all the seductive vices extant, I regard that of gambling as the worst. It captivates and ensnares the young, blunts all the moral sensibilities, and ends in

utter ruin." Dutifully, the assembly ruled that violators of the prohibition of all games of chance were subject to two years imprisonment and/or a $500 fine. The law was promptly dismissed by the vast gambling public, ignored by marshals, and forgotten by legislators.

In 1864, President Abraham Lincoln wanted Nevada to become a state. He needed Comstock silver to finance the Civil War. He needed two additional anti-slavery votes. And he needed to keep a check on the "secesh" leanings of California. The law required 120,000 certified residents, but Nevada had less than 40,000. When Congress voted, the outcome was Nevada one, the law zero. Thus Nevada became a state. Nye remained governor, but a new legislature was elected, which passed a bill allowing wide-open gambling. Governor Nye vetoed it, but the lawmakers overrode his veto. In 1869 they instituted license fees for all gambling houses—of which Virginia City claimed 120 (and one library).

As mining in Nevada declined, then died, during the last two decades of the nineteenth century, the state became more and more dependent on gambling taxes. But with a new and major gold, silver, and copper mining boom at the turn of the twentieth century, revenues from gambling decreased in importance. John Findlay points out that "the return of prosperity in mining enabled the state to afford to follow the nation's progressive impulse. Seeking greater respectability in the eyes of other states, Nevada outlawed gambling in 1910." This time, again, the law succeeded primarily in moving the games into back rooms, turning front rooms into cigar stores, barber shops, and candy counters. Combined with national liquor Prohibition, the laws created a "brotherhood" of drinkers and gamblers. In *Gambler's Money*, Wally Turner writes, "One of the by-products of all this was the creation of a lawlessness in attitude for a whole generation of Americans, and a class of dishonest law enforcement officers and public officeholders such as the nation had never known before."

Furthermore, the state *and* society turned out to be the big losers. Fees and taxes declined, payoffs and corruption increased, crooked games and rigged equipment boosted Nevada's notoriety, and undesirable characters provided the muscle. In 1913 and 1915, the law was watered down slightly to allow social card playing, but matters generally stood pat for another 16 years, until the height of the Great Depression.

It's often been repeated that re-legalizing wide-open gambling was Nevada's answer to the collapse of the nation's economy. But Wally Turner argues effectively

(opposite) Roulette means "little wheel."

that distaste for the system that had produced speak-easies and back-room gambling prepared Nevadans to accept legal gambling. On February 13, 1931, Republican Philip Tobin introduced a bill in the state legislature, which provided for the licensing of gambling houses, and the collection of fees ($25 per gaming table and $10 per slot machine) by the county sheriffs. Licenses could not be granted to non-citizens. Cheating was forbidden, minors prohibited, and applicants had to pay three months' fees in advance. That was it.

Again, Wally Turner: "How is the program to be controlled? Who is responsible for seeing that no cheating occurs. The sheriff? Who keeps the sheriff honest? Where is a provision barring ex-convicts? Who licenses the dealers? Who sees that the gambling house is financially capable of paying off winners? In short, who is responsible?

"The answer. Nobody."

"The legislature of Nevada turned loose a group of professional gamblers on its people and their guests, and then spent the next three decades trying to control them."

For another 15 years, the state seemed content to allow the gambling industry to evolve organically, with no additional taxes or regulations. Those were the days! Exactly like the first few wildcat years on the Comstock. Before big business, the law, and civilization installed their dampers. Gambling was so wide-open that notorious operators such as Guy McAfee and Tony Cornero from Los Angeles, Benny Binion from Texas, and Ben Siegel from New York were handed licenses with barely a question asked. Downtown Las Vegas was almost completely transformed into wall-to-wall casinos, and two casino-resorts occupied the new Strip, with two more under construction. Still, in 1945, when the state finally delegated taxation and licensing responsibilities to the Nevada Tax Commission, the reasons had more to do with the end of World War II and the loss of federal funding than with any squeamishness about a pariah industry or boss gamblers. It finally required the national headline splash of Siegel's gruesome murder in 1947 to shake the state out of its innocent lethargy.

In 1949, the Nevada Tax Commission assumed greater powers in the investigating of applicants and enforcing of stricter regulations; its agents were granted the authority of peace officers. Also in the late 1940s, the downtown casinos and Strip hotels got caught up in a fierce price war. They competed with each other by offering better house advantages and higher limits at the table games, along with higher and more frequent slot jackpots. The struggle for players reached cutthroat proportions. Finally, the operators convened, and agreed to standardize the house percentages.

That clinched it. Las Vegas thereafter would come under increasing control of the state regulators and the casino cartel. Of course, it took another 35 years until all the undesirables had been driven out (or so far underground as to render the point moot). But finally the industry achieved a respectability nearly unknown in gambling history. And today it's a giant corporate numbers game—high volume, quick turnover, and an absolute reliance on the One True God: the Percentage, the P.C., the Edge, the Vig or Vigorish. The omnipotent House Advantage.

■ NEGATIVE EXPECTATION

"Gambling experts estimate that less than one person in a hundred wins money from gambling in the long run. The paradox is that although most people are consistent losers, they continue to gamble over and over and over again," observe Humble and Cooper. Alan Wykes writes, "Gambling gratifies an urge more often sought than material gain. The true gambler is notoriously open-handed. Only professional swindlers and cheaters are motivated by greed." John Findlay adds that Americans "look upon betting as a commodity for sale by respectable retailers, as an experience worth purchasing with losing wagers. The thrills from taking risks become almost as important as winning; the excitement of the speedy games and unusual surroundings makes even the losses seem worthwhile." Concerning the house advantage, Caesars pit boss, Bart Carter commented, "Gambling is considered entertainment, and modern casinos define the house advantage as the price of admission."

Indeed. In 1989, Las Vegas's gross gaming revenues (the "hold") amounted to a little under $3.3 billion; in the first quarter of 1990, visitors to southern Nevada lost nearly a billion. Four billion dollars a year translates into nearly a thousand dollars in profit every second! From whom do the casinos win $60,000 a minute? Losers. How do the casinos win it? Favorable odds. Since the casinos make the rules of the games, they simply give themselves a mathematical advantage.

The game of roulette best illustrates the house advantage. There are 38 numbers on the wheel: 1 through 36, plus a zero and double zero. If the ball drops into number 23 and you have a dollar on it, the correct payoff would be $37 (37 to 1, which equals the 38 numbers). However, the house only pays $35. It withholds 2 out of 38 units, which translates to a 5.26-percent advantage for the house. Now, this 5.26-percent advantage can be looked at in different ways. For every $100 you bet on roulette, theoretically you can expect to lose $5.26. Or, out of every hundred spins of the roulette wheel, you can expect to lose 52.63 of them. Or, you're more than 10 times more likely to lose at roulette than you are at craps, at which some wagers have a half-percent advantage. But don't make the mistake of thinking that for every $100 you carry into the casino you'll only lose 5 bucks. Because your $100 *bankroll* can quickly buy thousands of dollars worth of *action*—with the "vig" taking its nickel from every winning bet.

The house advantage is the single most important concept to be aware of in order to understand the secret behind casino gambling, and in order to determine how much "admission" you'll pay for the various forms of "recreation."

■ WHEEL GAMES

Some form of wheel wagering has been in existence since the earliest "spin the stick" games for choosing contestants, combatants, victims, and the like. The Big Six, or **Wheel of Fortune**, or Money Wheel is one of the oldest carnival games. The Wheel is partitioned into 54 slots of different denominations: 24 $1 slots, 15 $2 slots, seven $5 slots, four $10 slots, two $20 slots, and two slots with a joker, casino logo, American flag, or other symbol. You lay your bet on the corresponding unit on the layout; the odds are the same as the denomination. For example, a $1 bet on the $20 pays $20, and the joker pays 40 to 1. The house advantage starts at a prohibitive 11.1 percent for the even-money bet and rockets to 24 percent on the joker. This explains why most Wheel attendants could compete with the Maytag repairman for loneliness on the job.

In Las Vegas, one Wheel of Fortune, at Vegas World, is notable: 26 feet (8 meters) in diameter, rotating on a four-and-a-half-inch (11.4 centimeters) steel shaft, and weighing in at 3,000 pounds (1,360 kilograms), more than all the other Las Vegas wheels combined. This wheel has a $5 minimum bet, which doesn't affect the percentages but certainly impacts on the expectation! *Do* lose a Lincoln here, though, for the unique thrill in knowingly making the biggest sucker bet in town!

(opposite) The Starship Enterprise-sized Wheel of Fortune at Vegas World.

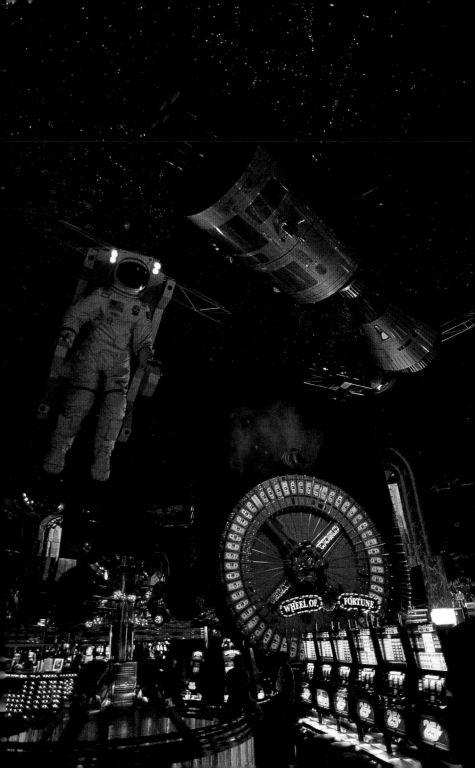

Keno, like the Wheel (and roulette), is a slow-paced, bad-odds, easy-to-learn numbers game for first-timers, suckers, drinkers, long-shot artists, and the walking wounded. This "solitaire bingo" dates from the Chinese Han dynasty, when it had 120 ideograms to choose from. Immigrants brought it to Nevada in the 1860s, where the choices were reduced to 80 and the ideograms were replaced by numbers. Pull up a public school-type desk under the big numbers board in the easily identifiable keno lounge, then simply mark your numbers (one to 20 of them) with the black crayon on the paper ticket according to the instructions in the ubiquitous instruction booklets. Be sure to understand about minimum bets (usually 70 cents or $1) and the variety of tickets (straight, way, and combination).

CASINOS TO SEE

Do you think that all casinos look alike? Or that they all equally cause an advanced case of casinility? Or would you like to sightsee casinos but don't know what to look for? The following are some fine points to enhance your experience of Gambleville.

At the southeast corner of Fremont and Sixth is the original casino wing of the **El Cortez**, built in 1941. The exterior has remained unchanged for 50 years, though the big old sign was added several years later.

When it opened in 1946, the **Golden Nugget** was the classiest joint downtown, with a Barbary Coast motif, carpeting, and large nudes gracing the walls. Since Steve Wynn remodeled the casino in the mid-1980s, it has been returned to its former glory, and is once again *the* elegant establishment on Fremont Street. Don't miss the largest gold nuggets in the world, displayed across from Lillie Langtrey's.

At the **Horseshoe** across Glitter Gulch is an unmistakable contrast between the solid Wild West motif of the early 1950s and the predominant glitz of the mid-1960s. The casino in the original Horseshoe is connected now to the casino in the old Mint via a hole in the wall next to the poker pit. The old wing's wood, brick, and ornate chandeliers clash a bit with the new wing's brass, glass, and flickering lights. But in either casino you can still, after 40 years, place a million dollars on one roll of the dice or deal of the cards. And even if you don't have that kind of money, you can still *see* a million dollars on display in back of the old casino.

The **Lady Luck** has by far the brightest and airiest casino in downtown Las Vegas, with large picture windows lining two sides, and the biggest Big Bertha slot machine you've even seen, facing the corner of Ogden and Third.

The venerable **Las Vegas Club**, Fremont and Main, has the best blackjack rules in the state. You can double down on any two, three, or four cards. You can split and re-split any pairs. You can surrender half your bet on the first two cards. And you win on any six cards that don't bust. Although the card counters bemoan the thin penetration, non-counters are about as even with the house as they'll ever be.

The **Four Queens** casino, on the other hand, receives the highest rating from professional blackjack players. Its single- and double-deck games are dealt right down to the sweet by-and-by.

The **California** caters quite single-mindedly to the Hawaiian market, and this casino has a distinctive aloha vibration. Many islanders stay and play, and the Cal Club Snack Bar serves excellent saimin (noodles) soup, fried saimin, bento, and teri sandwiches.

Circus Circus, with veritable hordes of grinds, tinhorns, low rollers, suckers, and kids, is one of the best casinos in town for people watching.

The **Riviera** across the street is the Strip's equivalent to the Lady Luck downtown: bright, airy, comfortable, friendly—and three times the size. At 125,000 square feet (11,600 square meters), this is the world's largest casino. Fun place to play. Even the single- and double-deck pits reportedly don't sweat the counters.

At the **Desert Inn**, you can easily pretend to be in Monte Carlo, or even Las Vegas in the jacket-and-tie 1950s. Crystal-clear TV sets front the sports book and the bar.

The **Mirage** *casino* is ordinary; getting in and out is all the fun. The race and sports book is the indoor equivalent of the volcano out front.

You can spend at least several hours ogling the internationally renowned **Caesars Palace**, which is, truly, a palace for all Caesars, the Casino of Casinos.

The million-dollar, 4,000-square-foot (370-square-meter) leaded stained-glass dome at the **Tropicana** is the great Las Vegas casino breathtaker. It's suspended on pneumatic shock absorbers to withstand building vibration from the air conditioning; the ceiling remains stationary and the building vibrates around it. The casino is also literally the ultimate carpet joint. Fifty-five-thousand square yards of the 28-color carpet was manufactured on looms found only in a small town in England. Even the neon palms in the slot atrium are amazing.

Tasteful stained-glass signs and a 30-foot (9-meter) Tiffany-style mural, "The Garden of Earthly Delights," set the **Barbary Coast** apart from the madding crowd. This casino, along with **Bourbon Street**, **Maxim**, and **Rio**, are favorites of the blackjack pros.

But by far the most eye-popping, jaw-dropping, crowd-stopping, smile-swapping casino of them all is **Vegas World**. Words fail. Go see for yourself.

According to John Scarne in *New Complete Guide to Gambling*, the range of the vigorish is from 18.9 percent on the 12-spot ticket to 26.4 percent on the three-spot (though the spectrum of best to worst odds can be wider). This all adds up to an average hold of 28 percent. Since each keno "race" takes about 10 minutes to run, this is a good game to play in the coffeeshop, or if you're killing time in a casino, or if you want to rest from other games in relative stress-free comfort, or if you want to drink (cocktail waitresses are usually attentive to the keno-lounge drinkers), or if you're looking for a shot at a jackpot risking only a small spot.

Roulette is French for "little wheel." The invention of roulette as we know it today is often attributed to the French philosopher-mathematician Blaise Pascal, who is also credited with originating probability theory and the laws of perpetual motion. But the forerunners of roulette—called *hoca, boule,* and even-odd—were in use throughout Europe in the pre-Pascal 1600s. The earliest gambling action in Monaco consisted of two roulette wheels in a barn. European wheels utilized (and still do) one zero, which put the players at a 2.7 percent disadvantage; they also offer another concession, called *en prison,* which lowers the casino edge to 1.35 percent.

At craps, you have a manual connection with the primary equipment.

You can make a total of 14 bets on a roulette layout, 13 of which carry a disadvantage of $5.26 out of every $100 bet. You can bet on one number ("straight"), two numbers ("split"), three numbers ("street"), four numbers ("corner" or "square"), five numbers (this bet covers 1, 2, 3, 0, and 00, and has a house advantage of 7.89 percent), six numbers ("line"), 12 numbers ("column" or "dozen"), high or low (1-18, 19-36), red or black, and even or odd. Though you can play roulette with regular casino checks (chips), you can also buy "wheel chips," which come in half a dozen different colors—to differentiate between players. You must specify to the dealer which denomination your personal wheel chips represent, and you *must* redeem them for regular checks before you leave the table.

Countless systems have been in use for centuries to try and beat the wheel: the famous Martingale, which doubles the wager after a loss, and its counterparts Reverse and Great Martingales; the D'Alembert; the Biarritz; Cuban; Cross-Out or Cancellation; Third Column or Perfect; and the Biased Wheel. This last was used successfully by an English engineer named Jaggers in Monte Carlo in the late 1800s. He noticed that a slight inaccuracy in the wheels would favor certain numbers, and he employed half a dozen assistants to watch and note the numbers.

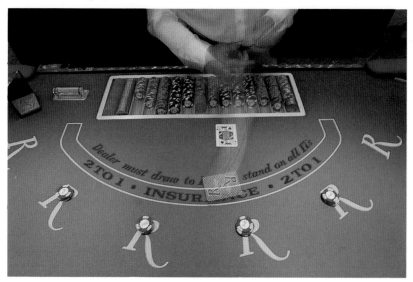

Pitching cards.

Then he analyzed the results, used them as a basis for betting, and walked away a $180,000 winner after five days of casual gambling.

A modern variation on this theme was developed by a group of physics graduate-student hippies at University of California, Santa Cruz in the late 1970s. They undertook to predict the outcome of each spin of the wheel by determining the dozen or so variables that make up the physics of roulette. They wrote a computer program which would analyze the various physical elements of any wheel at any casino, and then project, in two seconds, the quadrant into which the spinning ball would drop 15 seconds later. Then they built a tiny computer that fit into a shoe, which could be programmed and decoded by means of the big toe of the programmer, who would then transmit the signal to the bet placer. The whole scheme, as well as everything else you ever wanted to know about roulette, is covered in *The Eudaemonic Pie*, by Thomas Bass. Shortly after the book was published in 1985, the Nevada Legislature passed a law prohibiting the use of any device that could project the outcome of any casino games—punishable by up to 10 years and $10,000.

Various methods have been employed to "gaff" or rig roulette wheels. Magnets and steel-centered balls have controlled the outcome, as have tiny needles that pop up in all the red or black cups or around the back track to steer the ball toward the zeros. Other techniques include "screening out"—blocking the view of the wheel while a dealer uses sleight-of-hand to switch the number—and the old standby of short payoffs. One of the most prevalent myths of cheating at roulette, however, is entirely spurious: that the dealer can control where the ball will drop into the wheel. Forget it.

Even though the house advantage is 5.26 percent, the hold for roulette tends to hover at upwards of 30 percent. You can see for yourself why this is true by just observing the game for a few minutes. Watch how the dealer marks the winning number of a spin with a pointer, and then shovels in, with both hands and arms, the ton of losing bets on the layout. John Scarne concluded, "The best way to avoid losing at roulette is to stop playing." But most gambling experts simply recommend that if you play for small stakes, you can relax and enjoy the leisurely pace, the pageantry of the wheel and layout, and the history and glamour of the game.

■ SLOTS

At the same time that the San Pedro, Los Angeles and Salt Lake Railroad was envisioning a company town in the middle of Las Vegas Valley, and a French chemist was discovering the illuminating properties of neon gas, a Bavarian immigrant to San Francisco was inventing a machine that would ultimately dominate the Nevada gambling industry. Charlie Fey, the 21st (and last) offspring of a West German family, hit the road to adventure in 1876 when he was 14, winding up in England as an apprentice scientific-instrument maker. In 1882 he continued west to Wisconsin, where he worked on delicate measuring equipment, and dabbled in gambling equipment such as punchboards and wheels. Finally, his restless spirit carried him to San Francisco in the mid-1890s, where the Barbary Coast gambling clubs inspired him to invent the mechanical three-reel slot machine.

The slot's instant popularity created a new industry in San Francisco, and soon slot machines proliferated in the city's saloons. Though some of the machines' gimmicks changed slightly over the years, the basic concept and design (single coin, stiff handle, fruit symbols) remained firmly in place until as recently as the mid-1960s, when Bally's introduced electrical slots with light-and-sound effects, multiple-coin betting, and triple-pay lines. The new machines finally attracted action from participants other than the proverbial "wives of crap shooters and twenty-one players." Still, these quarter slots held a substantial 20 percent of the drop, paying off in sporadic, though sizable, jackpots—perpetuating their reputation as sucker bait. Slots accounted for a minimal 30 percent of gambling revenues up until 1975.

Then dollar slots appeared on the casino scene. Since these machines handled much larger action, they could be set on a much lower hold, starting at 10 percent, and even dropping down to five without compromising the house advantage. (Five percent of a buck is equal to 20 percent of a quarter.) With more frequent and bigger payoffs, slots began to account for higher percentages of the gross (42 percent in 1980), and more space on the casino floor.

But the ultimate transformation occurred, not surprisingly, with the introduction of poker video slots in the late 1970s. Finally, here was an interactive machine with which one could make decisions, play hunches, and have a whole level of enjoyment beyond the "idiot pull." Video poker immediately carved a large class of slot hounds out of local Nevadans, and greatly swelled the ranks at Gamblers

(top) Arrivals lighten their loads at McCarran Airport ... (bottom) but in Las Vegas, it all comes out in the wash.

Anonymous meetings, especially of women, who seem to be having an intense love affair with the machines. Today, video poker is a mainstay in bars, lobbies, supermarkets, laundromats, and convenience stores, in addition to casinos.

In the last several years, microchips have added an incredible variety of slots. Poker comes in penny, nickel, quarter, $1, $5, and $25 denominations; straight draw; deuces, sevens, or jokers wild; and second-chance machines which allow a side bet to draw up. Video keno, blackjack, roulette, even greyhound racing these days contribute to the slot machines' average of 60 percent of casino floor space, and more than 50 percent of revenues, which means more profits for the casinos than all table games combined. Progressive machines, such as Quartermania and Megabucks, are linked throughout the state by telephone modem, and have multiplied jackpots into the millions of dollars, competing with state lotteries. And new models now take tokens worth $100, and rumor has it that $500 machines are on the horizon.

Slots are particularly popular with first-timers, as well as players somewhat intimidated by the fast pace and high pressure of the table games. They're particularly unpopular with old-timers and professionals, who consider them machines to take your money. The main dilemma is that you simply can't fathom the odds against you, which can be anywhere from two to 50 percent. So how do you locate a "loose" slot? First, generally, the higher the bet, the lower the hold. Nickel machines keep an average of 20 percent, quarter machines around 10 percent, dollar machines roughly five. So, depending on your bankroll, play the dollar slots for an increased expectation, and the nickel slots for more action or less risk. Secondly, you might wander, watch, and wait for a slot that looks promising—though it's a myth, a mathematical impossibility, that any slot is "due" for a jackpot. Some people ask a slot attendant or change person for a recommendation. Others believe that machines with a captive audience, such as those near waiting lines for coffeeshops, buffets, or showrooms, are tight, and those near front doors or heavy traffffic are loose. If you see a woman holding a hand up to a machine, she's testing the theory that loose slots literally feel warmer than tight slots! Actually, you *can* pretty much determine, after the first few dollars, if a machine is cooperative or not; trust your intuition! Finally, and probably the most foolproof way, is to be around, usually at 7 a.m., when the hard-count crew empties the change buckets below all the slots. The buckets with the least quarters are loosest!

■ CRAPS

Walk into any casino anywhere in the world and follow your ears toward the locale where humans (as opposed to machines) are making the loudest or rowdiest sound —you can bet the rent money that it emanates from the craps tables. Craps generates the most action and excitement of all casino games, for several reasons. It's extremely fast. Selected bets have one of the lowest house advantages in the casino, and the variety of wagers, odds, and strategies is extremely enticing. Craps is a game in which the players, especially the shooter, have a personal connection with the primary equipment, the magical dice. And it's a *group* game, in which you can bet with or against the shooter, and hot streaks can literally change the temperature throughout the casino. When a new shooter steps up to roll, one who looks like he or she couldn't "make a point with a pencil sharpener," you can bet against. But when the dice keep rolling and the players keep winning and the crowds keep gathering (on both sides of the pit), there's no excitement like it in the casino, the city, and possibly Clark County.

Dice, in one form or another, have been used for gambling for thousands of years. But America's game of "bank craps" evolved from Hazard, a dice game that gripped Europe for a thousand years. Hazard was introduced to Europe in the eighth century by Saracens, who conquered Corsica; from there it spread quickly through Italy, and over to Spain, France, and England. The French word *hasard* derives from the Arabic *az-zahr*, which means "dice." The French also referred to the two spot and three spot as "crabs." Hazard entered the United States through New Orleans in the early nineteenth century and was transformed into a primitive form of "private craps" by Southern slaves. The game spread up and out from the Mississippi River. Around the turn of the twentieth century, a dicemaker, John Winn, introduced the craps bank, wherein the players, instead of betting against each other, bet against the bank. Winn collected a half-percent commission on each bet, and allowed wagers with and against the shooter. Other dice players immediately booked craps games, and additional refinements were made. According to John Scarne, by 1910, bank craps had overtaken faro as the most popular casino game in America.

Craps is a complicated game to learn completely, and the hardest to step up to the first time. Luckily, with only a partial knowledge of the rules and percentages, you can still play an intelligent and exciting game of craps. By making the first and

(opposite) Stickman, boxman, and yo'leven—your odds are almost even at craps.

simplest wager (on the pass or don't-pass line), and backing the bet with odds (usually single and double), you're bucking one of the lowest percentages in the house: .6 percent. (A few die-hard casinos still offer triple odds, with a .4 P.C., and the Horseshoe downtown is famous around the world for 10-times odds, with a remarkable vig of .2 percent.) Simply placing your checks on the "line," you also remain blissfully ignorant of all the sucker bets, while still participating in a fast and fun game.

Other wagers include come and don't come, field, big six and eight, place and buy, and proposition. To fully understand the game, it's necessary to spend a couple hours reading about the bets, rules, and procedures, a couple more hours practicing with the dice and memorizing the odds, and a few more making tinhorn bets at the live action (though preferably at a relatively quiet table) while familiarizing yourself with the well-defined craps subculture.

Craps, like the Wheel of Fortune, keno, roulette, and slot machines, falls under the "independent-event" category of gambling. In plain English, this means that the Wheel, reels, ball, and dice have no memory. Each roll of the bones has nothing to do with the roll preceding it, nor the roll following. The roulette ball simply does not have the capacity to say to itself, "Well, I haven't hit number 23 for 114 spins, so it must be time." The same is true for slots, which immediately dispels a myth in which the majority of slot players, even those who understand gambling theory, believe: that "this machine is *due* for a jackpot." The theoretical odds of a poker slot dealing a royal flush remain the same for every hand—whether it hasn't hit one in a million plays or paid off the progressive total two hands ago. Thus, "systems" at craps, like roulette, are mostly wishful thinking. The craps-systems literature tends to record and analyze thousands of consecutive rolls, instructs how to follow hunches, and describes various money-management strategies, from conservative stakes at a "cold" table to aggressive betting on a long roll. The final word on craps systems was delivered by Nick "The Greek" Dandelos, one of the all-time great gamblers. "The best long-term attack I know of at craps," he said, "is to play the don't pass line and lay the odds. Using that system I've lost millions of dollars."

On that note, a final caveat. In spite of the low house advantage, craps still retains nearly 20 percent of the drop. Why? Sucker bets, certainly: proposition wagers have a 9.09- to 16.7-percent advantage. But also, the game is played so fast and the betting reaches such precipitous elevations with Old Man Percentage collecting his commission on every last check, that you can lose your bankroll faster, though arguably with more enjoyment, than probably any other game in the casino. To ensure the enjoyment, and reduce the risk of ruin, study the odds carefully, and do not deviate from a strict and well-planned betting strategy based on the size of your bankroll.

■ BLACKJACK

If craps is the hottest and most extrovert game in the casino, then blackjack is the coolest and most cerebral. Blackjack is the only game in the casino that has a memory, which means that cards removed from play can be remembered, and cards remaining to be played can be determined. In fact, the house advantage for twenty-one actually changes after every hand, depending on the cards already used. Thus, blackjack is the only casino "bank" game (played against the house) that invites various levels of skill into play. In fact, the house advantage itself is measured against the level of skill which the player brings to the game. Blackjack is the only casino game in which, with enough skill, the player can have an advantage over the house. Consequently, blackjack has been analyzed, computerized, theorized, strategized, advertised, epitomized—in short, *scrutinized*—by a legion of hackers, mathematicians, writers, and professional players down to its last obsessive detail. If craps and slots are subcultures, blackjack is an entire universe.

Naturally, the casinos have a difficult time tolerating a game at which they can be beaten, and at the edge of the blackjack universe, the player-pit relationship has become extremely polarized. Card counters (skilled players who can track the cards and calculate the corresponding advantages and disadvantages at a high speed and degree of accuracy) have been receiving the bum's rush since the advanced and highly effective systems showed up in the early 1970s. But even if you have no interest in casing the deck, a lesser level of skill, known as basic strategy, can be learned in just a few hours of study and practice. Basic strategy reduces the house advantage to near, or even below, the best odds at craps. In a massive study of players and hands conducted during the blackjack card-counting controversy in Atlantic City in the early 1980s, players were categorized as novice, experienced, basic strategist, and card counter. Players using basic strategy bucked an average .5 percent edge, while the best card counters enjoyed a 1-percent to 1.5-percent long-term advantage over the house, with some situations achieving mythical sure-

Some people look down on gambling.

thing status. Novice and experienced (or general public) were at a 1.5- to 2-percent disadvantage. So even if you don't count cards, don't practice basic strategy, and simply know the rules of the game, your expected loss per wager is less than half what it is at roulette.

The origins of twenty-one are as obscure as the origin of playing cards themselves. Some historians trace the symbols on cards back to the eighth-century Chinese T'ang Dynasty, whose paper money used pictures of emperors, princesses, and governors to signify value. The first mention of playing cards in Europe appears in the writings of a Swiss monk in the mid-fourteenth century, and by the late 1500s, a card game called bassette had taken the Continent by storm. Bassette was played with the Italian tarot deck, which consisted of 78 cards in four suits: four face cards in each suit (knight, jack, queen, king), 10 "spot" or numbered cards, and 21 trumps (from the French *triomphe*); this is generally considered to be the direct ancestor of today's 52-card deck. Bassette gave way to faro in Europe by the early 1700s, basically a guessing game as to which cards of the deck will appear next.

Faro made its way to America, as usual, via New Orleans and the Mississippi River following the Louisiana Purchase of 1803. Faro remained the all-time most popular betting game in the U.S. throughout the nineteenth century and into the twentieth; at the time of the Comstock, 300 faro banks were in operation in Nevada. There are as many theories as to why faro had died out in Nevada by the 1950s as there are why the Anasazi abandoned Pueblo Grande de Nevada in the early twelfth century. But by 1963, Major Riddle, then president of the Dunes, reported in his popular *Weekend Gambler's Guide* that only the Stardust sponsored a faro game, between midnight and 9 a.m., and the Fremont ran one for a few hours a day. The Reno Ramada tried to revive faro in 1987, to major indifference.

The French claim blackjack as a direct descendant of their *vingt-et-un*, the Spanish claim the same for their one and thirty, and the Italians consider blackjack to have evolved from their *baccarat*. Nevada-style baccarat is an adaptation of the game *chemin de fer*, or "shimmy," which made its way from Italy to France about the same time that Columbus was making his way from Portugal to Dominica. Originally played in private by only the highest of the French nobility, chemin de fer was already imbued with glamour and exclusivity by the time it appeared in public European gambling dens in the seventeenth century. The Nevada casinos, spearheaded by the Stardust just after it opened, imported shimmy and retained the aura by imposing high minimums, playing with cash instead of chips, segregating the table in a hushed pit off the main floor, costuming the dealers in tuxedos, and employing attractive, dressed-up shills. Recently, in some casinos a minibaccarat table or two have been placed on the edge of the main blackjack pit to accommodate lower rollers. Both versions are played by the same rules—participants bet on which of two two-card hands, Player or Banker, will come closest to the number nine. A third card may be drawn according to the player's total; tens and picture cards are valued at zero. The house advantage for the player hand is 1.36 percent, for the bank, 1.17 percent.

Anyway, French *vingt-et-un* arrived in America right on schedule and swept through the states in the nineteenth century. Modern-day blackjack has been traced to the early 1900s' back-room gambling dens at race tracks in Evansville, Indiana. Here, dealers paid a $5 bonus for a two-card count of 21 when one card was either the black jack of spades or clubs—hence the nickname. Blackjack made its first public appearance in Nevada casinos as soon as gambling was legalized in 1931, and within 15 years had replaced craps as the most popular bank game.

This is all the more remarkable since nobody—casinos, players, gamblers—knew much about the game or the odds. Early blackjack literature reflects this ignorance, and relies, for determining the unnumbered house advantage, on the rule that players draw their cards first, and if they bust they lose, even if the dealer also busts later on the same hand. John Scarne claims to have perfected a form of "card casing" in the late 1940s which effectively got him barred from several unnamed casinos; Scarne's basic strategy for playing blackjack was published in the first edition of his *Complete Guide to Gambling* in 1961. He also figured the house advantage at 5.9 percent (this number has been more accurately calculated to 5.5 percent) if players mimicked the dealer (simply drawing to 17). This could be reduced, he wrote, to 2.15 percent using proper doubling-down and splitting procedures.

But conventional history tends to favor the four Army engineers at Aberdeen Proving Ground in Maryland who played tens of thousands of blackjack hands and produced advanced calculations that determined "basic strategy" for blackjack; their results were published in the September 1956 issue of the *Journal of the American Statistical Association.* Mathematics professor Edward O. Thorp used the results to originate a card-counting technique, and published his notorious *Beat the Dealer* in 1962. The original Thorpe method was extremely difficult to master and implement, and the casinos, though they battened down the hatches and waited for the storm of red ink, actually profited handsomely from the "storm"— of black-ink publicity.

It's been nearly 30 years since the appearance in print of card-counting techniques, and the refinements, by both the counters and casinos, have been extreme. The counting systems themselves have been fine-tuned by the most powerful computers, simulating tens of millions of hands. A dozen or so competing systems have been developed, tested, and marketed. Most are based on a "plus-minus count" in which cards are assigned values of plus one, minus one, or zero, and are added or subtracted to determine the "running count." This is divided by the approximate number of decks remaining, for the "true count," which is used to calculate the amount of bets. Some systems manage to combine the true count with the running count. Others even employ a "side count," for figuring insurance-play odds, for example.

All the while, card counters must be acutely alert to the dealer, who can help or hurt the expectation, depending on his or her attitude. Whole books have been written on card handling: shuffling (zone, stutter, stripping), cutting and loading the deck, tracking the shuffle. Many chapters and essays have appeared concerning dealer "tells" (mannerisms that reveal the value of the hole card), spooking and front loading (glimpsing the dealer's hole card), and cheating (dealing seconds, clumping, palming). Formulas have been written to determine profit expectations (bet times advantage times hands per hour), and proportional bet-sizing methods developed to maximize bankrolls. Table hopping, depth charging, Wonging, single-, double-, and multi-deck strategies, toking guidelines, team play, credit manipulation, and camouflage have all been applied to the twenty-one pit. Every minute variable of the entire experience has been dissected and corrected and perfected—much of it to avoid being detected.

The casinos, of course, haven't been idle in the meantime. Sophisticated detection techniques have been added to the pit personnel's typically intense scrutiny of players, along with tightened security and heightened countermeasures: multi-deck shoes, lowered table limits, unbalanced shuffling, fewer hands between shuffles, intimidation, scrutinized table statistics, dealer resistance, barring, and blacklists. Many casinos feel they're at war with counters. Others are more patient. All casinos are observed and rated by periodicals, such as *Blackjack Monthly*, for levels of card-counting cooperation.

Doubtless, the myriad hoops that card counters must pass through discourage even serious blackjack players. But learning basic strategy is only slightly more challenging than learning the rules and options of the game itself, and can quickly, legitimately, and painlessly reduce your disadvantage from 5.5 percent by mimicking the dealer or nearly 2 percent calculated against the general public to an average .8 percent—without in the least jeopardizing your enjoyment of the game. After all, isn't that what gambling is all about?

SEX, LIES, AND LAS VEGAS

(**Note:** In this chapter, the term "girl" has been selected in an effort to use the least offensive label for women who practice prostitution.)

CASINO GAMBLING IS ACCESSIBLE, ACCOUNTABLE, accurate, and accepted. With books and videotapes, and lessons provided free by the casinos themselves, you can participate in the games, manage your bankroll, and maintain the proper attitude —in short, *play intelligently*—in a very short time. On the other side of the tables, the house advantage, that intractable swindle behind your predictable dwindle, is the worst-kept secret in Nevada. The second worst-kept secret is that sex is nearly as prevalent an illegal business in Las Vegas as gambling is a legal one. But there's one main contrast. The mathematically exact and publicly acknowledged gambling business is inversely proportional to the profoundly enigmatic and unspoken scope of the business of sex in Las Vegas.

■ BLOCK 16

At the turn of the century, red-light districts were common throughout the country. They were confined and adequately policed. By the time Las Vegas was founded in 1905, Nevada's tradition of flesh peddling in boomtowns was nearly 50 years old, as old as the state itself.

Las Vegas's original sex market, known as Block 16 (downtown between First and Second, and Ogden and Stewart streets) was typical. A mere block from the staid and proper First State Bank, the Block was established in 1905 by conservative town planners working for the San Pedro, Los Angeles and Salt Lake Railroad, as the predictable byproduct of the company's liquor-containment policy. Immediately after Block 16 lots were purchased at the railroad auction, two saloon owners hitched their establishments to freight teams and dragged them from McWilliams's Old Town over to the Block—with the working girls trailing right behind. Hastily erected lean-tos were replaced by cribs out back, then by rooms upstairs, all in a "line" facing Second Street. The Block, sleepy and deserted during the daytime, woke up at night, when its well-known vices, gambling and whoring, temporarily banished the dried-up, small-town desolation. When the train pulled in, no matter what time of day, savvy travelers used the 45-minute stop, as the engines were serviced with coal and water, to refuel themselves. This group of men daily huffed the few blocks to the Block for a couple of drinks, a little faro, maybe even a quickie.

In a twilight zone not quite illegal, Block 16 was not quite legal either. In the earliest years, saloons operating brothels were required to buy $500 licenses. Later, regular raids and shakedowns helped finance local government. The 40 or so "darlings of the desert" were required to undergo weekly medical exams; at $2 per, the city physician held a plum position! Law and order were maintained by the steely eyes and quick fists of six-foot-three, 250-pound Sam Gay, the one enduring character from the Block, who went from bouncer to five-term sheriff.

Even with an occasional spirited campaign to eliminate it, Block 16's activities were barely interrupted by the state's 1911 ban on gambling. It also managed to survive the tidal wave of shutdowns nationwide during the Progressive years of this century's second decade. The wave did touch Las Vegas in the 1920s, however, when a grand jury instructed city commissioners that "occupants of houses of ill fame not be allowed on the streets, unless properly clothed." On hot summer nights it wasn't uncommon to see scantily clad women sitting in second-floor windows along the Line while young boys on bikes rode by for a peek. The Block fared well during the tricky years of Prohibition, with booze provided by bootleggers from the boonies of North Las Vegas. And even during the federal years of Boulder Dam and the New Deal, amorality thrived, and Block 16 housed more than 300 working girls without undue interference.

Ironically, the re-legalization of wide-open gambling in 1931 foreshadowed an end to the Line, and kindled the enduring opposition of casino operators to blatant prostitution. The clubs, casinos, and hotels along Fremont Street were bright, boisterous, and (mostly) benign, but the Second Street approach to the Line was suitably subdued, sequestered, slightly sinister. Respectable residents now only ventured into the Block while acting as guides to visiting friends. At least one practical joker arranged for a shady lady to emerge and greet, familiarly, the visiting friend, wife at his side! To the dismay of local boosters, the prosaically named Block 16 began to gain a measure of fame, as word spread about this last holdout of the Wild West, and tourists to the dam site and Lake Mead visited Las Vegas to rubberneck the saloons and casinos and bordellos. It was no accident that the downtown sawdust joints, and even the first two hotels on the Strip, adopted strictly frontier motifs.

Rare photo taken in the Thirties of Block 16's working ladies outside the Arizona Club.

What finally killed Block 16, after a 35-year run, was World War II. The War Department had many reasons to want open prostitution closed. With soldiers at the gunnery range coming up for off-duty passes in rotations of hundreds per night, the road to downtown Las Vegas could become a "coital express," and Block 16 would turn into the "pubic center of the West—this at a time when syphilis took weeks to check, and when gonorrhea could cripple a company," Gabriel Vogliotti writes in his seminal *Girls of Nevada*. The voices of the wives of men assigned to bases near notorious Las Vegas (and Reno) were heard loud and clear in Washington: by allowing uninhibited sex for sale in the vicinity, men who were called to arms were, in effect, receiving federal help in sex betrayal; thus the War Department would be "debauching men and cheapening womanhood." The commander of the Las Vegas Aerial and Gunnery Range simply threatened to declare the whole city off-limits to servicemen, and local officials immediately revoked the liquor licenses and slot-machine permits of the casinos on Block 16. These fronts financed the prostitution, which by itself could not finance the fronts, and the Block's illustrious 35-year alternating current finally ran out of juice.

■ Roxie's

Las Vegas's era of centralized and destigmatized prostitution was officially eulogized, but another 30 years would pass before it would become unquestionably illegal. In fact, many Las Vegans opposed the Block's demise. A petition was submitted to city officials, with 395 signatures, to reopen it—not only to satisfy clients' needs and the best interests of the community's economic health, but also to contain and control the "service crime." Some of the girls relocated to Skid Row a block away on First Street, while others settled at the Little and Kit-Kat clubs out on Boulder Highway.

After the war, some of the old proprietors attempted to revive the Block, which had gone to seed with cheap rooming houses, but the city condemned most of the buildings in 1946. Another nail in the coffin of brothel prostitution in Las Vegas was hammered into place in 1949, only two years after Bugsy's untimely demise. State Senator A.V. Tallman of Winnemucca introduced legislation totally legalizing brothels in Nevada. The measure passed both houses, but Governor Vail Pittman vetoed it after powerful prodding by the increasingly influential hotel-casino owners. The veto fell short of being overturned by only a few votes.

Meanwhile, Las Vegas brothels refused to be laid to rest. Organized prostitution expanded beyond the city limits. The Kassabian Ranch and C-Bar-C were located in Paradise Valley a little off the Strip, while Roxie's squatted on Boulder Highway (near the intersection of today's Sahara Avenue) in a section known as Formyle. The Kassabian was shut down by the county vice squad in 1946, and the C-Bar-C burned to the ground in a mysterious fire shortly thereafter. But Roxie's survived well into the 1950s. The owners, Eddie and Roxie Clippinger, surrounded themselves with strong juice by paying off, for years, the county sheriff, two county commissioners, and a law firm, one of whose partners was the state lieutenant governor.

The FBI finally raided Roxie's in April 1954, charging the Clippingers with violation of the Mann Act (transporting girls across state lines for immoral purposes). Disclosures during the trial in Los Angeles, combined with a sting operation contrived by local crime reporter Ed Reid (covered in detail in *Green Felt Jungle*), produced indictments against the sheriff and a county commissioner, disgraced the lieutenant governor, contributed to the governor's subsequent defeat, and revealed Jake Lansky's hidden ownership in the Thunderbird, which led to the revocation

(previous page) Inside the Mirage.

of its license by the Tax Commission a year later. Among other revelations about Roxie's were payoffs to the county vice squad to discourage prostitution on the Strip and eliminate competition, a dollar-a-head kickback to cabbies who delivered tricks to Roxie's (members of Teamsters Local 631, the cab drivers once officially petitioned Eddie Clippinger for $2 a head), and TV cameras in the cribs—every trick's nightmare—to tape the writhings of the beast with two backs. When Roxie's was finally driven under, another nail had been hammered into the coffin of Clark County's quasi-legal and semi-clement brothel business. But it was by no means the last.

Because meanwhile, a new system of kopecks-for-sex was evolving as Las Vegas developed into the city with the most hotel rooms—all those beds!—in the world. And it all started, naturally enough, in the feverish dreams of that prominent pioneer and private pimp, Benjamin "Bugsy" Siegel.

■ MOE, BUGSY, AND GIRLIE

The sex business had been part of Siegel's overall vision from the beginning. An inveterate ladies' man, he instinctively provided easy sex to seduce, service, and presumably satisfy the suckers. His Flamingo established two traditions of sex, Las Vegas-style. First, he designed the hotel with separate modular wings, accessible without ever having to pass through a lobby or main entrance. This was at a time, in the late 1940s, when the men who ran hotels actively barred pros: grim, gray-haired matrons guarded elevators, and Mack Sennet-type house detectives roamed the halls, listening for the telltale language that is common to all people. At the Flamingo, a guy could spend every night with a different girl and never be seen by anybody.

The second tradition was that casinos should be "dressed up" with girls. Young and pretty. Suggestively attired. Everywhere! Coat-check girls. Hat-check girls. Cigarette girls. Shills. Escorts. Loungers. Showgirls. And the ultimate juice girls: the pit cocktail waitresses. Some working girls were hired as hotel help, at the beck and call of the house; they quickly and quietly introduced other receptive workers to the lucrative sideline and simple system of being procured. Unfortunately, Bugsy left the hotel business before he had the opportunity to extend and fine-tune his sex agenda. But he laid the foundation of a program that would develop quickly and manage to maintain a delicate balance between passionately opposing policies over the next 20 years.

Though many operators no doubt contributed, it's conceivable that Moe Dalitz, owner of the Desert Inn and the man who organized Las Vegas, administered the ultimate methods of supplying sex to guests. Dalitz was 50 when he came to Las Vegas, and he knew many things. He knew, like Bugsy, the sexual excitement implicit in gambling, and that girls were an integral "accessory to the world's most sophisticated, most flattering larceny." But Dalitz also faced down the Kefauver Committee during his second year as an owner, and he observed the growing distaste of the public for prostitution. So he knew the imperative of keeping it discreet. Still, he also knew that countless girls, all kinds of girls, a veritable city of girls, swarmed to Las Vegas, and that uncontrolled prostitution became very dangerous in urban areas because of its association with pimps, drugs, white slavery, theft, and violence.

Finally, Dalitz knew that the conflicting realities all boiled down to two basic truths. First, gamblers needed sex: the suggestion of it, with girls parading around on stage and decorating the floor, generally part of the casino scenery; the mysterious, slightly sinister glamour and myth of its ready availability with gorgeous and expensive pros; and the eventual consummation—prescribed, safe, discreet—that gets the guy to sleep or wakes him up, makes him feel lucky when he wins or consoles him when he loses, keeps him around the tables a little longer, and sends him home having experienced what has been called the "Las Vegas total." But second, the sex trade had to be directly and carefully choreographed, from start to finish, in order to avoid any chance of offending the millions of straights that filled the hotels, of becoming so obvious or vulgar or hazardous that it menaced in any way the smooth and consistent workings of the great god Percentage.

So Dalitz passed the word. Around the Desert Inn. Through his managers. To the front-line staff—the hosts, the pit bosses, the dealers, the bell captains, the bartenders. And to the other owners, to be passed down to their staffs. The rules, as usual, mostly revolved around juice. The girl had to be connected. She had to work for the hotel, be hired as a hooker and given a straight job for a front, or asked, after being hired, whether she was interested in turning tricks. Or she had to be recommended by a trusted employee who could vouch for her. The girl had to be cooperative. Her main objective was to see that the player spent more time at the tables and less time in the hotel room. She had to be reliable. And she'd better be honest. After all, the money that wallet thieves and chip hustlers stole belonged, in the words of Mario Puzo, "to the gambling casinos, and was just being temporarily held by the john." In the attitude of the gaming bosses, "larcenous girls were really stealing casino money."

Charges were standardized, from a quickie French up to the full trick, which was to cost no more than a "honeybee," "a bill"—a hundred dollars. Any deviation would be immediately and summarily rectified, by any one of the number of private and public security forces that surrounded, in concentric circles, the casino counting rooms. Similarly, freelancers were actively discouraged. Any girl found hanging around the casino, restaurants, or lounges too long was earnestly apprised of the rules and either driven away or registered, as the case might be. Streetwalkers, part-time call girls, divorcees doing their "friendly forty-two," swinging coeds or housewives, cocktail waitresses, showgirls—any woman with enough beauty, body, or appeal to sell, and the capability of successfully compartmentalizing sex into a purely business transaction—all translated Bugsy Siegel's vision, and Moe Dalitz's version, into a vast and well-managed sex market in Las Vegas, throughout the 1950s and 1960s.

The personal connection extended to the solicitor as well. A man who wanted sex, from a high roller to a tinhorn, had to know and use the proper channels. The major plungers, well known to owners and executives, were supplied with a showgirl or a high-class courtesan as a matter of course. Lesser players, if well known to the cocktail waitresses and registered cruisers, could have their pick of the pit girls. Hotel guests were "fired on" by the bell captain or one of his boys; casino customers could become familiar enough with a pit boss or bartender to make a circumspect inquiry. Cab drivers and motel clerks carved their own niche within the system, but professional pimps were quickly discouraged. The word spread among the legions of male Las Vegas patrons: follow established protocol. Accrue some juice and use it judiciously. Thus the whole path was a procession of pedigree, from the whispered word to the soft knock on the door. Man to man. After all, the subject here, the matter at hand, happened to be the most intimate act known to man and woman.

If you didn't know the procedure, however, you might walk away thinking that Las Vegas's fabled copious copulation was one of the great myths of the day. Because above all, the pandering, procuring, and coupling had to be *illegal.* Herein lay the true beauty of the system, and the unmistakable signature of Siegel, Dalitz, and all the other racketeers-turned-executives. For propriety, for privacy, and ultimately to protect the reputation of legal gambling, the whole delicate system, its makeup, mechanics, and management, had to operate outside the law. One false step, one loose lip, and the whole precarious structure could collapse like a house of cards.

■ IS THERE OR ISN'T THERE?

This code of silence, second nature to the gamblers, was imposed upon the vast industry of commercial sex in Las Vegas, one that continued to invite equal measures of fascination and condemnation. The system reigned supreme for almost 20 years, and worked so well that wildly differing impressions of it were reported. Writing in 1953, Paul Ralli commented naively, "One of the best proofs that Las Vegas is reasonably outside the control of mob influence is the almost total absence of organized prostitution. Ten years ago, prostitution constituted the town's main attraction, next to gambling. But today, it's as though the call of Las Vegas is to the appetite of the pocketbook rather than that of the flesh." Hillyer and Best, otherwise far from priggish or censorious, wrote in 1955, "Las Vegas today is probably as clear of professional female enterprise as any other resort area its size. Maybe more so. Gambling is the greatest deterrent to sex since man invented the chastity belt."

Other writers, however, had different ideas. Typically, *Green Felt Jungle* established the negative extreme. "Money mysteriously breeds prostitutes the way decaying flesh breeds maggots. Where there's easy money there's whores; it's that basic. And where there's gambling, there's easy money." Reid and Demaris claimed that of Las Vegas's 1962 population of 65,000 residents, "a conservative 10 percent are in one way or another engaged in prostitution. Cabbies, bartenders, bellhops, newsboys, proprietors of various establishments (liquor stores, motels, etc.), gamblers, special deputies, and professional pimps make a sizable income by procuring for a veritable army of prostitutes."

In *Gambler's Money*, Wally Turner saw the system, in 1965, a bit more objectively. "Every night lovely long-legged dancers appear on stage, contributing to the air of suppressed excitement that the gambling operators seek to create. Are there prostitutes among them? Las Vegas being what it is, undoubtedly some of the girls sell themselves for money on occasion. To some of the [bosses], sex is just another commodity and they would insist that it be sold. But prostitution in Las Vegas has changed in the past few years. There are no houses where prostitutes live together. There are no streetwalkers. But there are many call girls, and frequently they do business only through the staff of one or more of the casinos. Some share their fees with the employees who called them. Others may be called directly by management to deal with a heavy winner and distract him, or at least keep him in town until the pendulum of the percentages swings again to the house and he is relieved of his winnings."

Vogliotti reported that a magazine writer came to Las Vegas to do a story on prostitution at the height of the Dalitz system, but didn't get very far. His parting judgment? "Only a Senate investigating committee could extract any truth." The writer found that "call girls, showgirls, cocktail waitresses all gave the same 'Who me?' as did the owners, lawyers, and police. It is a vast, smooth mendacity, a universal conspiracy to deny." Vogliotti declared that "the amount of prostitution in Las Vegas is, safely, that of Paris or Amsterdam, but the whole thing has been so beautifully distorted by writers that few men really know the picture."

But to the rest of the world, the picture *was* as the magazine writer painted it, and that was how the few men in the know wanted the picture to appear. Then, Howard Hughes entered the picture, and all the careful construction, all the distinct lines, bled together like a watercolor in the rain.

■ HOWARD AND JOE

On one hand, it's possible to ascribe a direct cause and effect from the Hughes whirlwind to the Great Las Vegas Whore Invasion of the 1970s. Certainly the owners of the Desert Inn, Sands, Frontier, Castaways, and Silver Slipper were bought out, and Hughes's staff was in. Certainly Hughes's ultimate Las Vegas chief of staff, Robert Maheu, installed a security team so huge that it constituted a sort of private army, and he took many emergency steps to erase anything even remotely notorious—skimming, cheating, bribing, racketeering, aiding and abetting, and of course, girl-running. Certainly the old rules were deteriorating, and the new rules, strictly enforced, were less than permissive.

On the other hand, the owners may have changed at the Hughes properties,

but many bosses stayed on as advisors. And the management of the many non-Hughes hotels—Trop, Stardust, Riviera, Dunes, Sahara, Hacienda, Fremont, Horseshoe, Mint, and a dozen other small casinos and hotels—remained, except for the usual turnover, the same. In 3,000 phone conversations with Hughes during his four years in Las Vegas, Maheu claimed he never once received instructions from his boss on the working-girl situation. Finally, documents exist written by aides to Maheu that read, "When you get into the hotel business, you back into the whore business. Every man who enters the business must decide how he feels about pandering or, at least, supplying the furniture of love."

Maheu subsequently retreated from his staunchly puritan position concerning prostitution in his hotels, but the die had been cast; a strangeness and uncertainty, similar to the period just after the closing of Block 16, crept into the sex business. Into the vacuum stepped Joe Conforte, without whom no chapter on sex in Nevada could be complete. Conforte, who owned the world-famous Mustang Ranch in northern Nevada, had been crusading for more than 15 years for prostitution to emerge from its twilight zone of quasi-legal status into full acceptance within the law. By this time, houses of ill repute had been servicing Nevada for more than 100 years, and nearly 50 rules and regulations had been entered into the state statutes governing the brothel business. For example, no brothel can operate on a main street, or within 400 yards of a church; no advertising is permitted; minors may not be employed in brothels, nor anyone with venereal disease; public opinion may be used by city councils and county commissioners to close brothels as a public nuisance, or to tax and regulate them. In short, 50 convenings of the state legislature continually added to the control of whorehouses, without finally outlawing them altogether.

Conforte had fought for legalized prostitution in Washoe County's Reno for many years, doing battle with another crusader, District Attorney Bill Raggio (now majority leader of the State Assembly), who finally succeeded in jailing Conforte for a number of years on charges relating to their disagreements. After serving his time (and running a prostitution ring inside the Carson City prison!), Conforte set up shop at a ranch, known as Mustang, just across the Washoe County line in tiny Storey County (population 1,500), and did a booming business in relative peace and quiet—until charges of "paying off" the county officials started to rankle him. By then, Mustang Ranch was the county's largest taxpayer, which gave Joe a certain amount of juice in local politics. In 1971, Conforte convinced the commissioners to pass Ordinance 38, which legalized, once and for all, prostitution in Storey, the first county in the country to do so.

Meanwhile, a young politician named Roy Woofter, whom Conforte had befriended and staked to a law-school education, was elected district attorney of Clark County. Woofter quickly introduced an ordinance allowing one brothel to operate in Las Vegas in a high-walled security compound in a specified area of town, with experienced management, and medical, police, and community clearance—in short, all the features that recommended legalized prostitution. Woofter actually managed to gather a fair amount of local support for the bill, including that of more than one county commissioner, and a surprising number of locals. Immediately, however, the hotel owners and convention bureau officials let out a howl that was heard all the way to the state capital. The owners wanted prostitution to be available but discreet, so as not to tarnish the already questionable image of the world's gambling capital (they also believed that a brothel would compete with a casino). The convention managers, similarly, insisted that nothing could be more detrimental to their business than a legalized whorehouse nearby (though the illegal working-girls' connection to conventions across the country is truistic).

State legislators sought to keep Conforte out of Las Vegas, to safeguard the image of and revenues from gambling, and to bolster the will of local officials to enforce the law (and remove the potential for their corruption), by passing Statute 244-345 (8), rendering prostitution illegal in counties with a population of more than 250,000—which applied, in 1971, only to Clark County. This effectively ended the local brothel movement, gave jurisdiction to state law-enforcement agencies, and once and for all pounded the proverbial last nail in the 20-year-old coffin. Conforte's Mustang Massage operated for a year and then folded.

■ MEANWHILE, JUST NEXT DOOR . . .

The ruling also triggered a sordid little episode in Nye, the county next door to Clark, where traditional Nevada prostitution remained undisturbed in the eyes of the law. A veritable war erupted between an established brothel owner in Beatty, 90 miles (145 km) northwest of Las Vegas, and a newcomer whose dream was to open a brothel only 60 miles (97 km) west of Las Vegas, just over the Clark County line. Walter Plankinton, a retired truck driver from Texas, opened a new Chicken

Ranch outside Pahrump in 1976, with artifacts from the famous old Chicken Ranch, which had operated for 130 years in LaGrange, Texas, only to be closed in 1973. Plankinton unwittingly shook up the powers-that-be in Nye County, including the sheriff and a number of deputies, the district attorney, the district court judge, and the entrenched brothel owners. The chain of events included intimidation, corruption, extortion, conspiracy, white slavery, racketeering, arson, and attempted murder. Ultimately, the case was resolved by the FBI, U.S. District Attorney in Las Vegas, and federal courts, with several convictions, a fair amount of disgrace, and a Pyrrhic victory for the embattled Plankinton and the Chicken Ranch. (This saga is im-

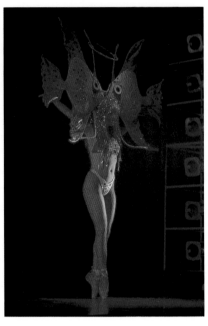

Fish bliss at "Splash"

mortalized in Jeannie Kasindorf's excellent *Nye County Brothel Wars*.) Today, five brothels around Pahrump compete for the nearest legal sex trade to Las Vegas.

■ THE SIXTIES CATCH UP TO LAS VEGAS

Certainly the Hughes presence, not to mention the quarter-billion dollars he pumped into his dream of a futuristic spaceport and company town in the great Southwestern desert, helped stimulate a boom period, in which the Aladdin, Caesars Palace, Landmark, Circus Circus, Four Queens, International, Holiday Inn, and MGM Grand opened in a five-year period, and nearly every existing hotel expanded. Increased tourism and gambling revenues reflected the prosperity and full employment of Lyndon Johnson's Great Society and the Vietnam War. Social upheaval, the sexual revolution, and the drug culture also contributed to the transformation of Las Vegas during the short, intense, and uncertain Hughes era.

Suddenly, thousands of new hotel workers—bellmen, bartenders, dealers, cocktail waitresses, showgirls—joined the picture, possessing as little idea about the traditional dynamics of the sex industry as did the vast new wave of visitors. Driven to distraction by the tons of female flesh surrounding him in Las Vegas, a male tourist now found himself in a quandary when deciding whether to ask a bartender, cab driver, or bell captain about how to hire a girl. Vogliotti described it best. He calculated that in 1974, there could be 600 bartenders at work on the evening shift, and "they have no single attitude on procurement. If a visitor hits one by chance who is sympathetic, the bartender may solve his problem by asking what he thinks of the little redhead six stools down. But the man mopping the bar may be one of the great majority who is content with his $220 a week and irritated that so many glassy-eyed jerks think he will pimp. He may shrug and explain, deadpan, that being married himself, he often wonders just what the hell you *do* do. On the other hand, he is maybe one of a few who work a quiet second business with a string of girls, or even one who, after long and friendly discourse with a customer, figures him good for a few hundred and goes to a phone to call his wife."

With the demand swelling and the old rules increasingly relegated to history, a dilemma of supply suddenly surfaced. Maybe the conventional wisdom that Hughes had bought out the mob opened the door, or maybe the radical Sixties finally arrived in Las Vegas. Suddenly, hard-core streetwalkers came out of the woodwork. In addition, weekend warriors—California secretaries, Utah Lolitas, and the like—descended on Las Vegas like locusts. Today, residents still recall the time, in the late 1970s, when a man couldn't walk the long block from the Sahara to the Riviera *with his wife* without getting a couple of bold and lurid solicitations. The corner of Flamingo Avenue and the Strip was so overrun that streetwalkers took turns directing traffic. Some were freelancers; many had pimps. Some were clean, while many were drug addicts and thieves. It was what the cops, the casinos, and Carson City had feared all along: obvious, rampant, defiant, and dangerous prostitution in the city that could now, with some accuracy, be called Sin Central.

Finally, in the early 1980s, John Moran was elected Clark County sheriff on a platform of ridding the county of its highly visible prostitution problem. In 1982, police arrested 13,000 pros, as Moran's vice squad rounded up busloads of streetwalkers, apprehending many of them two or three times a night. The campaign proved mostly successful; in 1984, a little over 6,000 arrests were made, and in 1985, a little over 5,000. In 1986, 90 percent of prostitution-related arrests were made *inside* the hotels, as undercover vice cops collared the freelancers in lounges.

Once again, Las Vegas was relieved of its unsavory image as a whore capital, by removing the most visible evidence. But by then, other systems had been renewed, or invented, to ensure that prostitution stayed alive, well, and out of harm's way.

■ TODAY'S MARKET

The best features of the Dalitz system continue to thrive in the casino context, though it's difficult to notice, even if one is on the lookout for it. The lists of available and trustworthy call girls have become more exclusive, managed by select executives to service the most deserving customers (often the highest rollers who wouldn't need the help), in the strictest privacy. The hotel staffs, as well, could easily have fingers in the vast and lucrative sex pie. In *Prostitution, Business, and Police: Maintenance of an Illegal Economy,* James Frey quotes a vice officer as saying: "Bellmen run broads, pitmen run broads, baccarat runs broads, shills are sent upstairs. Everyone's aware it's happening, but you can't admit you're aware of it." This report, and a similar one—*Analysis of a Prostitution Network*—describe the system for "bellgirls." Bell captains maintain a private list of between 20 and 70 names of every size, shape, color, and age of reliable pros who've accrued the necessary juice. A bellman makes the initial contact with a guest ("Care for some company?"), and informs the captain, who can have a girl to the door in 20 minutes. The split is 60 (girl) to 40 (bell staff). Frey writes that it's a "low-cost, low-risk, high-utility" network, which provides maximum protection for all parties concerned.

The main rule for the customer is that he must be a guest of the hotel, prefer-ably paying with an out-of-state credit card (cash guests could be undercover vice). But for the other millions of male visitors, still intent on the Las Vegas total, the freelance market is accessible and convenient. Today's intercourse industry has evolved from a variety of influences, but mostly reflects the dominant local service economy. The seminal year was 1975, when getting your head, straight, full French, Greek, English, Roman, Around the World, half and half, golden shower, S&M, B&D, binaca blast (or crème de menthe, or Alka Seltzer), fetish, even Ker-mit the Frog became simply a matter of letting your fingers do the walking through —where else? The Yellow Pages!

In 1971, the first sex ads appeared under Escort Services—two small display ads with girls in discreet, two-piece bathing suits. The other ads in the Escort cate-gory were for detective agencies! But by 1975, three whole pages of Escort Services left nothing to the imagination, with companies named Lusty Women, Party Girls, Swinging Companions, and Suzi Wong's Matchmaking. In 1977, Escort Services filled five pages and Massage Parlors also filled five. In 1981, Dating Ser-vices was added, with one full page, and a half page of Adult Maid and Butler ser-vices even appeared. In 1982, however, as part of new Sheriff Moran's crackdown, Massage ads disappeared entirely (except for the legit bodyworkers), Dating disap-peared, but seven pages of Escorts remained. By 1987, the continuing crackdown had mostly eliminated Escort Services, but a new listing had emerged: Entertain-ers. Twenty-seven pages worth in 1990! And when this category is closed? Sex might move to such listings as Bed Accessories, or Temporary Services, or even the all-purpose Rentals.

Another current wrinkle comes in the form of anonymously published, garage-printed, girlie rags found in vending boxes that line the Strip from the Trop to the Sahara, which exhibit pictures of girls in suggestive poses and list local phone numbers. Other cheap newsprint advertises the Nye County legal brothels outside of Pahrump. These fliers and tabloids and even Yellow Page ads are all technically illegal; state law prohibits the advertising of prostitution. On the other hand, tacit Las Vegas tradition is tolerant to that extent. After all, even in the age of AIDS and wholesome Convention and Visitor Bureau ad campaigns, as long as there's gam-bling, and parading showgirls and cocktail waitresses and keno runners, and hotel rooms, and a man and a woman. . . .

DAY TRIPS
SLIPPING THE GRIP OF THE STRIP

FOR MOST VISITORS, THE AREA ENCLOSED BY FREMONT STREET, from Main to Fifth, and by Las Vegas Boulevard South, from Sahara to Tropicana, delineates the limits of most tourists' Las Vegas—the boundaries beyond which 15 million of roughly 20 million visitors never venture. The hotels, gambling, signs, and sex create an electromagnetic field that most first-timers, and many long-termers, simply can't, or don't want to, escape. Why bother? You can drink for free, take in a lounge act or floor show, scarf the cheap food, people-watch till your eyes pop, and gamble at that place and time where and when you feel luckiest. It's exactly what Las Vegas expects and wants you to do.

According to a recent Las Vegas Visitor Profile Study, 15 million of 18 million visitors stayed in Las Vegas for four nights or less. A full 75 percent of visitors' trip time was devoted to the big three: eating, sleeping, and gambling (with an average betting budget of $390). Another eight percent of trip time went to entertainment (though only three of ten visitors attended a headliner or floor show), and only seven percent went sightseeing. Of the five million people who got out of town, two million went to Hoover Dam, one and a quarter million to Laughlin, and only half a million to stunning Red Rock Canyon, less than a half hour's drive from the heart of Glitter Gulch.

These surprising statistics certainly confirm the irresistibility of the Las Vegas magnet—especially since within a mere hour of city center are some of the American Southwest's most spectacular natural and man-made scenery and attractions. The variety, as well, is plentiful enough to supply even the most fast-lane sightseers with new experiences every day for weeks. Historical, cultural, and educational venues, as well as recreational sites, are found all over town. In addition, high mountains and low deserts, vast lakes and canyon-rimmed rivers, fiery red hillsides and bucolic green valleys, a massive dam and an Old West theme park, ancient Pueblo ruins and Nevada's newest boomtown, all beckon from just beyond the fearsome force field. See "Useful Addresses" in the back of the book for addresses and phone numbers.

(previous pages) Lazy, hazy sunset over Las Vegas Valley.

■ THE OLD FORT

This tiny museum is the oldest build- ing in Las Vegas and a true "soul sur- vivor." The adobe remnant was part of the original 150-square-foot (14-square- meter) "fort" constructed by Latter-day Saints' missionaries in 1855, first non- Indian residents in Las Vegas Valley. The Mormons abandoned it in 1858. The remnant served as a storage shed on the original Las Vegas Ranch. After buying the ranch, the San Pedro,Los Angeles, and Salt Lake Railroad leased the old fort to various tenants, including the Bureau of Reclamation, which stabilized the shed, and rebuilt parts of it to use as a concrete-testing laboratory for Hoover Dam. In 1955, the railroad sold the old fort to the Elks, who in 1963 demolished all the buildings except for the little remnant, which was bought back by the city in 1971. Since then a number of preservation societies have helped keep the Old Fort in place. It's immensely re- freshing to see some preservation of the past in this city of the ultimate now.

Tiny remnant of the Mormon fort, oldest building in Nevada.

■ MARJORIE BARRICK MUSEUM OF NATURAL HISTORY

This is a good place to bone up on local flora, fauna, and artifacts. First study the vegetation in the arboretum outside the museum entrance, then step inside for the wildlife: small rodents, big snakes, lizards, tortoises, gila monster, iguana, chuck- walla, gecko, and spiders, beetles, and cockroaches. Wander through the art gallery into some graphic Las Vegas history. Display cases are full of native baskets, kachi- na dolls, masks, woven goods, pottery, and jewelry. Mojave Desert fossils and min- erals are exhibited, with a huge polar bear incongruously standing in the middle. The centerpiece is a rough skeleton of an ichthyosaur, a whale-sized sea lizard, which is Nevada's state fossil.

■ NEVADA BANKING MUSEUM

Exhibits here trace Nevada banking history, from checks written before statehood (1864) to consolidation in 1981 of 16 original Farmers and Merchants, and Nation, banks into First Interstate Bank of Nevada. Examine currency issued by local Nevada banks in the early 1900s, plus collections of letterheads, passbooks, liberty bonds, cds, financial statements, silver commemorative bars, gaming tokens and chips, Carson City coins, and old teller machines.

■ LAS VEGAS ART MUSEUM

One of several enjoyable facilities at Lorenzi Park, this is a valiant attempt to maintain an art museum in Las Vegas. The museum has nearly 200 permanent pieces. The three galleries turn their exhibits over every month; the displaying artists are introduced at an open house from noon to 3 p.m. the first Sunday of the month. Most of the art is for sale. Admission is free, but donate what you can to this definite contribution to cultural Las Vegas.

■ LIBERACE MUSEUM

Liberace embodies the heart and soul of Las Vegas, in life and in death. Born in Wisconsin in 1919, third of four children in a musical family, Walter Valentino Liberace (who legally assumed the one name, Liberace, in 1950, and was known as "Lee" to his friends) was a prodigy pianist at age seven, a concert boy wonder at 14, and first played Sin City at 23. From then on, he was a one-man walking advertisement for the extravagance, flamboyance, and uninhibited tastelessness usually associated with the town he loved so much. Like Las Vegas's surface image, Liberace's costumes began as a means of standing out; then he had to keep topping himself with increasingly outrageous gimmicks. Along the way, he became one of the most popular entertainers of all time. "Mr. Showmanship" racked up six gold records, and is entered in the Guinness Book of World Records as the world's highest-paid musician.

The Liberace Museum is the most popular tourist attraction in Las Vegas, outside of the casinos. You can bet the rent that at least two tour buses will be parked out front with hundreds of retirees paying tribute to the man who, his passable playing and uncontrollable clothing notwithstanding, was possessed of a certain charisma, generosity, and genuine rapport with his audiences that inspired mass displays of devotion. "People fainting, sobbing, too stunned to talk" is how Dora Liberace, sister-in-law and museum administrator, describes some reactions of her customers.

The main building preserves Liberace's costumes: Uncle Sam hot pants, suits made of ostrich feathers, rhinestones, and bugle beads, and capes customized from 100 white fox skins (75 feet/23 meters long, $700,000) or 500 Black Glama minks (125 pounds/57 kilograms, $750,000). Also on display are the world's largest rhinestone (50 pounds/23 kilograms, $50,000) and a grossly ornate rolltop desk from his office. The library building on the other side of the Tivoli Restaurant houses family photos, miniature pianos, silver, china, cut glass, gold records, and historical data. Across the parking lot the piano and car gallery contains several antique pianos, Liberace's 50,000-rhinestone Baldwin, his million-dollar mirror-tiled Rolls, a custom rhinestone car (with matching toolbox), and a 1940s English taxi, among others.

A gift shop in the main building sells Liberace albums, tapes, videos, postcards, 8x10 glossies, song books, autobiography ($30), and doll ($300).

■ SOUTHERN NEVADA ZOOLOGICAL PARK

This could be the "wildest" place in Las Vegas. And it's a very personal little zoo, with an offbeat charm and a lot of heart—taking its engaging character directly from the long-term manager, Muffie. First, say "hello" to Ronald Raven, who will return the greeting in perfect pronunciation. (You'll be saying "hello" throughout your visit to this zoo, and for a couple of hours after, too.) Arnie the lion and Zara the tiger were donated by local owners when they started getting too big for comfort; several of the primates are on permanent breeding loan from the San Diego Zoo. Another eye-opener: two big golden eagles perch atop a post in the (open!) deer pen; they were both injured and can't fly. The zoo's most precious animal is Cougie, born in September 1988, whose mother, weak from the birth, was killed by a car near Elko when the cute cougar was only three weeks old.

The cages are cramped, of course, and not much is labeled, but any animal you care to inquire about has a long story, which the friendly staff is only too happy to relate. In business for 10 years, committed and growing, this is the only public zoo in Nevada.

Where else but at the Liberace Museum?

■ NEVADA STATE MUSEUM AND HISTORICAL SOCIETY

A comfortable and enjoyable place to spend an hour or two studying Mojave Desert and Spring Mountains ecology, Southern Nevada history, and local art. Three rotating galleries exhibit anything from photographs of the neon night or desert to Nevada textiles or early telephone technology. The Hall of Biological Science has interesting exhibits on life in the desert. Learn how the mighty Spring Mountains are a "biological island surrounded by a sea of desert." The Hall of Regional History has graphic displays on mining, nuclear tests, Hoover Dam construction, politics, ranching, and Indians.

■ RIPLEY'S BELIEVE IT OR NOT

One of the world's all-time greatest travelers, Robert Ripley visited almost 200 countries between the 1920s and late 1940s, and became a collector of the strange, the incredible, the bizarre, the macabre. Nobody believed his travel stories, so in 1918 he began documenting them in a daily cartoon which, at its peak, reached 80 million people in 17 languages! Ripley also hosted some of the great radio shows (1930-46), and pioneered on-location broadcasts (Grand Canyon, North Pole, underwater)! A million pieces of mail a year was not unusual; he once received as many in a month! This museum houses some truly astounding items, which could explain the exclamation points at the end of almost every sentence in the display descriptions!

Marvel over the Human Smokestack, Philadelphia Garbage Elephant, seven-foot roulette wheel made of 19,000 jelly beans, and the world's smallest cameras. Don't linger too long near the medieval castrater and chastity belt, wrist-bone crusher, or eye spikes! You definitely *won't* believe the Human Unicorn, two-headed calf, gallery of sickest eaters, or the tallest, thinnest, and most-kissed men in history! But by far the most eye-popping, heart-stopping, drawer-dropping sensation of sight and sound is walking out of the museum into the video arcade!

■ GUINNESS WORLD OF RECORDS MUSUEM

A slightly sedate version of Ripley's, this small establishment features photographic, typographic, video, audio, and slide-show exhibits of world records: the tallest, fattest, oldest, and most-married men; longest neck, and smallest bicycle; videos of dominoes; slides of the greatest engineering projects; and an informative display of Las Vegas firsts and foremosts.

■ ETHEL M'S DESSERT AND DESERT

That's Ethel *Mars*, as in Mars Bars (Milky Ways, 3 Musketeers, and m&m's). If you feel like taking a ride after lunch or dinner, the free tour takes you past big picture windows overlooking the bright factory, with workers and machines turning and churning, then out into the tasting room. Sample a nut cluster, caramel, butter cream, or liqueur candy, so rich that one piece is a whole dessert. Outside is an enjoyable 2-acre (.8-hectare) cactus garden, with indigenous desert flora.

■ SOUTHERN NEVADA MUSEUM

On the way to Hoover Dam, your first stop out of the city should be this extensive and interesting complex. The main museum houses an incredible collection of history, tracing Indian cultures from the prehistoric to the contemporary, and chronicling exploration, settlement, and industry. Step outside and into the rail cars for a full course on Nevada's railroads, then stroll down to historical Heritage Street, with its four original houses and print shop. Finally, wander out to haunt the ghost town, little more than ruins in the desert. You'll leave with a complete lesson in the background of the Las Vegas area, especially your next stops—Boulder City and Hoover Dam.

■ RED ROCK CANYON

West of Las Vegas, stretching across the sun-setting horizon and hemming in the valley, are the mighty and rugged Spring Mountains. Smack in the center of this range is Red Rock Canyon, a multicolored sandstone palisade so close to Las Vegas that it competes with, or better yet complements, the electrified cityscape. Less than 15 miles (24 km) from the world's greatest concentration of indoor recreation awaits 62,000 acres (25,100 hectares) of outdoor splendor—as dramatic a contrast as might be imaginable. The transition from city and suburb to expanding sprawl and then wilderness is unforgettable. A mere 10 miles (16 km) from downtown Las Vegas on West Charleston Boulevard, you're on open road through the outback Mojave; the view—thick stands of Joshua trees, backdropped by the precipitous Spring Mountain walls, with Red Rock Canyon standing sentinel—has been known to leave even *National Geographic* photographers speechless. In 20-30 minutes, you take a right into the Bureau of Land Management's southern Nevada showcase.

Start with the enormity of the semicircular scenery, swallowing crowds and dwarfing climbers. Then superimpose the gorgeous colors of the sandstone—yellow, orange, pink, red, purple—all overlaid by the stalwart and tempered gray of older limestone. Then add the narrow, steep-walled canyons, moist, cool, lush gashes between the cliffs, for wonderland hiking, and the contoured, inviting boulders that have turned Red Rock Canyon into an international climbing destination. Finally, tack on the cooperative year-round climate, close proximity to the city, and the excellent visitors center, and it's safe to say that the nearly 17 million yearly tourists who don't make it to Red Rock Canyon simply don't see Las Vegas.

Red Rock Canyon clearly reveals the limestone formed when most of Nevada lay under a warm shallow sea, and the massive sand dunes which later covered this desert. Chemical and thermal reactions "petrified" the dunes into polychrome sandstone; erosion sculpted it into strange and wondrous shapes. When the land began faulting and shifting roughly 100 million years ago, the limestone was thrust up and over the younger sandstone, forming a protective layer which inhibited further erosion. Known as the Keystone Thrust, the contact between the limestone and sandstone is as precise as a textbook illustration, and accounts for the bands of contrasting colors in the cliffs. Except for the spectacular canyons carved from runoff over the past 60 million years, the 15-mile-long, 3,000-foot-high (400-meter) sandstone escarpment today remains relatively untouched by the march of time.

The BLM Visitor Center is nestled in the Calico Hills at the lower end of the wide oval that encompasses all this glowing Aztec sandstone. Take a while and ori-

ent yourself to the area at the center's excellent 3-D exhibits of geology, flora and fauna, and recreational opportunities, then walk along the short nature trail out back. A 13-mile (21-kilometer) loop road is open 9-5 and features half a dozen overlooks, picnic sites, and trails leading to springs, canyons, quarries, and *tinajas* (tanks). With any luck, hikers and climbers will be dotted along the rock to demonstrate the amazing scale of the fiery walls. And if you're riding a lucky streak, they'll be wearing red!

You can easily spend an entire day exploring the edges of the loop road. Be sure to stop at both Calico Vista points, with humongous 6,323-foot (1,927-meter) Turtle Head Mountain leaning high and limy over the Calico Hills. A short trail from the second vista gets you into the territory. Another trail enters Sandstone Quarry, where red and white sandstone for Southwestern buildings was mined from 1905 to 1912. Absorb the view of the Madre Mountains, a dramatic limestone ridge line of the Spring Range, then swing around south past the White Rock Hills, Bridge and Rainbow mountains, and Mt. Wilson. Hikes enter Lost Creek, Icebox, and Pine Creek canyons. You could then spend another six days hiking around the 16- by 10-mile (25- by 16-kilometer) park, or devote a lifetime to climbing the 1,500 known routes up the red rock.

Icing on the cake.

(opposite) Hikers and climbers dot Red Rock Canyon.

■ Spring Mountain Ranch State Park

Watch for wild burros along the stretch between Red Rock Canyon and the state park; it's easy to tell the males from the females. Pay at the gate to enter the ranch, nestled at the base of the Wilson Cliffs, sheer buff-colored sandstone bluffs. The area's cooler temperatures, plentiful water, bountiful land, and gorgeous setting have attracted travelers since the 1830s. By 1869, a ranch had been established with a stone cabin and blacksmith shop (both still standing). Three generations of Wilsons owned the land from 1876 till 1948, after which it was sold several times, once to Vera Krupp, and once to Howard Hughes. The State Parks Division finally acquired the 528-acre (213-hectare) ranch in 1974; by then, it was worth more than $3 million.

The long green lawns, bright white picket fences, and New England-style red ranch house make an idyllic setting for picnics, football or frisbee tossing, daydreaming, and snoozing, as well as for concerts, musicals, and kids' events put on in summer. Stroll around the grounds, and up to the reservoir, which waters the ranch via gravity-fed pipes. The main Ranch House doubles as the visitors center; pick up a self-guiding tour brochure. Sunsets here are incomparable.

You might think you're in New England at Spring Mountain Ranch State Park.

A half mile (.8 km) south of the state park are two commercial establishments. Bonnie Springs, originally a cattle ranch, now includes a motel, cocktail bar and restaurant, petting zoo, and stables. Old Nevada is a Western theme park with a mini-train ride along the outside of town, two museums, a beer hall, mine, saloon, opera house, and shops, plus an 1800s melodrama and hangings.

■ BOULDER CITY

In 1930, when Congress finally appropriated the first funds for the Boulder Canyon Project, the Great Depression was in full swing, and the country was embarking on its most massive reclamation effort to date. The dam would be one of the largest single engineering and construction tasks ever undertaken. Urbanologists across the country were exploring large-scale community planning. Boulder City was born of these unique factors. Sixty years later, it remains the most unusual town in Nevada.

Construction of Boulder City began in March 1931, only a month before work commenced at the dam site. Boulder City became the first "model town" in the country, a prettified all-American oasis of security and order in the midst of a great desert and a Great Depression. The U.S. Bureau of Reclamation controlled the town down to the smallest detail. A city manager, who answered directly to the Commissioner of Reclamation, oversaw operations, and his authority was nearly total.

After the dam was completed in 1935, many thought Boulder City would become a ghost town, but visitors to the dam and Lake Mead began to turn the town into a service center for the new tourist attraction and recreation area. For 30 years, the government owned the town and all its buildings, but in early 1960, an act of Congress established Boulder City as an independent municipality. A city charter was drawn up, the feds began to sell property to the long-term residents, and alcohol was no longer prohibited. Gambling, however, was, and remains, illegal.

Coming into Boulder City is like entering a town in Arizona or New Mexico, with Indian and Mexican gift shops, and a number of galleries, as well as crafts, jewelry, antique, and collectibles stores along the downtown streets. And no casinos. Stop first at the Chamber of Commerce and collect two excellent fliers, one with walking tours of the historic districts in town, the other a map keyed with scenic, recreational, artistic, and historical sights. Continue into town and stop at the Boulder City/Hoover Dam Museum. Watch a stunning 30-minute movie on the dam's construction. Across the street, peek into the lobby of the 55-year-old Boulder Hotel. Make sure to use your walking-tour brochures and stroll up Arizona Street, then down Nevada Highway, to get a feel for this Depression-era model city.

■ HOOVER DAM

The 1,400-mile (2,250-kilometer) Colorado River had been gouging great canyons and valleys with red (*colorado*) sediment-laden waters for nearly 10 million years. For the past 10,000 years, Indian, Spanish, and Mormon settlers coexisted with the fitful river, which often overflowed with spring floods, then tapered off to a muddy trickle in the fall. But in 1905, a wet winter and abnormally severe

(left) View of Black Canyon, looking upstream, on December 1, 1932, after the Colorado River was diverted. (right) Same vantage point downstream of Hoover Dam, on March 26, 1935—a year ahead of schedule.

(opposite) Giant electrical turbines inside Hoover Dam.

spring rains combined to wreak havoc: flash floods actually changed the course of the river to flow through California's low-lying Imperial Valley, greatly enlarging the Salton Sea. For nearly two years, engineers and farmers fought the water back into place. But the message was clear. The Rio Colorado must be tamed.

Enter the U.S. Bureau of Reclamation, established only three years earlier. Over the next 15 years, the Bureau narrowed the list of possible dam sites from 70 to two: Boulder and Black canyons in southern Nevada. It took another three years to negotiate an equitable water distribution among the affected states and Mexico, and another six for Congress to pass the Boulder Canyon Project Act, authorizing funds for "Boulder Dam" to be constructed in Black Canyon (it was finally named after Herbert Hoover, then Secretary of Commerce).

The immensity of the undertaking still boggles the brain. The closest civilization was at the sleepy railroad town of Las Vegas, 40 miles (64 km) west. Two hundred miles (320 km) of poles and wire had to be run from the nearest large power plant, in San Bernardino, California. Tracks had to be laid, a town built, men hired, equipment shipped in—just to prepare for construction. And then! The mighty Colorado had to be diverted. Four tunnels, each 56 feet (17 meters) across, were hacked out of the canyon walls. Thousands of tons of rock were loosened, carried off, and dumped, every day for 16 months. Finally, in November 1932, the river water was routed around the dam site. Then came the concrete.

For two years, eight-cubic-yard buckets full of cement were lowered into the canyon, five **million** of them, till the dam—660 feet (200 meters) thick at the base, 45 feet (14 meters) thick at the crest, 1,244 feet (379 meters) across, and 726 feet (220 meters) high—had swallowed 40 million cubic yards, or seven million tons of the hard stuff. The top of the dam was built wide enough to accommodate a two-lane highway. Inside this Pantagruelian wedge were placed 17 gargantuan electrical turbines. The cost of the dam exceeded $175 million. At the peak of construction, more than 5,000 workers toiled day and night to complete the project, braving the most extreme conditions of heat, dust, and danger from heavy equipment, explosions, falling rock, and heights. An average of 50 injuries per day, and a total of 94 deaths, were recorded over the 46 months of construction.

The largest construction equipment yet known to the world had to be invented, designed, fabricated, and installed on the spot. Yet miraculously, the dam was completed nearly two years ahead of schedule. In February 1935, the diversion tunnels were closed, and Lake Mead began to fill up. The dam was dedicated eight

HOOVER DAM HYPERBOLES

- Nine million tons of rock excavated, roughly enough to build the Great Wall of China
- One million cubic yards of river bottom removed, the equivalent of digging a trench 100 feet long (30 meters), 60 feet wide (18 meters), and a mile (1.6 km) deep
- 165,000 railroad cars' worth of sand and gravel for cement, enough to stretch a single train from Boulder City to Kansas City
- Nearly seven million tons of concrete poured, enough to pave a two-lane road from Miami to Los Angeles
- 18 million pounds (eight million kilograms) of steel, enough to build the Empire State Building
- A thousand miles (1,600 km) of steel pipe
- Nearly 50 trillion pounds (22.7 trillion kilograms) of water retained in Lake Mead
- No predictions have been calculated for the dam's life span; it's 55 years old in 1990

months later, by President Franklin D. Roosevelt. A month after that, the first turbine was turned, and electricity started flowing as the Colorado River water finally came under control. Today, Hoover Dam supplies four *billion* kilowatt-hours of electricity annually (enough for half a million houses).

Find a parking space nearby, and visit the small exhibits room near the tour entrance: black-and-white photos, brochures, and special displays. Buy tickets for the 35-minute dam tour. A 75-second elevator ride whisks you to the bottom of the dam (like descending from the 53rd floor of a skyscraper). Tunnels lead to a truly monumental room housing the monolithic turbines. Next you step outside, where a hundred necks crane to view the top of the dam—looking very much like a daredevil skateboarder's wet dream. Next you walk through one of the diversion tunnels to view a 30-foot-diameter (10-meter) water pipe. The guide packs hours of statistics and stories into the short tour, and at a buck a shot, this is one of the true bargains in the Las Vegas area. Also, during the hot months, the dam's interior temperature of 55-60 degrees (13-15°C) provides exquisite relief. Back on top, a small Snackateria serves hot dogs, popcorn, muffins, and frozen yogurt, across from a gift shop with the usual souvenirs. Across the dam is Arizona.

GRAND CANYON FLIGHTSEEING

Las Vegas is the gateway to the Grand Canyon—one of the world's greatest natural wonders—and half a dozen flightseeing companies offer excursions from McCarran Airport, over the city, Boulder City, Hoover Dam, Lake Mead, and the western edge and south rim to the canyon airport. From there, ground transportation covers the 12 miles (19 km) to the south rim services where, depending on the tour, you have from two to four hours for sightseeing, photography, hiking, lunch, the museum, or an IMAX movie.

To say that the Grand Canyon is a mile deep, 4 to 18 miles wide, and 277 miles long, would be to deny this vast chasm its poetry and timelessness. Ever since García Lopez de Cárdenas laid eyes on the Canyon in 1540, great authors have struggled to find words that adequately describe the mindboggling formation. Said naturalist John Muir, "It is impossible to conceive what the canyon is, or what impression it makes, from description or pictures, however good. . . . The prudent keep silence." President Theodore Roosevelt, who declared the canyon a national monument in 1909, cautioned, "Leave it as it is. You cannot improve it; not a bit. What you can do is keep it for your children, your children's children, and all who come after you, as one of the sights every American, if he can travel at all, should see."

Alas, the Hoover and Glen Canyon dams have reduced the once-mighty Colorado River to a mere trickle of its former self; it once carried an estimated 500,000 tons of sediment daily through the canyon. Aside from the river, its tributaries, and the flooding of side gullies, the canyon has also been etched by snow, rain, air, water from melted glaciers, volcanism, and faults. Geologists believe that parts of the canyon are one-third as old as the planet Earth, having been formed roughly two billion years ago, in the Precambrian Era.

Viewing the canyon's multicolored peaks, buttes, pinnacles, and ravines, and pondering its ancient history, make for an inspiring side trip and thought-provoking diversion from the glitter and gambling of Las Vegas. Slightly expensive, but worth its weight in philosophical musing. Five companies can take you there:

Scenic Aviation Services, tel. 739-5611, offers a Freedom Tour, which provides a round-trip flight and three to four hours at South Rim for hiking and sightseeing, for $139. They also do a Deluxe Tour, which includes a lunch buffet, IMAX viewing, and guided bus excursion, for $169. With Scenic, you can also fly one-way to the canyon for $109, or better yet, go standby on their 2:30 flight for $25 cash.

Air Nevada, tel. 736-8900, does a three-and-a-half hour, air-only tour for $119, and a seven- to eight-hour trip, with hotel pickup and drop-off, lunch at Bright Angel Lodge, and museum admission, for $176.

Sierra Nevada Airways, tel. 736-6770, offers the full-day package, leaving at 7:30 a.m. and 1:30 p.m., for $155.

Lake Mead Air, tel. 293-1848, flies out of Sky Harbor Airport, 6 miles (9.5 km) south of Las Vegas on Nevada State Highway 146. They do a one-hour-and-forty-minute fly-by, without landing, for $79 scheduled, or $99 per person unscheduled with two or more passengers.

You can also climb aboard one of the **Helicop-Tours** choppers, tel. 736-0606, for a thrilling two-and-a-half-hour ride over the city, Hoover Dam, and Lake Mead, then halfway down into the canyon to land on a private plateau, where cheese and champagne are served. Then you're whisked back to the Quail Air Center (behind the Tropicana) by way of the Strip, and shuttled back to your hotel. Their two-hour trip is $200, their 90-minute tour $160.

■ LAKE MEAD RECREATION AREA

Hoover Dam began detaining the Colorado and Virgin rivers in 1935. By 1938, Lake Mead was full: three years' worth of river water braced by the Brobdingnagian buttress at Black Canyon. Largest man-made lake in the West, Lake Mead measures 110 miles (177 km) long and 500 feet (152 meters) deep, has 822 miles (1,323 km) of shoreline, and contains 28.5 million acre-feet of water (or just over nine trillion gallons). The reservoir irrigates two and a quarter million acres (900,000 hectares) of land in the U.S. and Mexico, and supplies water for more than 14 million people. The dam received its 26-millionth visitor on Feb. 7, 1989. Millions of people each year use Lake Mead as a recreational resource. For all this, Lake Mead is only a sidelight to the dam's primary purpose: flood and drought control. In addition, Lake Mead is only the centerpiece of the 1.5-million-acre (600,000-hectare) Lake Mead National Recreation Area, which includes Lake Mojave, and the surrounding desert from Davis Dam to the south and Grand Canyon National Park in the east, all the way north to Overton—the largest Department of Interior recreational acreage in the country.

And recreation it certainly provides! Swimming is the most accessible, and requires the least equipment: a bathing suit. Boulder Beach, only 30 miles from Las Vegas and just down the road from the Alan Bible Visitor Center, is the most popular swimming site. Over a mile long, it's rarely too crowded. And the water, which can reach 85 degrees (29°C) in July, is so inviting that even divers can wear just bathing suits (down to 30 feet/10 meters; in winter, it's wet suits). Also for divers, visibility averages 30 feet, the water is stable, and sights of the deep abound. The yacht *Tortuga*, doomed and possibly haunted, rests at 50 feet (15 meters) near the Boulder Islands, and Hoover Dam's asphalt factory sits on the canyon floor nearby. The boat *Cold Duck*, in 35 feet (12 meters), is an excellent training dive. The old Mormon town of St. Thomas, inundated by the lake in 1938, has many a watery story to tell. The clamming is worthwhile near Saddle Island. Wishing Well Cove has steep canyon walls and drop-offs, caves, and clear water. Ringbolt Rapids, an exhilarating drift dive, is for advanced only, and the Tennis Shoe Graveyard, near Las Vegas Wash, is one of many footholds of hidden treasure.

Boating on the vast lake is even more varied. Power boats skip across the surface—racing, pulling water-skiers, or just speeding hellbent for nowhere. Houseboats putter toward hidden coves for days of sunbathing, fishing, partying, relaxing, and staying wet. Sailing is a year-round thrill, with conditions described as "between paradise and panic." Spring is fine but fall is king: the blistering heat's gone, the wind's steady, and the water's warm. Winter winds are fluky, characteristic of large inland bodies of water, and ferocious summer storms can roar across the canyon with little mercy and less warning, only to disappear without a trace 30 minutes later. Likewise, windsurfing on sailboards is exciting and unpredictable, with the strong thermals in summer, good conditions and solitude (not to mention polypropylene underwear and dry suits) in winter.

Fishing is eventful and changeable, too. Largemouth bass, rainbow, brown, and cutthroat trout, catfish, and black crappie have been the mainstays for decades. These days, though, striped bass provide the sport, especially since tens of thousands of gallons of phosphorous fertilizer were added to the lake to replenish nutrients depleted by the Glen Canyon Dam (topped off in 1963). Phosphorus nourishes algae, which feeds plankton, which is consumed by threadfin shad, which is dinner for the striped bass. Striper popularity has also allowed the largemouth bass, fished out in years past, to regenerate. Five marinas in Nevada provide camping, restaurants and bars, fishing supplies, and boat rentals. Two of these offer showers, houseboats, and motels.

Recreation is also abundant at Lake Mojave, created downstream by Davis Dam in 1953. This lake backs up almost all the way to Hoover Dam, like an extension of Lake Mead. The two lakes are similar in climate, desert scenery, vertical-walled canyon enclosures, and a shoreline digitated with numerous private coves. Lake Mojave, however, is much smaller, and thus not nearly as susceptible to Lake Mead's mongrel monsoons; and narrower, so the protection of shore is never too far away. Still, it offers excellent trout fishing at Willow Beach on the Arizona side, where the water, too cold for swimming, is perfect for serious angling. Marinas are found at Cottonwood Cove just north of the widest part of the lake and at Katherine Landing just north of Davis Dam. For all that, it's a much better-kept secret than exalted Lake Mead.

Finally, the desert enclosing all this incongruous water furnishes a sharp contrast worthy of the proximity to its other anomaly—Las Vegas. From the mammoth granite outcroppings in the wild and surreal shapes of Christmas Tree Pass, just uphill from Laughlin, to the 1,500-year-old petroglyphs chiseled white into the psychedelic scarlet sandstone of Valley of Fire, 100 miles (160 km) north of

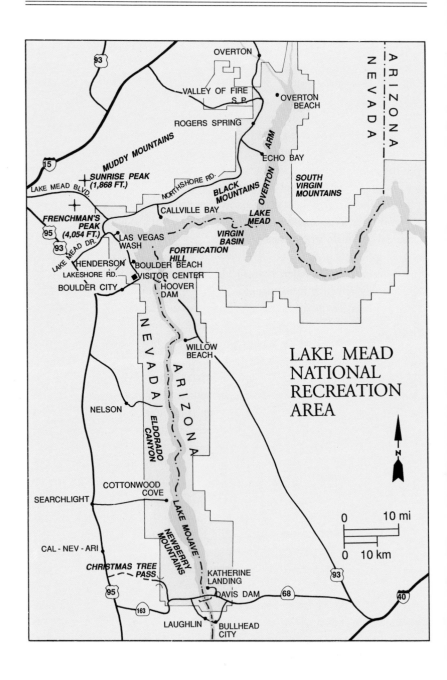

LAKE MEAD
NATIONAL
RECREATION
AREA

Lake Mead's moody blues.

Laughlin, you can get as high and dry (and awry) as in any wilderness area in the country. The only way to place Las Vegas in its proper perspective, to truly recognize that the city and the dam embody one of the world's greatest efforts to spruce up a desert, is to get away and look back. Climb a mountain and survey the city, the valley, the dam, the lakes, and the desert—all in the indivisible panorama. Experience the contrast. That's what traveling is all about.

■ VALLEY OF FIRE STATE PARK

At this stunning piece of Olympian sculpture, the gods had miles of fire-red rock to carve, and 150 million years to fill in the details. Like Red Rock Canyon, this valley, 6 miles long and 3 to 4 miles (4.8 to 6.4 km) wide, is another spectacular ancestral hall of the Navajo Formation, a continuum of Mesozoic sandstone that stretches from southern Colorado through New Mexico, Arizona, Utah, and Nevada. Its monuments, arches, protruding jagged walls, divine engravings and human etchings, all in brilliant vermilion, scarlet, mauve, burgundy, magenta, orange, and gold, more than any other characteristic are representative of the great American Southwest.

The highest and youngest formations in the park are mountains of sand deposited by desert winds 140 million years ago—the familiar Aztec sandstone. These dunes were petrified, oxidized, and chiseled by time, sun, water, and chemical reactions into their magnificent shapes and colors. Underneath the Aztec is a 5,000-foot-deep (1,524-meter) layer of brown mud, dating back 200 million years, when uplift displaced the inland sea. The gray limestone below represents another 100 million years of deposits, from the Paleozoic marine environment.

Unlike Red Rock Canyon, where uplift slipped older limestone over the sandstone, here it all remains exactly as it was stratified, and the red rock provides an incomparable lesson in erosion. One of the best and most photographed examples is along the road just beyond the eastern entrance, at Elephant Rock. Continue west to the Cabins, built for travelers out of sandstone bricks by the Civilian Conservation Corps (CCC) in 1935, when the valley became the first state park in Nevada. Seven Sisters are stunning, but the visitors center has a truly spectacular setting under a mountain of fire. Inside is a good place to pick up a map of the park and trail guides, books of local interest, slides, and postcards. From here, take the spur road to Petroglyph Canyon Trail, and dig your feet into some red sand. A trail guide introduces you to the local flora. Mouse's Tank is a basin that fills up with water after a rain; the fugitive Indian, Mouse, hid here in the late 1890s. The spur road continues through the towering canyon and dead-ends above Rainbow Vista; jeep trails continue beyond.

Heading west again on the through road, you come to a quarter-mile loop trail to fenced-in petrified wood, the most common local fossil. On the other side of the highway, another spur road goes past the high staircase up to petroglyphed and sheer Atlatl Rock and into A and B campgrounds. There's a walk-in section to the rear of A Campground, but the back of B Campground has some of the most spectacular campsites in Nevada. The Beehives, a little farther west along Nevada State Highway 40, are worth the look. Head from there back to Las Vegas, or turn around and continue to Overton.

◼ LOST CITY MUSEUM

Over a rise beyond the eastern entrance to Valley of Fire awaits the Muddy River Wash, at the mouth of Moapa Valley. Lake Mead terminates here, and a thin strip of rich agricultural green escorts the road up the river valley. The Anasazi Indians

PETROGLYPHS AND PROTAGONISTS

Petroglyphs are prehistoric rock carvings representative of the culture and religion of ancient Indians. Though some of the shapes and figures of the artwork are recognizable today, their significance has mostly been lost with the ages. Scientists speculate that rock incision was one of the rituals performed by shamans before a hunt, special event, or life passage, or that the renderings served as graffiti, or a sort of community bulletin board.

The petroglyphs in Valley of Fire are particularly numerous and noticeable. The sandstone is coated with a layer of oxidized iron and magnesium which, when carved, becomes white, so the artistic possibilities were propitious. It's not hard to imagine how a smooth, flat, and high-hanging face such as Atlatl Rock would have been irresistible to the graffiti artists of the day, though one does wonder how the ancients *reached* it. The petrogylph of a ladder might shed some light on the question, and would point to a more recent Anasazi carver. But the incised *atlatl* above it returns the aura of mystery; this "spear-launcher" long predates the bow and arrow, which arrived here around A.D. 500.

Experts recognize certain "totems," or clan signs, in the petroglyphs; in fact, some Hopi clan symbols appear in Valley of Fire, supporting the theory that the Anasazi who migrated into Arizona and New Mexico intermingled their culture with their eastern cousins.

Some of the artwork's symbolism seems obvious: suns, snakes, animals, people. But you'll also see hieroglyphs that could represent mushrooms and cacti (with renderings reminiscent of the psychedelic peyote cultures farther south), butterflies, octopi and starfish, Greek letters, menorahs, tic-tac-toe games, spermatozoa, trebel clefs, even the Great Prophet foretelling the arrival of 747s, roller coasters, and basketball. Road maps? Advertising? Headlines? Interpretations are only limited by imagination.

One of the Valley's more recent claims to fame involves the filming of a movie, during the fall of 1965, called *The Professionals*. Burt Lancaster, Lee Marvin, Robert Ryan, and Woody Strode portray mercenaries fighting revolutionaries, led by Jack Palance, in the rugged wastelands of northern Mexico in 1917. Written and directed by Richard Brooks, Ralph Bellamy plays a Texas oil tycoon who foots the bill for this private little skirmish in the war; Claudia Cardinale plays his wife. The star-studded cast and crew stayed at the Mint during filming, and it's from this time that the apocryphal story of Lee Marvin using a bow to shoot arrows across Fremont Street to silence Vegas Vic ("Howdy, pardner—welcome to Las Vegas!") originates. The movie provided great publicity for the state park.

were farming successfully here a thousand years ago, and built the Pueblo Grande de Nevada, or Lost City, on the fertile delta between the Muddy and Virgin rivers. The Mormons began to colonize the valley in 1864, and today this well-tended plot is their legacy.

A glimpse of the Anasazi ("Ancient Ones") legacy is found at the Lost City Museum, just south of the small farming town of Overton, 50 miles (80 km) northeast of Las Vegas. The museum houses an immense collection of Pueblo artifacts, including an actual pueblo foundation, and a fascinating series of black-and-white photos covering the site's excavation in 1924. In a brilliant article (*Nevada Magazine*, November 1976), David Moore makes the point that the "Lost City" wasn't so much lost as simply overlooked; Jedediah Smith sighted and cited the site during his travels through southern Nevada in the 1820s, and another expedition reported these "ruins of an ancient city" in the *New York Tribune* in 1867. But it was Nevada Governor James G. Scrugham, a mining engineer who, in 1924, initiated the official dig. Some of the Anasazi ruins were drowned by Lake Mead, but even today, the Overton-Logandale area of the delta remains one of the country's "finest bottomless treasure chests of ancient history," according to Moore. Residents who

Famous Elephant Rock at Valley of Fire.

(opposite) The sandstone Cabins provided accommodation for travelers to the state park in the Thirties.

rototill their yards or replace septic tanks uncover scads of shards: in 1975, an entire ancient village was revealed by workmen digging a new leach line.

The exterior of the museum, reminiscent of an adobe pueblo, was constructed by the Civilian Conservation Corps in 1935; climb down the log ladder into the authentic pit house in front. Stroll around back for petroglyphs, more pueblos, picnic tables, and a pioneer monument.

■ MT. CHARLESTON

Twenty miles (32 km) north of Las Vegas on US 95 along the Mojave Desert floor is a turnoff west into Kyle Canyon, one of many short, narrow, and sheer cuts into the northern Spring Mountain Range, which hems in the western Las Vegas Valley for 50 miles (80 km). The range's highest point is Mt. Charleston, named after Charleston, South Carolina, by Dixie crew members of an Army survey team which mapped this mountain's forest reserve in 1906. Eighth-highest point in Nevada, Mt. Charleston's propensity for capturing precipitation from the westerlies gave rise to the name Spring Mountains. The rain, snowmelt, and runoff percolate through the porous limestone, spurtle to the surface in numerous springs, and finally gurgle through the natural aquifers into the deep artesian system below Las Vegas Valley. Being high and wet, and surrounded by low and dry, the Spring Mountains approximate "a garden island poking out of a sea of desert." In fact, the local flora and fauna have become biologically isolated; 30 species of plants are endemic. Additionally, these mountains support a system of five distinct life zones; ascending from Las Vegas to Charleston Peak in terms of altitude is the equivalent of traveling from Mexico to Alaska in terms of latitude.

Most of this range is administered by the Bureau of Land Management, though the elevations above 7,000 feet (2,300 meters) are managed by the Las Vegas Ranger District of the Toiyabe National Forest. And like the Park Service's Lake Mead Recreation Area, Mt. Charleston offers year-round outdoor activities—from cool alpine hikes in the blistering summers to fine snow sports in the mild winters.

A little more than 10 miles (16 km) from US 95, the Kyle Canyon Road (Nevada State Highway 157) climbs steeply into the forest. First stop is Mt. Charleston Hotel, which has a large lodge-like lobby complete with roaring fireplace, bar and big dance floor, and spacious restaurant. Built in 1984, this is one of the most romantic spots in southern Nevada, a perfect place to propose (and then return to Las Vegas to get married an hour or two later). Up the road is Mt. Charleston village, with a few residences and a U.S. Forest Service district office. The road ends at Mt. Charleston Lodge restaurant; from there the half-mile Little Falls Trail is easy-going, the three-quarter-mile Cathedral Rock Trail is moderately steep, with sheer drops but great views, and the North Loop Trail covers nine hard miles (14.4 hard km) to the peak.

Backtracking on Nevada Highway 157 to just before the hotel, Nevada Highway 158 heads off to the left and connects in 6 miles (9.6 km) with Nevada Highway 156, the Lee Canyon Road. Robbers Roost is a short easy hike to a large rock grotto which once sheltered local horse thieves. The South Loop Trail starts just past Hilltop Campground (13 hard miles/21 hard km to the peak).

At the top of Lee Canyon is the Lee Canyon Ski Area, or "Ski Lee." Operated since 1962 by the Highfield family, the base altitude is 8,500 feet (2,590 meters) and the top of the chairlift is another 1,000 feet (300 meters) higher. Thin air. But cliff walls towering above the slope protect skiers from biting westerlies. A beginner chairlift (and ski school) feeds the bunny slope; a T-bar ferries bodies to the intermediate Strip; and the double chairlift delivers Las Vegans (80 percent of skiers are locals; another 10 percent are their guests) to runs called Keno, Blackjack, and Slot Alley.

Down the mountain a bit from the ski area are plentiful places for tubing, sledding, snowmobiling, and cross-country skiing. Best nordic is on north-facing slopes, in open meadows above 8,000 feet (2,438 meters). Scott Canyon, Mack's Canyon, and the Bristlecone Pine Trail are popular. Next nearest skiing to Las Vegas is Brian Head, Utah, four hours away. Where else in the world can you scuba dive a drowned asphalt factory at sea level in the morning, slalom an advanced ski slope at 9,000 feet (2,740 meters) in the afternoon, propose and get married in the evening, and then shoot craps all night long?

■ LAUGHLIN

The Colorado River flows out of Mojave Desert country, into Sonoran Desert country, where the southern wedge of Nevada splits the Arizona-California border. This is the lowest point in Nevada—450 feet (137 meters) above sea level—and the hottest. The country's highest temperatures are recorded here more than 20 days a year. Other than Tristate City, a minor mining town that lived and died in the 1920s, the wedge remained untouched by human hands until the early 1950s, when Davis Dam was built. A prominent rock shaped like a bull's head was buried beneath Lake Mojave, but not before it gave a name to the dam workers' base of operations: Bullhead City, Arizona. After the dam was topped off, Bullhead City clung to the banks of the Colorado, as it clung to life, a tiny retirement community and fishing service center. Across the river in Nevada, a bait shack squatted on Sandy Point beach, frying to a crisp in the fierce Sonoran sun.

Enter Don Laughlin. Like many an optimistic prospector before him, Laughlin saw a gold mine where everyone else, even the ravens, saw a lunar wasteland. Thirty-three years old, in his pocket cash and a gaming license from a dozen good years

(opposite, and above) The Colorado Belle, a riverboat casino actually on a river!

in the heady Las Vegas of the 1950s, he purchased 6 acres (2.4 hectares) of land at the end of a sandy road for $250,000, $35,000 down. On it sat the bait shop, an eight-room motel (half of which was occupied by his family), and a six-seat bar. But it was his gaming license that put Laughlin in the black, and he slowly began to expand his Riverside resort. (An Irish postal official put "Laughlin" on the map. According to legend, the inspector, O'Reilly, listened to Laughlin's suggestions of Riverside and Casino for the name of the town, but settled on Laughlin instead, liking the Irish ring of it. Today Don Laughlin jokes that the town was named after his mother.)

Both Laughlins struggled for the first decade or so. Banks laughed at his loan applications. But Southern California Edison built a coal-fired power plant just up the hill from the river, expanding the population base. And slowly, people from Needles, Kingman, Lake Havasu, and even as far away as San Bernardino and Flagstaff began frequenting the friendly little river resort-casino as an alternative to Las Vegas. By 1976, the Riverside Hotel had expanded to 100 rooms with 300 slots.

The growth of Bullhead City, Arizona, right across the Colorado River, kept pace. Its population increased from 600 in 1966 to more than 6,000 by 1976, as employees, retirees, and snowbirds moved in, attracted by the weather, the water, and the wagering. By 1984, the Riverside was a 14-story, 350-room hotel, and a half-dozen other casinos lined the river. But little else existed there. The same year, Laughlin boasted a grand total of 95 residents—the temperature still higher than the population, and one casino for every 16 people! The rest of Laughlin's 3,000 employees lived on the Arizona side (by then Bullhead City had surpassed the 15,000 mark), commuting across the river by way of the Davis Dam bridge or the casino ferries.

But the mid-1980s was just the beginning of the boom. Don Laughlin proceeded to spend more than a million of his own dollars in road improvements, more than three million to build the new bridge from Bullhead City to his hotel, then finally convinced Nevada to take it over. He also spent $6 million to expand the airport across the river. Meanwhile, developers like Bob Bilbray (whose 1978 investment of a couple million dollars in 430 town-site acres/174 hectares has increased by 250 percent) have been building condos, apartments, shopping centers, a school, and a library. And the casinos keep coming: Circus Circus's 1,238-room Colorado Belle opened in July 1987, right next door to its Circus Circus sister, the

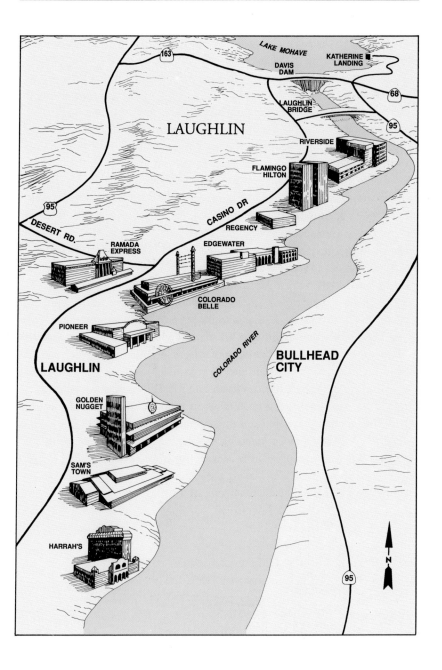

600-room Edgewater. Harrah's gorgeous 1,000-room Del Rio Hotel opened in mid-1988. And a huge Flamingo Hilton recently opened between the 660-room Riverside and the little Regency Casino. Steve Wynn paid $40 million for Del Webb's Nevada Club (now the Golden Nugget), and construction is underway on a thousand-room tower. Price tags attached to riverfront land along Laughlin's "strip" are now twice as high as those along that other Strip 100 miles (160 km) north. In fact, for all of Las Vegas's monopolizing of the great Nevada boom, Laughlin registers a resonant cannonade all its own.

Consider the statistics. Occupancy rates in 1988 averaged an astounding 97.2 percent, with March, April, and June surpassing 99 percent. Seven out of ten visitors arrived from Arizona and California, with eight out of ten having no plans for onward travel. The other two of ten originated from Las Vegas. Surveyed visitors spent an average of seven hours a day gambling, with a betting budget of $353— just under that of Las Vegas. In plain English, not only do Californians and Arizonans come to Laughlin to gamble, but Las Vegas residents and visitors as well!

The reasons become clear as you tour the town. You'll immediately notice how airy and bright the casinos are, thanks to the big picture windows overlooking the river. Their more comfortable and less claustrophobic atmosphere makes you wonder what Las Vegas has against natural light. Also, inside the Riverside and Del Rio casinos, you can snap pictures to your heart's content. The hotel rooms can be 50 percent cheaper than comparable ones in Las Vegas, which accounts for vacancy rates that you need a micrometer to measure. And food here, like the cheap hotel rooms, expansive casinos, cooperative weather, and playful river, is user-friendly. All seven major hotels have 24-hour coffee shops, restaurants, and inexpensive buffets. Fishing in Lake Mojave (*big* striped bass), cruising the Colorado in ferries and tour boats, taking the self-guided walk through Davis Dam, swimming, camping, and hiking round out the activities.

PRACTICALITIES
GETTING THERE, GETTING AROUND, GETTING AWAY

(**Note:** For complete lists of addresses and phone numbers of hotels, restaurants, museums, and other attractions mentioned in the following pages, please refer to the "Useful Addresses" chapter in the back of this book.)

■ TRAVEL GUIDES

Just as Las Vegas's many "fronts"—lights, signs, themes, promises, seductions, surfaces—mount a staccato assault on your senses yet still coalesce into a coherent whole, so do the sources of information on the city and vicinity seem fragmented at first, but then merge into the big picture. The process is a large part of the pleasure—like resolving a connect-the-dots rendering. Most visitors are satisfied by booking a package weekend through a local travel agent at one of the big-name resorts, then gambling, eating, and show-going nearby, and maybe glancing through a visitors guide for one or two further possibilities. But to really understand Las Vegas, to see through and around and beyond the fronts, requires some deeper digging, some invested investigating. The image is always enchanting, confounding—and fleeting. As soon as you think you've framed the final form, it dissolves and changes into something new.

Start with a travel guide. *Nevada Handbook*, by none other than yours truly, has an 85-page chapter on Las Vegas and environs. The practicalities, travel tips, and charts will get you organized and *thinking* about Las Vegas, if you're so inclined.

The American Automobile Association has a 95-page tour-guide on Las Vegas and Laughlin.

Frommer's *Guide to Las Vegas* mostly shills for the top 20 hotels—their rooms, restaurants, floor shows, casinos—and includes a few day trips and casino tips. Doesn't get too far off the beaten track, but not bad for where it goes. Although this guide has been through 10 editions and at least four different authors, the 1990 background material remains identical to 1971's.

Fodor's, on the other hand, finally has a new *Las Vegas*, written by Jefferson Graham, a reporter for *USA Today*, and author of *Las Vegas—Live And In Person*. Graham had help from experts for the chapters on gambling and dining.

■ VISITORS GUIDES AND MAGAZINES

No less than nine free publications for visitors are available in various places around town; motel lobbies are the best bet. They all cover basically the same territory—showrooms, lounges, dining, dancing, buffets, gambling, sports, events, coming attractions—and most have numerous ads that will transport coupon clippers to discount heaven.

Las Vegas Advisor, a monthly newsletter, is a must for serious and curious Las Vegas visitors. Written and published by Anthony Curtis of Huntington Press (Box 28041, Las Vegas, NV 89126, $30 per year), the *Advisor* takes a close and objective look at important local trends, events, tournaments, shows, meal deals, and coupons, and includes a Top-Ten Values rating worth the entire price of admission. All this, and more, packed into six attractive pages. Highly recommended.

Today in Las Vegas is an 80-page weekly mini-mag bursting its staples with listings, coupons, 20 pages of restaurants, and a good column on free casino lessons. For a free copy, write or call Lyconia Publishing, 3225 McLeod Dr., #203, L.V.,

The ladies and the tramp.

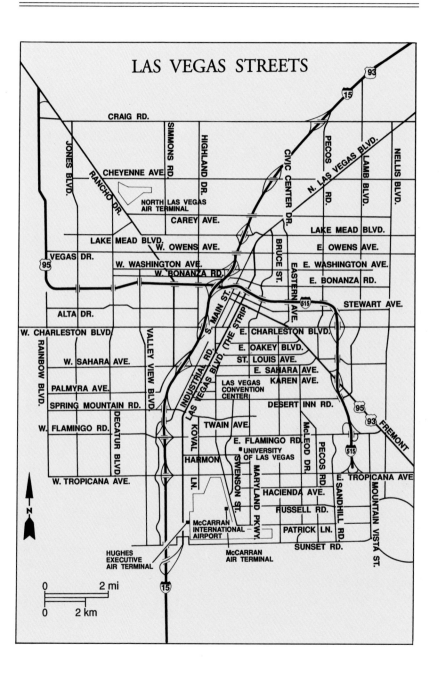

NV 89121, tel. (702) 385-2737. Just as good for listings, though with very few coupons, is the 48-page weekly *Tourguide of Las Vegas,* available Fridays from Desert Media Group, 333 N. Rancho #330, L.V., NV 89106, tel. (702) 873-2300.

What's On provides comprehensive information, plus articles, calendars, phone numbers, and lots of ads—recommended. It's Las Vegas maps are by far the best of the lot. Send $2.50 to Las Vegas Magazine, 610 S. 3rd, L.V., NV 89101, tel. (702) 385-5080.

The 100-page *Showbiz Magazine* spotlights performers, and has listings and ads for shows, lounges, and buffets, plus television and movie times; available from Total Entertainment, tel. (702) 383-7200.

Players' Panorama mostly covers gambling, with a little about mainroom shows, but they have an excellent listing of a dozen or so hotel package deals—the only one in the bunch that has anything about packages. Cover price is $2, but it's given away free in motel lobbies. Also available from Players' Panorama, 3111 S. Valley View, Blvd., #S-102, L.V., NV 89102, tel. (702) 367-2114.

Las Vegan magazine has come up with a successful mix of contemporary and historical articles, with a little art, fashion, gossip, humor, restaurant listings, showrooms, lounges, and a two-month daily calendar of happenings. Even the ads are tasteful. Definitely pick up a copy for $2.50 at Readmore Books and Magazines or a hotel gift shop when you're in town. Or get a subscription ($15 for six issues a year) from *Las Vegan City Magazine,* 2929 Industrial Rd., L.V., NV 89109, tel. (702) 733-8080.

■ LIBRARIES

The **Clark County Library** main branch is at 1401 E. Flamingo, tel. (702) 733-7810. The Nevada section is on shelf seven against the front wall.

The **James Dickinson Library** at UNLV is an odd and initially confusing structure, and very red. Study the two buildings, one rectangular and the other circular, with tunnels connecting them from outside, then wander around inside a bit to get your bearings. The rectangular building houses the circulation desk (first floor); periodicals, video, audio, and computer labs (second floor); and Special Collections (fourth floor). Go through the tunnels on the second and third floors to the round building for reference and the stacks.

Special Collections has hundreds of computer entries under Las Vegas—everything from Last Frontier Hotel promotional material (1949) and mobster biographies to screenplays for locally filmed movies and the latest travel videotapes. And that's just what's catalogued. Ask the supremely solicitous staff to help you find photographs, manuscripts, theses, records, archives, phone books, diaries, private collections—all on Las Vegas and environs. If this place had a kitchen and shower, I could live there.

Also in Special Collections is the **Gaming Research Center**, largest and most comprehensive gambling research collection in the world. It covers business, economics, history, psychology, sociology, mathematics, criminology, and biography, all contained in books, periodicals, reports, promo material, photographs, posters, memorabilia, and tape.

■ BOOKSTORES

Las Vegas is not renowned as a literary town. In fact, the word "book" around here, 90 percent of the time, is a verb. One books reservations, rooms, tickets; "to book" also means to accept and record wagers. "Book" as a noun generally refers to the room, counter, or big board where wagers on sports events and races are recorded. Probably the only place in town where bookmaking has anything to do with publishing is at the **Gambler's Book Club/Shop**. This cramped space is crowded with all the books on every form of wagering extant, from craps to video machines, from jai alai to dog racing. They also have a large case devoted to Mafia books and biographies, lots of local fiction, history, travel guides, books on probability theory, casino management, gambling and the law, magic, and a room in the back full of used books. Eavesdrop on the animated discussions around you! And be sure to pick up their 26th annual, 28-page tabloid catalog. But beware! If you're at all into print media about the local passions, this place will clean your pockets faster than the Wheel of Fortune.

B. Dalton has two branches, one at the Meadows Mall and one at the Boulevard Mall. **Waldenbooks** has three branches, within the Fashion Show and Meadows Mall, and across the street from the Boulevard Mall. **Barnes and Noble** in the Moyer Student Union on the UNLV campus has a good regional section; textbooks fill the rest of the store. **Readmore Books and Magazines** is found in four locations around town; they carry an amazing amount of magazines—no reason to go anyplace else for them. **Amber Unicorn** is a great used bookstore, with some excellent deals on classic Nevadana—unless *I've* bought them all already.

■ MAPS

Front Boy sells state-by-state Rand McNally maps, raised reliefs of Las Vegas and southern Nevada ($15 each), and United States Geological Survey topographical maps in different scales ($5). Ask for the stunning USGS Landsat photo ($5) of Las Vegas and Lake Mead. They also sell a street-map book of the city ($18.95), and poster-size maps of Las Vegas, the U.S., and other places.

■ INFORMATION BUREAUS

The **Chamber of Commerce** has a wall of commercial brochures, general fact sheets, and a Teleguide computer terminal—nice graphics and colors, a little information, discount coupons you can print out. They also have good info on a computerized phone line.

The **Las Vegas Convention and Visitors Bureau** also dispenses fliers in their Brochure Room inside the Convention Center to the right of the rotunda. One of the LVCVB's priorities is filling up hotel rooms—call their reservations service at (702) 383-9100. The marketing department is around the corner on Desert Inn Road off Maryland Parkway next to the firehouse; they have reams of information about visitors and conventions. The LVCVB has one of the biggest budgets of any visitors bureau in the country—the large, plush, busy marketing department is the proof.

■ ACCOMMODATIONS

With 55 major hotels and 215 motels, Las Vegas boasts a grand total of nearly 75,000 places to sleep. Steve Wynn's Mirage, opened in November 1989, accounts for 3,000 rooms of the total. Circus Circus's Excalibur, which came on line in June 1990, adds another 4,000. Recent expansions at the Sahara, Holiday Inn, Lady

(opposite) The people mover at Caesars takes you to your every fantasy.

Luck, and Vegas World have boosted the room count by 2,000. The Sands is adding a new tower with 1,300 rooms, the Stardust is constructing a 33-story tower with 1,500 rooms, and the Riviera, which recently completed an expansion making its casino the largest in the world (yes, it's even bigger than Trump's Taj Majal in Atlantic City), has also begun construction on an 1,800-room, 43-story skyscraper, which will be the tallest building, by 10 stories, in the state. Finally, the new MGM Grand, due to open in 1992, will contain 5,000 rooms, making it the largest hotel in the world.

With so many to choose from, if it seems like easy money to find that one perfect room with your name on it, think again. Nearly 20 million visitors are expected in Las Vegas in 1990; that's roughly 55,000 a day. Weekend occupancy rates averaged 93.5 percent in 1988 (mid-week rates averaged 81.4 percent). In addition, 681 conventions, with a total attendance of more than 1,700,000, often (twice a month) dump between 10,000 and 100,000 delegates on the town in one fell swoop. And many people, especially in winter, stay for weeks and months at a time in motels.

In short, this town fills up fast—especially the top hotels and best-value motels. But even if you show up on New Year's Eve or during the 104,000-participant Winter Consumer Electronics Trade Show, some kind of room, somewhere, should be available. Besides, your hotel or motel room is where you'll spend the *least* time during your wild Las Vegas weekend or vacation. One way to look at accommodations in Las Vegas is to remember the old traveler's axiom: eat sweet, pay for play, but sleep cheap. Otherwise, as always, it's best to make your reservations far in advance to ensure the appropriate kind, price, and location of your room.

HOTELS AND PACKAGES

The cheapest hotel rooms are found weekdays, downtown. Rates rise rapidly on the Strip, and ascend again, both places, on the weekends. Occupancy rates, however, are consistently higher downtown than on the Strip. If you don't have to ask the price of a room, or if you want to splash out in ultra luxury, or if you just received a large insurance settlement or hit a progressive slot jackpot, try a four-bedroom suite with a complete bar, sunken marble tub, swimming pool, and Kuala Lumpur theme at the Desert Inn ($850); or a 1,000-square-foot (93 square-meter), 23rd-floor corner suite in the Island Tower at the Trop, complete with rock-façade jacuzzi, eight-person steamroom, sauna, and cushion-carpeted bedroom ($400); or even a mini-suite at Bally's with round bed, mirrored ceiling, and pink champagne on ice ($100). Otherwise, if you're staying for the typical three or four nights, and you're on a budget with a limit that you'd prefer to max out in some other way (a hotel room, after all, is a hotel room, even in Las Vegas), get yourself the best package deal you can find. These usually include one or two meals, several comp cocktails, funbook, tickets to the hotel's showroom or revue, free trip to the spa, discount coupons, and bellman's gratuities. Simply call the 800 numbers in "Useful Addresses" in the back of this book for up-to-date information and reservations, check with the reservations services (see below), or call your local travel agent.

WEEKLIES

The most affordable way to get your fill of Las Vegas is to take a motel room by the week. Most motels give sizable discounts for these rates; many contain refrigerators or entire kitchenettes. This can save you a lot of money in both lodging and food costs, allowing you to spend it on other pleasures of the senses. The only challenge is *finding* one. Several factors conspire to make the search discouraging. First, not all the motels have weeklies. And those that do often allot a limited number of their total rooms for the discounted rate. Secondly, every winter a flock of snowbirds migrates to Las Vegas, some of whom squat in these weeklies till it gets too hot. It's not uncommon to hear in early December that the Desert Paradise Motel, for example, won't have a weekly room rate available till the Ides of March, or that Tod Motor Lodge is taking applications to be put on a waiting list, or that Hop's will be full forever. These snowbirds reserve their same rooms for the following November right when they depart in spring. Third, with 1,000 people moving to Las Vegas every week to start a new life, and with apartment occupancy rates hovering just below 100 percent, these wanna-be Las Vegans often wind up monopolizing the few vacant weeklies.

Where there's life, though, there's hope (in fact, hope is quite a profitable product in this town). If you plan to eat all your meals in restaurants and don't need a refrigerator or stove, you can get weeklies for as low as $85 (New West), and you'll have a much easier time locating one. You can also bring your own hotplate and cooler (don't forget an extension cord or two) for your coffee, tea, hot cereal, and sandwiches. The more prepared you are the better—bring all the kitchen stuff you'll need: pots, plates, cups, silverware, spices, toaster oven, sponge, dish soap, can opener.

GETTING MARRIED IN LAS VEGAS

Nearly 75,000 marriages are performed in Las Vegas every year, close to 200 every day of the year. In Nevada, there's no waiting period, no blood test, and the minimum age is 18 (16 and 17 need a notarized affidavit of parental consent; under 16, a court order). All that's required is a license. Simply appear at the County Recorder's office, 200 S. 3rd St. downtown, tel. 455-3156, with your money ($25), your ID, and your fiancé. It's open 8 a.m. to midnight Monday through Thursday, and 24 hours Friday, Saturday, and holidays. Then, if you want a no-frills, justice-of-the-peace nuptial, walk a block over to 136 S. 4th St., to the office of the Commissioner of Civil Marriages, open same hours as

Minister administers nuptials.

above, where a surrogate-J.P. deputy commissioner will unite you in holy matrimony for another $25-30. No appointments, no waiting, just "I now pronounce you . . ." and it's done.

But a more traditional setting, with flowers, organ music, photographs, and a minister awaits at the renowned wedding chapels of Las Vegas. Most are grouped around the courthouse, or on Las Vegas Boulevard South between downtown and Sahara Avenue. Within a 10-block stretch are a dozen or so; wander in, talk to the receptionist, tour the facilities, and if you're lucky you might be able to observe a ceremony or two in progress. Within an hour you'll have a good impression of the Las Vegas wedding industry: the concept lovely, the execution a matter of taste.

You have your choice of ceremonies: "civil" means no mention of God, "non-denominational" uses the word. You can also supply your own text—much depends on the minister. The basic chapel fee is $40-60, and $35 is the recommended donation to the minister. Spring for a $5 silk boutonniere and $45 bouquet, and throw in $50 worth of snapshots, plus the limo ride to the courthouse for a license or back to your hotel ($25 toke to the driver—worth it for the stories alone!). You can really start to add up a tab by arranging to have live organ music, having an audio or video tape made of the wedding, renting tuxes and gowns, buying rings, cakes, garters, and wedding certificate holders, right there on the premises.

The spring wedding season starts in February, around Valentine's Day, and continues through June, the monster month. New Year's Eve is the biggest wedding night of the year. Weekends are always busiest. Most chapels like to book weddings at half-hour intervals, so even without reservations, you can probably squeeze "a beautiful ceremony" into an available slot. But to reserve in advance a time convenient to the convention, contact the Las Vegas Convention and Visitors Bureau, 3150 Paradise Road, Las Vegas, Nevada 89109, tel. (702) 733-2323, for their list of three dozen marriage parlors.

The granddad of all the wedding chapels, in fact one of the oldest buildings in Las Vegas, is the **Little Church of the West**, 3960 Las Vegas Boulevard South. This historic chapel opened in 1942 at the Last Frontier Village, the western theme park next to the Last Frontier Hotel. It was designed by the Last Frontier's architect and manager Bill Moore, as an exact, half-size replica of a famous church built in Columbia, California in 1849, with redwood walls and gas lamps. The Las Vegas chapel remained in place for almost 40 years, even after the village was dismantled, and the Last Frontier Hotel was reincarnated as the New Frontier, then came back again as the Frontier. Finally, it was moved to its present grassy and shady location, next to the Hacienda Hotel, in the early 1980s.

Wee Kirk o' the Heather and the **Hitching Post** have been operating since the late 1940s; they both moved to their present locations, 226 and 231 Las Vegas Boulevard

Candlelight Chapel.

South, in 1959. The **Little White Chapel**, 1301 Las Vegas Boulevard South, has been in the same location since 1954; Joan Collins was married there once. The **Candlelight**, 2855 Las Vegas Boulevard South, right in the heart of the Strip, is probably the most popular chapel, with a 24-hour-a-day conveyor belt of ceremonies. **L'Amour Chapel**, 1903 Las Vegas Boulevard South, has red-velvet love seats in the chapel, a store full of wedding gowns for rent or purchase, and a 36-foot (11-meter) RV, Weddings on Wheels, for getting married outside the Mirage, for example, just as the volcano blows. Possibly the most tasteful is **The Chapel of Love**, 1431 Las Vegas Boulevard South. Only one of the four lovely rooms to choose from is booked at any given time, which eliminates the discomfort of rushing one wedding party out to make room for the next.

Once you land a room, there are several variables which you'll need to understand and make clear with the management. Be sure their week is as long as yours! Some Las Vegas motels have redefined "week" into *six* nights. It's true. Something having to do with Saturday rates. Try not to leave any deposit; in Las Vegas, once the money is gone, it rarely comes back (though toward the end of your stay, a deposit might be as much a security for *you* as the motel!). The telephone situation can also be tricky. Some motels charge 25 cents for local calls; some have free local calls but don't offer long-distance; where available, long-distance might need to go through the front desk. Find out if the room is cleaned every day, or every week, or at all; sometimes linen is extra. Always look at the room first! Make sure the heat or air conditioning works; it's never a bad idea to have a small space heater or fan just in case. Make sure the windows lock and there's at least a chain on the door; a deadbolt is even better. If there's a kitchenette, test the stove/oven, and see that the refrigerator is cold. You might have to take the room regardless of its flaws, but if you point them out to the front desk, you could try bargaining down the price a little. Or another room might mysteriously appear.

Use the chart in "Useful Addresses" to call around for availability and reservations. Most motels with weeklies operate on a first-come, first-served basis. In this case, ask about the price and amenities, and whether a weekly room is available *today*. Management doesn't really know if people are going to leave, except from day to day after it happens. Some, however, will hold a room for you, such as the Fun City and the Crest. Another possibility is to take your chances and breeze into Las Vegas, grab a room for one night, then get on the phone the next day. Best time to call is around noon. In this case, it's wise to arrive on a weekday, when single-night rooms are readily available, and rates are 20 to 50 percent lower than on a Friday or Saturday. With diligence and luck you'll find a weekly and wind up saving a substantial amount of dough by the weekend, which you can then blow in some other way.

MOTELS

Motels cluster in five general areas of town. The groups that are consistently least expensive and most available are north of downtown on North Main, Las Vegas Boulevard North, and the north numbered streets; and east/southeast of downtown on East Fremont. The north locations are slightly iffy for walking around securely after dark, but are fine for daytime strolling and driving to and from anytime; the closer to downtown, the safer. Some charge as little as $20 nightly and $85 weekly. The East Fremont motels line up one after another on the wide straight strip toward Boulder City. It's a "fer piece" to the casinos (except the venerable Showboat at the west end and Sam's Town at the east), but it's a good place to cruise if you don't have a reservation and most No Vacancy signs are lit.

The two groups south of downtown along Las Vegas Boulevard South are good for location, though a bit more expensive. Most convenient are the motels between Charleston Boulevard and Sahara Avenue, right between downtown and the Strip. Another line of motels stretches down the lower Strip between Bally's on Flamingo Avenue and the south edge of the city just beyond the Hacienda Hotel.

Finally, a good group of motels surrounds the Convention Center along Paradise Road, Desert Inn Road, and Convention Center Drive.

CASINO CAMPING AND RV PARKING

The nearest campgrounds to Las Vegas are **American Campgrounds**, about five miles (eight km) north of town, and **KOA**, about five miles southeast. Otherwise, camp at **Red Rock Canyon**, 20 miles (32 km) from town, **Lake Mead** campgrounds, 20-40 miles (32-64 km) from town, or Mt. Charleston, 40 miles from town.

Hotels that have RV hook-ups include **Circus Circus**, **Stardust**, **Hacienda**, and **Sam's Town**. Most charge between $9-11 for a space and hook-up, with full hotel facilities at your disposal.

Other camper parks include **Hitchin' Post**, and **Lone Palm**.

RESERVATION SERVICES

These services reserve blocks of rooms at large hotels downtown and on the Strip. If they don't sell them before a certain cutoff date (from 2 to 20 days in advance), the hotels cancel the service's reservations and sell the rooms themselves. Depending on the cutoff date, you can book a room with a service at an otherwise "sold-out" hotel. The services also book two, three, and four-night packages. Some handle tours and shows. Others book air and hotel combination packages as well. Some offer rooms at a lower rate due to the block discount (the hotel pays the service's commission). Often the services (and the hotels themselves) require a two-night minimum over the weekend at the premium price; the hotels are reluctant to sell for Saturday night only, and hold out till the last minute before they release any one-night weekend rooms. Also, weekends often require reservations far in advance, especially during holidays and high season. You confirm your room with a credit card number, so make sure that you understand the cancellation policy; usually you can get all your money back with 48-hours' notice, but at some places you forfeit your first night's deposit.

■ WHERE TO EAT

Las Vegas is both a gourmet's kingdom come and a gourmand's hog heaven. You can max out the lines on two of your credit cards at some of the finest dining west of New York City and east of Paris, or you can stuff yourself silly for under $5, shoveling home sheer tasteless volume at any one of 27 buffets around town. Most major hotels have a gourmet room with four dollar signs next to the name, as well as a $5 steak or prime rib in the coffeeshop, some combination of Italian, Japanese, Chinese, Mexican, and steakhouse restaurants under the same roof, plus snack bars, fast food, and ice cream parlors. A handful of restaurants around town have survived 30, 40, even 50 years, while trendy Cajun, Southwestern, and nouvelle cuisine meals are served fresh from the latest high-tech kitchens. Familiar fast food is around every corner, as well as plenty of exotic ethnic eateries. More than 700 restaurants are listed on 35 Yellow Pages, with this writer's favorite 60 or so covered below.

LAS VEGAS'S TEN
OLDEST RESTAURANTS

Green Shack. Not only is this the oldest, continuously operating restaurant in Las Vegas, but it's also in the same location, even in the same building! Green Shack opened, as the Colorado, in 1929, when Jimmie Jones sold fried chicken from the window of her two-room house. In 1932, she purchased a barracks from Union Pacific, hauled it to her house, and called it the Green Shack. This barracks is still the dining room, hosting chicken dinners, birthdays, anniversaries, weddings, divorces, wakes, and hearty parties for nearly 60 years—ancient history for Las Vegas! The bar and kitchen have since been added, but the Shack is still run by Jimmie Jones's great-grand-nephew. There is simply nowhere else in this town to go for chicken—white meat, dark meat, fried, roasted, gizzards, livers, $8.50-

10.75. They also serve some fish, steak, and tasty bread pudding. The Green Shack has it all—informality, friendliness, great food, and best of all, a long history.

Fong's. In 1933, J.S. Fong, a cook at the Rainbow Club downtown, opened the Silver Café at 106 North First Street next to the Silver Club. He advertised American food, with 25-cent breakfasts and 35-cent dinners, and was the only Las Vegas café serving Chinese food, by request, till 1941. In 1955, the Silver Café changed its name to Fong's when it relocated to the present site on East Charleston. You can't miss it: big neon pagoda-roof signs grace the entrance. Inside are mandarin-size red booths, large paintings, and a rock shrine, along with the same American and Chinese food this family has been serving almost as long as the Green Shack has been dishing up its chicken.

Wimpy's. This Fifties-style drive-in began as a small café at 306 Fremont Street in 1935, then moved a block down to 210 Fremont in 1948 and changed its name to Wimpy's Drive-In. It disappeared for a while in the late 1950s, then resurfaced at its present location in 1963. Pull up and grab the Servus Fone to order your $1.50 burgers, 75-cent corn dogs, turkey sandwich or specials for $3.50, the best chili dog in the state for $2, plus banana splits, milkshakes, etc. Very busy place—classic cheap food, great atmosphere, a time capsule.

El Sombrero has been in the same location since 1951, when it was opened by Uncle Clemente Greigo; his nephews Jose and Zeke Aragon are now in charge. The best thing about El Sombrero is that this stucco cantina, with six booths, six tables, and a completely Mexican jukebox, looks its age, and has certainly seen it all, but retains its baby-boomer vitality and devotion to service and quality. Small dinners are $5, combo dinners are $6.45, and the service is no-nonsense!

Alpine Village began serving German food to Las Vegans in a downtown location in 1952, and moved four times before settling into its present location in 1970. The main dining room is reminiscent of a Bavarian village square, with wrought-iron grillwork, sloping roofs, a staff wearing *Sound of Music* costumes, and a truly festive atmosphere. The Rathskeller downstairs is a bar and sandwich shop, with peanuts and popcorn on the tables and oompah piano playing. A gift shop sells German dolls, mugs, glassware, etc. Schnitzels, bratens, chicken, and daily specials go for $12-16. Valet parking available.

The Venetian. This restaurant began as the Pizzeria Restaurant, down the block from the Green Shack, in 1955, one of the first pizzerias in Las Vegas. It moved to its present site in 1966 and changed its name to the Venetian Pizzeria; the Pizzera was eventually dropped, though the pizza is still served in the bar or with a dinner. The Venetian is very popular, wins awards, and has interesting interior and exterior murals of Venice. Spaghetti dinners $10, chicken $17, veal $19, fish $21, and five pages of wine on the menu.

The Venetian is one of the oldest, and best, restaurants in Las Vegas.

Macayo Vegas. Across from the new Charleston Plaza, the Macayo opened here in 1960, and has been so successful that today it boasts four other locations in town, plus several others in Arizona. It has a bright and cheery atmosphere, with *typico* Tex-Mex food, like fajitas and chimichangas. $6-10.

The Flame. The red and blue flickering neon flames have been attracting carnivores since 1961. The server brings around a tray of meat, from which you pick your steak; the set price of $17.95 includes fries or a baker, salad and onion rings. Three-dollar breakfasts and four-dollar lunches are also served from 2 a.m. to 5 p.m. This place is small, very crowded, noisy, old, and fun—about as far away from the Strip as you can be, for being right on the Strip.

Sultan's Table. In 1961, Dunes Hotel owner Major Riddle sold a large chunk of his hotel to locals Charlie Rich and Sid Wyman, and used part of the cash to finance its first major expansion. Sultan's Table opened in March 1961, and has been one of Las Vegas's top gourmet rooms ever since. Its decidedly French menu features such delicacies as frog's legs ($22), Long Island duck l'orange ($24), beef bourguignon ($26) and crepes suzette ($10). It's a big, quiet, beautiful room, with stained glass, piano, and impeccable service. Recommended.

Golden Steer. You wouldn't recognize it from the unremarkable exterior, but this steakhouse, in the same location since 1962, is one of the most popular and elegant restaurants in Las Vegas, usually jammed with locals, and visitors in the know. In the front room is the spectacular woody, glassy bar surrounded by comfy living room furniture. The three dining rooms are no less inviting. And the food?

Well, the filet mignon is truly the Aristocrat of Tenderness, and the N.Y. pepper steak is the best in town. Dinners start at $17. Reservations a must at prime time.

H O T E L   F O O D
■ Pageantry And Panorama

Benihana. This spectacle of a restaurant, at Las Vegas Hilton, consists of a cocktail lounge out front, with musical waters, a Las Vegas tradition, and an animated bird show with stuffed-animal entertainers, which is reminiscent of Chuck E. Cheese. Hibachi tableside and *robata* barbecue rooms feature similar menus, with dinners from $12 to 33, mostly meat, fish, and veggies. For just the show, though, sit in the lounge and sip some steaming *sake* (performances on the hour starting at 5 p.m.).

Bacchanal. Walk past the stone lions guarding the door for Caesar and down to the sunken room with a lighted pool and statue at center stage. This fixed Roman feast of seven courses—appetizer, soup, salad, fish entrèe, main meal, vegetables, and dessert—is accented by toga-clad wine goddesses who serve all the juice of the vine your heart desires and your liver can stand, and massage male guests' necks and shoulders just before dessert. At $60 per person, it's one of the most expensive meals in town, but worth it for the experience, especially in a group.

Dome of the Sea. The Dunes's subterranean seashell, serving sumptuous piscatory delicacies, is bathed in a soothing soft-blue light, with fish swimming along the walls. A mermaid might even swim up and play the harp in a mid-room lagoon. Mahi mahi $18, salmon hollandaise $21, lobster tail $36.

Ristorante Italiano. This room at the Riviera is known for its wall-length mural behind glass and its veal: osso buco, saltimbocca, piccata, and scallopine ($18-20). Pasta $11-12, chicken $15-16, steaks $25, lobster $35. After dinner, see "Splash" or gamble in the world's largest (and brightest) casino.

Kokomo's. This Continental restaurant sits under hut-like canopies within the rain forest of the Mirage's domed atrium. It's slightly noisy from the casino and the waterfalls, but the hubbub quickly becomes part of the unusual atmosphere. Try the Dungeness crab cakes ($16), salmon ($18), filet mignon ($16-22), prime rib ($18-28), or lobster tail ($34).

Next door to Kokomo's is **Moongate.** In fact, all the Mirage's restaurants are in the same wing, served by a single, 29,000-square-foot (2,735-square-meter) kitchen. The Moongate replicates a Chinese village square, with a big lilac tree in the middle, pagoda roofs, scalloped walls, and great curves. The food is as pleasing as the environment, and the prices are reasonable. Satay beef, moo shu pork, tea-smoked duck, and strawberry chicken all go for $14, and scallops, shrimp and lobster are under $20.

Centerstage. This restaurant is a combination steakhouse and coffeeshop, a very effective concept for its location. Without a doubt the room with the best neon view in town, the Centerstage sits in a tinted dome looking straight down Glitter Gulch, with the lighted Union Plaza Hotel tower soaring above. When you make reservations, specify seating at a front-window table.

Down Fremont Street is the **Skye Room**, on the 24th floor of the old Mint tower (now the Horseshoe). The restaurant and bar also have great views, the restaurant facing south (Strip) and west (Spring Mountains), while the bar looks south and east (you *almost* think you can see Lake Mead—but not quite). Salmon, sole, scampi, chicken, duck, or steak Diane flambé for $18; filet, sirloin, prime rib, or porterhouse for $19. Like the Centerstage, great downtown prices for good food and an incomparable view.

The only view that compares, actually, is at **Visko's of New Orleans**, on the 27th floor of the Landmark Hotel. Newly remodeled, this pastel room is quiet and sultry, and the view is pure ambrosia. Blackened catfish starts things off at $10, catfish is $11, trout $14, lobster $20. After dinner, head up to the Lambada Club on the 31st floor for a drink and a dance, and enjoy a 360-degree view—you won't believe how large the Desert Inn country club and golf course are!

■ Gourmet Rooms

Of a dozen or so very fancy hotel restaurants in Las Vegas, the following four are representative. **Pegasus**, at the Alexis Park Hotel, is one of the only restaurants in town that consistently receives a four-star rating from Mobil Travel Guides. The Mobil judges must have major expense accounts! Start with a little goose-liver pâté or truffles ($25), or fresh clams ($12), then move on to some chicken (cheapest entrée at $23), shellfish fettucine ($28), quail in madeira sauce ($35), or one of seven lobster dishes (starting at $36). The room is large and bright, with pleasing peach pastel decor and brass trim, and a piano on center stage. It's elegant and understated—comfortably unpretentious. Best of all, the Alexis Park has no casino.

Similar in price, though opposite in ambience, is **Michael's**, at Barbary Coast. Start off with a little coquilles St. Jacques ($15) or vichyssoise ($8), then tuck into a nice spinach salad ($8). Prime rib is $30, veal piccata is $34, a filet is $39. Finish off with fresh berries ($9) and espresso (a whopping $4.50!). Plan on at least $50 per person without wine—and renowned for being worth it. Unlike the Pegasus, this is a small, dark, intimate room, with a stained glass dome, great for a romantic interlude, or a very private *tête à tête*.

Similar in ambience but less expensive is the **Burgundy Room**, at the Lady Luck downtown. Good-looking fish dishes start at a reasonable $18, lobster for $19, filet for $20. Popular, intimate, satisfying.

Finally, combining the airy brightness of the Pegasus with the downtown prices of the Burgundy Room is **Rhapsody**, at the Tropicana. Salmon and grilled capon breast go for $18, snapper and duckling with raspberry sauce for $20, veal for $23, and filet $26. Sunday champagne brunch (9 a.m. to noon) is $15. The semicircular room, decked out in burgundy velvet booths, big vases, silk flowers, and chandeliers, overlooks the Island water park—most conducive to relaxation and digestion.

Along with the Bacchanal and Sultan's Table (covered earlier), other gourmet rooms of note include **Delmonico's** at the Riviera, the **Regency Room** at the Sands, and **Le Montrachet** at the Hilton.

■ Steakhouses

Perhaps the essence of the Las Vegas steakhouse can be experienced at Circus Circus's aptly named **Steakhouse**. Wind your way through the permanent crowds of grinds and kids toward the buffet and tower elevators; walking into the Steakhouse, cow portraits lead to the meat locker where sides of beef can go hang. The split-level dining area surrounds the grill, which lends an authentic, slightly smoky air to the room. Perfect for charcoal freaks. Chicken for $12, top sirloin for $15, filet $20, surf and turf $20.

Similarly, the large mesquite grill and line area of the **All-American Bar and Grille**, at the new Rio Hotel, faces the downstairs dining room; upstairs are additional tables, along with a quite unusual collection of antique slot machines. Order your meat—top sirloin for $14, New York for $18, filet for $19—and then choose your sauce—bernaise, dijon, peppercorn, mushrooms, horseradish.

The Charcoal Room at the Hacienda Hotel, also has a grill fronting the dining area, but the setting and service are more like a gourmet room's. Your dinner begins with a relish tray, followed by black bean soup, salad and raisin bread, then a sorbet and champagne *intermezzo*, and then the entrée—chicken ($15), sole ($17.50), or prime rib ($21.50).

Wellington's at the Aladdin has some of the most reasonable steakhouse prices: T-bone or barbecued ribs or chicken for $9, catch of the day $10, prime rib $11-13, filet $17.50.

BUFFETS, STEAKS, AND MEAL DEALS

Buffets are one small step up from fast food, and one giant leap down in price. For the cost of satisfying a Big Mac attack, you can shovel home, on average, 23 choices of chow. Breakfast presents the usual fruits, juices, croissant, steam-table scrambled eggs, sausage, potatoes, and pastries. Lunch is salads and cold cuts. Dinner is salads, steam-table mook, vegetables, and potatoes, and usually either a baron of beef, shoulder of pork, leg of lamb, saddle of mutton, or breast of turkey. Prices have little to do with quality; the $6 lunch at the Las Vegas Hilton might not be noticeably better than the $2 lunch at the Trop. Unless you're really starving and must have food!—now!—check out the buffet first by asking the cashier if you can sneak a peek.

The buffets are cheap: Circus Circus's cudfest goes all the way up to $3.89 for 36 different dinner dishes, and even the Golden Nugget's dinner buffet, the most expensive in town, is only $9.50. Buffet times and prices are listed in most of the free visitors' guides, and in the Friday *Review-Journal.* Generally, breakfast is served from 7-10, lunch goes 11-3, and dinner 4-10, give or take an hour earlier or later.

The best buffet in Las Vegas is at **Palace Station**, 2411 W. Sahara Boulevard. The quality here is superior, plus the buffet line surrounds an open prep area, where cooks keep the food stocked, and prepare dishes to order (eggs, sandwiches, meat, and fish).

For the fabled cheap steaks and prime rib, just read the large print on the hotel marquees around town. Or look at the ads in the visitors' guides. Nearly all these meat bargains are served in the hotel coffeeshops. If none are listed on the marquee or menu, ask. **Circus Circus**, the **Frontier**, and the **Sands** have long-running $6 slab specials. Some hotels serve their meal deals at unusual times. The **Horseshoe**, for example, offers a $2 steak or prime rib dinner from 10 p.m. to 5:45 a.m., and the **California** and **Fremont** also serve late-night steaks.

Other Las Vegas food specials include 50-cent shrimp cocktails and hot dogs, $10 lobsters, and dollar beers.

Downtown, **The Steakhouse** at the Horseshoe has good meat and prices. **William B's** at the Stardust has a great reputation with the locals. And **Diamond Lil's** at Sam's Town covers the meat-and-atmosphere department.

■ Italian

By far one of the best hotel restaurants in Las Vegas, consistently in the Top-Ten Values of the "Las Vegas Advisor," is **Pasta Pirate** at the California Hotel downtown. A wonderful meal can be made of the dinner salad, which comes with baby shrimp ($3), and the toasted ravioli appetizer ($4). But for the same money, you can get a nice slab of filet mignon, with a baker, veggies, garlic bread, and glass of wine! Or try the mesquite-broiled mahi mahi ($8) or snapper ($9). Designer pasta is an alternative: first "you picka you pasta, then you picka your sauca," as the menu instructs. The grill is out front, and those cooks *move*. The decor is early rustic—vents, pipes, shelves, neon. Highly recommended.

Also downtown is **Chicago Joe's** at Fitzgerald's. This is an expansion of one of downtown's favorite little hole-in-the-wall Italian restaurants, opened in 1975, at

When this line cook, at the Palace Station's Action Buffet, was asked if he could flip two pans of eggs at once, he replied matter-of-factly, "Yes—one winds up on the floor."

820 S. Fourth, and the quality remains consistent. Weekdays from 2-9 p.m., all-you-can-eat spaghetti is $4; lasagna, ravioli, and sausage and peppers are $6.25. Pasta dinners go for $6-8, Chicago hot shrimp or shrimp parmigiana for $10.

Andiamo's at the Hilton is beautiful, bright, and comfortable, with the big kitchen facing the room. Roast duck and noodles $15, pasta with cream sauce $11, veal scallopine marsala $17.

Portofino at the Desert Inn, is on the second floor of the DI overlooking, obliquely, the casino (the view, of the round brass chandeliers, is slightly surreal). Pasta goes for $10-14, trout $18, filet $28.

Primavera at Caesars Palace overlooks the stunning Garden of the Gods swimming pool. Poolside dining, too. The thing to have here, naturally, is the Caesars salad ($12.75 for two), but also try anything from eggs for breakfast and hamburgers for lunch to Maine lobster ($45) for dinner.

■ Oriental

Empress Court at Caesars Palace is the fanciest and most expensive Chinese restaurant you'll ever eat in.

Ah So, also at Caesars Palace, features a seven-course Japanese feast for $42.50 per person.

Lillie Langtrey's at the Golden Nugget offers Cantonese specialties—almond duck, lemon chicken, ginger beef—served in an 1890s' San Francisco atmosphere. Western desserts.

House of Szechwan, in a beautiful room at the Sands hotel, serves delicious and reasonable food. Try the moo shu pork.

RESTAURANTS AROUND TOWN
■ Breakfast

Poppa Gar's. "Poppa" Garland Miner goes about as far back as anybody in the Las Vegas restaurant business—50 years! He started out at the Round-Up Drive-In on the Strip in the early 1940s, then took over the food service at the El Cortez in 1945. After a few years he moved up Fremont Street to Bob Baskin's, where he and Bob put out the victuals till 1965, when he moved to his present location. The historical black-and-white photographs alone are worth the visit, and the quail and eggs, with fresh country sausage, are legendary.

Bagelmania. Thanks to Northeastern sunbirds (and the Jewish Mafia), Las

Vegas is a great town for bagels, lox, matzo brie, and designer cream cheese. This is one of the best.

Bagels N' More. Jewish deli with the best homemade corned-beef hash this side of the Hudson River, and fancy-schmancy omelettes.

Jamie's. Classic diner with great food and cheap prices.

■ **Brazilian**

Yolie's Steakhouse. The only place in Nevada to get marinated meat, mesquite-broiled, *rodizio*-style, which means sliced continuously from the skewer onto your plate by the waiter in the fashion of a true *churrascaria* (Brazilian house of meat). Sausage, turkey, brisket, lamb, pork, along with salad, soup, and sides come for a set price of $18.95. The room is soft and inviting, the bar is big and comfortable, or sit outside on the deck.

■ **Chinese**

Chin's has garnered both "the highest acclaim" and the "best Chinese restaurant in the city" from two impeccable sources. Eggroll $5, other appetizers up to $14, vegetable plate $8, and chicken, seafood, pork, beef start at $15.

Golden Wok. Many local Chinese frequent the Golden Wok. It has a typically varied menu, with spicy Szechwan dishes and fresh Cantonese-style vegetables, from $7-12. Lunch buffet for $6.

Szechwan. Very fast to-go service, in case you just want rice and veggies for dinner in your room (the Vegetable Delight, $5.95, is just that).

Chinese Gardens. In a massive pagoda-like building, this is the Oriental equivalent of the Venetian. The huge menu has everything from Szechwan kung pao ($8) and chef's specialties ($12) to chop suey and egg foo yong. Try the wonton roast-duck soup.

■ **Continental/Cajun**

Cafe Michelle is very popular with Las Vegans, for its patio dining (overlooking the shopping center parking lot), eclectic American and European dishes (crepes, spanikopita, veal), and extremely reasonable prices. Crowded at lunchtime; a bar next door has live music at night.

Ferdinand's. Don't be fooled by the unprepossessing gray-brick building with no windows. It's wonderfully dark inside—especially appealing in the summer to get out of the blinding sun. Bacon and eggs are $4, sandwiches $5, Cajun lunches $6-9. Get blackened anything (including Spam!) for dinner for $8-17, or try fish creole ($11-15), sausage and peppers ($11), jalapeño hushpuppies and sweet-pota-to-pecan pie.

The Tillerman is the number-one favorite of Jackie Brett, Las Vegas entertainment writer for *Nevada* magazine, and a longtime resident with truly discerning taste. Pleasant room with big ficus trees, menus on scrolls, and a dozen fresh-fish daily specials ($14-19).

Vegas Bayou, along with Ferdy's (above), serves the best Cajun in Las Vegas. Jambalaya $9, étoufé $15, blackened everything, lounge entertainment.

■ Italian

Battista's Hole In The Wall. Family-style meals (antipasto, garlic bread, mine-strone, all-you-can-eat pasta on the side, and all-you-can-drink red wine) start at $9.95 for spaghetti and meatballs and go all the way up to $26 for cioppino. Classic Italian restaurant decor.

Bootlegger. Cozy, family-run, great service, reasonable and tasty food; lunches $4-7, dinners $9-17.

■ Japanese

Ginza. This Japanese restaurant is always occupied by at least several tourists from Tokyo. Ten a la carte dishes, in true Japanese style, will run $40.

Osaka. A close second to the Ginza.

■ Mexican

Ricardo's has a well-deserved reputation for the best (and most) Mexican food in Las Vegas. A single tamale a la carte ($3.95) will fill you up, and a seafood enchilada ($8) is good for at least two-and-a-half meals.

Dona Maria's. Much lower-key than Ricardo's, with just as good and inexpensive food. The tamale with green enchilada sauce ($3) is a lip-smacker. You'll forget you're in Las Vegas inside Dona Maria's, serving the city faithfully since 1977.

El Burrito, like El Sombrero, is another hole-in-the-wall beanery—nine booths, no bar, no lobby, you wait on the congenial sidewalk with the other devotees for a table. One waitress, open kitchen, doing a great business since the mid-1960s.

■ Pizza

Boston Pizza. With four locations around town—check the Yellow Pages—this place will transport all Yankees right back to the famous Greek-style Houses of Pizza from Lowell to Provincetown, with its crispy crust and secret pizza sauce.

Terina's. Features Detroit-style, which is similar, but offers a choice of round, square, thick, or thin slices.

Battista's. Voted Las Vegas's best pizza.

Brooklyn's Best. Adequately holds down the New York-style tradition.

■ Vietnamese

Saigon Restaurant. With its classic plain Vietnamese interior, it could be right out of San Francisco. The incomparable Imperial rolls are $3, and try the long-simmered beef-noodle soup, and satay.

Visit Dr. Chin for pain.

■ ENTERTAINMENT

With a dozen arenas and concert halls hosting everything from headliners to prize fights and rock 'n' roll to rodeos, plus 18 Las Vegas-style floorshow extravaganzas, more than 50 lounges with Las Vegas-style combos performing every night of the week, and some afternoons, at least two dozen discos, nightclubs, and country-western saloons, a dozen topless or bottomless bump-and-grind joints, and regiments of private exotic dancers, half a dozen comedy clubs, plus light shows, people-watching, and cruising, bargain movies, amusement parks, and local theater, dance, music, and art performances and exhibitions—the only way to arrive in Las Vegas and not be entertained is in a coffin.

SHOWROOM DARWINISM

Bally's, Caesars, Desert Inn, Golden Nugget, Mirage, Riviera, Hilton, Stardust, and Tropicana all have large rooms (with a total seating of around 10,000) where Las Vegas performers earn Las Vegas wages in front of Las Vegas crowds. A recent lineup included Diana Ross, Ann Margaret, Don Rickles, Wayne Newton, David Brenner, Ray Stevens, David Copperfield, Bill Cosby, and Frank Sinatra. Also, 18 Las Vegas-style showroom revues seat another several thousand. Unless the performer is a perennial sell-out, such as Sinatra, Cosby, or Wayne Newton, you should be able to get into any show that's in town when you are. Check out the stars and revues as soon as you settle in, and make reservations immediately.

Most hotels don't sell tickets to the shows. You make reservations for general seating and either dinner or drinks; the waiters and waitresses collect a set price for admission and refreshments. Some hotels accept reservations a few days ahead, others only on the day of the show. Many hotels prioritize reservations for their own guests, so you might pick your hotel by the show you'd like to see—especially if it's included in a package deal. Otherwise, be persistent. If you can't get reservations, you could show up at show time and hope for a no-show. Or, consult your bell captain or motel manager, who might have the necessary juice, or at least a suggestion.

Seating begins 90 minutes to two hours before showtime. You're greeted by the maitre d' and escorted to your table by a captain. Here you enter into a Darwinian domain: "survival of the tippest." To begin with, it's not absolutely necessary to tip; no seats are in Siberia. At worst you'll be sandwiched into a banquet table on the floor right in front of stage with the other low rollers. Preferable, though, is to get a booth on the first or second tier near the center. At the revues, a party of four, a $10 toke to the captain, and an early arrival should do the trick. For the headliners, a $20 to $50 tip might be the ticket. Discreetly hand over the *baksheesh* to the greeter, and then talk it over with the seater.

If it's a dinner show (the exception), banquet service begins early, and a 15 percent toke to the server is the norm. If it's cocktails (the norm), two or three drinks per person will be brought all at once; a $5 to $10 toke is appropriate. One idea is to order a bottle of wine, which won't turn flat or warm while you wait for and watch the show. Another idea is to arrive just before showtime. You might have to split up, but single leftover seats can be great. Also, if you're solo, this is a fine way to avoid waiting by yourself for an hour and a half till showtime. Otherwise, strike up a conversation with the people who'll be stuffed in all around you.

Headliners can run anywhere from $25 to $50 depending on the star; most often you can expect to pay around $30. Weeknight shows are often less expensive than weekends, and sometimes the later show is less expensive than the earlier one. Most include two cocktails.

EXTRAVAGANZAS

This is the classic Las Vegas entertainment. These days there are five major floor shows and a dozen lesser revues, consisting of minor variations on the same theme. Most include elaborate song-and-dance production numbers with performers costumed in anything from the skimpiest five-ounce G-string to the most outrageous 20-pound headgear. A mix of live and taped music accompanies some combination of Broadway show tunes, Geritol oldies, cabaret classics, and dirty-dancin' disco. One variation is ice-skaters, another is female impersonators, and a third is superstar imitators. The sets are lavish, the costumes dazzling, the special effects surprising, and the exposed mammaries curious. Then there are the specialty acts: magicians and illusionists, often with large animals, jugglers, comics, daredevils, acrobats and aquabats, musclemen and musclewomen, marionetteers, and indescribable gimmicksters.

"Lido de Paris" at the Stardust has been running since 1958; "Folies Bergere" at the Tropicana is one year younger. "City Lites" at the Flamingo is now in its second decade. "Jubilee" at Bally's is the most extravagant (a $10-million production), and "Splash," one of three revues at the Riviera, was voted Best in 1989 by

Siegfried and Roy.

Las Vegans, and is highly recommended—you won't *believe* the motorcycle dare-devils. "Boylesque" at the Sahara with Kenny Kerr and "the most beautiful men in the world" has been around a long time, as have the "La Cage" female imperson-ators, with Frank Marino as Joan Rivers, at the Riv.

Tickets can range anywhere from $8.50 for the afternoon "Sex Over 40" at the Continental all the way up to $27.50 for "Jubilee," including the standard two cocktails. "Beyond Belief," the Siegfried and Roy show at the Mirage, costs $62 per person (includes all tips). A few shows still offer dinner at the earlier perfor-mance (typical meat-and-potatoes banquet food) which isn't that much more ex-pensive than the cocktail show, so be sure to ask for details when you make reser-vations.

LOUNGE ACTS

Another Las Vegas institution: several dozen of the major hotels have live enter-tainment in bars usually located right off the casino. These acts are listed in the tabloids and magazines, and if you look hard enough, you can usually find one or two that manage to be entertaining. Good bets are the nostalgia Fifties and Sixties groups—recently The Platters, the Guess Who, Classics Four, and Tony Orlando

Scenes from "Splash"

and Dawn were playing. Bourbon Street and the Four Queens often have Dixieland jazz bands. And groups at Caesars Palace's Cleopatra's Barge usually get the barge rocking a little. Mostly, though, these groups (boy-girl duos, techno-trios, classic foursomes) absorb more energy than they supply.

In fact, the "good old days," when up-and-coming stars earned $10,000 a week to hone their acts in the lounges on their climb to the showrooms, are over. Gone are the comedians doing a fourth show at three in the morning; gone are the singers sitting in with their friends in other lounges; gone is the Rat Pack, any one to six of whom could invade a performance and proceed to treat the crowd to a night they'd never forget. The stars and singers all work the headliner rooms, comedians appear at the clubs, and the novelty acts are incorporated into the extravanganzas. The show lounges of yesterday have been turned into the keno lounges of today. The show lounges of today are mostly meant to be Muzak to the slots.

COMEDY
So far four clubs have opened up in the recent past: **Comedy Store** at the Golden Nugget, **Catch a Rising Star** at Bally's, **Improv** at the Riviera, and **Comedy Stop** at the Trop. Las Vegas gets the top new talent from Nueva York and Los Angeles. Most clubs have two shows on weeknights and three on weekends; tickets run $10-15.

DISCO
As you might expect, disco is alive and kicking in Las Vegas. Half a dozen clubs around town roar every night of the week, and not one of them has a cover charge. This is extremely cheap entertainment, if you can live with the crowds, the drunks, and the often deadening beat. One caveat, however. Make sure to call up first—not only to find out what's happening but to ascertain that a club still exists at all. These places open and close faster than you can deal and draw a bum hand from a quarter poker slot, and even the *weekly* visitors guides and newspaper listings often fall way behind in keeping track of this pack.

CULTURAL LAS VEGAS
Allied Arts Council is the local arts agency that glues together the music, dance, theater, and visual arts of this rapidly expanding city. Before visiting, send for a complimentary copy of their classy black-and-white magazine, *Arts Alive,* if

you want to get beyond the "Strip tease" and into the entertainment that many of the enormously talented locals present to each other. Write 3710 S. Maryland Pkwy., L.V., NV 89119, or call (702) 731-5419 to see what's going on.

KIDS IN LAS VEGAS

Being under 21 in Las Vegas is a very safe bet, since state law prohibits minors from gambling in casinos (strictly enforced). On the other hand, for this reason Las Vegas traditionally had little to offer the impressionable youth of the nation. Recently, however, the city has been promoting itself as the "Family Place to Play," and a number of facilities have opened which cater primarily to the younger generation. Furthermore, now that Las Vegas has achieved a respectable population base, visiting youngsters can avail themselves of more and more opportunities geared toward the growing number of local offspring. Three museums, a zoo, chocolate factory, two amusement parks, a Youth Hotel, Circus Circus, miscellaneous activities, and family outings will keep the kids happily occupied in this previously adult oasis.

LIED DISCOVERY CHILDREN'S MUSEUM

This is Las Vegas's entry into the fastest growing trend in the museum biz: hands-on and interactive exhibits for kids (of all ages). Located in the new central library building (833 Las Vegas Boulevard North), the museum features 130 exciting, thought-provoking, and fun exhibits. Highlights include a human-performance area with ski, baseball, and football machines to test athletic skills; a money display to teach about savings accounts, writing checks, and using ATMs; telescopes await atop the eight-story science tower; at the What Can I Be exhibit, kids can look at and play with career ideas. A radio and TV station, newspaper office, bubble machine, space shuttle display, 120 other attractions, along with a museum store and restaurant are also contained in the 40,000-square-foot (3,716-square-meter) facility. For hours and prices, see "Useful Addresses."

IMPERIAL PALACE AUTO COLLECTION

Walk through the Imperial Palace casino, pass the elevators and go all the way to the back; other elevators whisk you up to the collection, on the fifth floor of the parking structure. Notable jewels in the imperial crown include the custom 1928 Delage limousine built for King Rama VII of Siam (Thailand), the 1947 Tucker with a third-eye headlight that turns with the steering wheel, and the 1955 Mercedes sports car which comes with factory-fitted luggage. You'll ho-hum over all the Rolls-Royces, Cadillacs, and Duesenbergs, but Hitler's bulletproof Mercedes parade car is unique as are the half-dozen prototype motorcycles.

AMUSEMENT PARKS

Wet 'n' Wild is a huge water park where the thrills and spills and chills are non-stop and never-ending. The Blue Niagara is a six-story, 300-foot-long (91-meter) slide of "blue innerspace"; the 75-foot-long (23-meter) Der Stuka gives you the sensation of free fall; the Wave Pool has four-foot-high (one-meter) surf. HydraManiac, Banzai Boggan, Raging Rapids, Bubble Up, Lazy River, and the Flumes will keep you, your kids, and your granny wet and wild all day long.

Scandia Family Fun Center is a bit drier and tamer than Wet 'n' Wild, but offers some variety for the kids, such as a creative 18-hole miniature golf course, race cars and bumperboats, automated pitching machines, video arcade, and snack bar. Miniature golf, on a good Las Vegas-style windy day, is hilarious.

YOUTH HOTEL

This unusual facility in the Las Vegas Hilton will keep the kids happy and busy and the parents free and easy. Built at a cost of $2 million in 1969, the 13,000-square-foot (120-square-meter) "hotel in a hotel" can accommodate 120 children (ages 3 to 18), but you have to be a guest at either the Las Vegas or Flamingo Hiltons. It has five indoor playrooms, an outdoor playground, and boys' and girls' dormitories. The entrance is in the Las Vegas Hilton's North Tower lobby. Meals (extra) are served at 8 a.m., noon, and 6 p.m., and a snack bar fills in between. There's a staff member for every eight kids, whom you can leave for anywhere from one hour to the whole weekend. No reservations are necessary for the hourly service, available 8 a.m. to midnight in summer. Reservations are necessary for overnight stays; call the Las Vegas Hilton at (702) 732-5705.

OTHERS

Waldenkids is a big store full of kids' games and supplies in the Meadows Mall, Meadows Lane at Valley Blvd. Souvenir stores are all over downtown and the Strip, for T-shirts, pendants, jim-jacks and knickknacks. For ice cream, there's a **Swensen's** in the shopping mall at Bally's, and the portions at **Leatherby's**, 2755 E. Sahara, are so big that the kids'll be at high revs for several hours, and then go into hypoglycemic shock for several more.

All the hotels have some sort of video arcade, but one of the best is right at the exit to Ripley's Believe It Or Not in the **Four Queens**. **Circus Circus**, of course, is the place for real Las Vegas-type excitement for the young ones. You can also take them bowling (**Arizona Charlie's, El Rancho, Gold Coast, Sam's Town**, and the **Showboat** all have lanes; at **West Hill Lanes**, 4747 W. Charleston, you don't have to walk through a casino); horseback riding (**Big Valley Riding Stables**, 6291 S. Pecos Rd.), or rollerskating (**Crystal Palace** rinks in three locations).

Don't forget **Ripley's** and **Guinness** museums, the **zoo**, and **Ethel M's** chocolate factory. Day-trips should definitely include the **Red Rock Canyon, Spring Mountain Ranch**, and **Bonnie Springs/Old Nevada** loop, as well as **Hoover Dam** and **Lake Mead**.

■ GETTING THERE

BY AIR

More than 600 daily scheduled flights on 17 major airlines and 19 charter companies service over 15 million people a year at Las Vegas's stunning McCarran International Airport. The wide-eye, rubber-neck amazement that this town is famous for kicks in the moment you step into the terminal, with its slots, palm sculptures, maze of people-movers, escalators, elevators, and sheer enormity. McCarran ranks 20th in U.S. airline traffic, even though Las Vegas is only the country's 79th largest city (1986). Based on the number of residents in the city, however, it supposedly handles a greater percentage of passengers per capita than any other airport in the world.

Las Vegas is one of the easiest cities in the world to fly to. And though flying to and from Las Vegas isn't the cheap junket it once was, the number of airlines keeps fares competitive. Package deals can be an especially good value, if you're only staying the usual three or four days; any good travel agent should be up on the latest. Or contact the Convention and Visitors Bureau, which can pinpoint packagers or wholesalers in your area. Also try reservations services (see "Useful Addresses") which handle hotel packages, often including airfare. The travel supplements of the Sunday dailies frequently list the latest special deals and fares and packages to Las Vegas.

Las Vegas Transit buses don't serve the airport. You can take a Gray Line airport shuttle van to your Strip ($3 one-way) or downtown ($4.25 one-way) destination; tel. (702) 384-1234 for reservations. A classier, regularly scheduled, more Las Vegas way is to catch a Bell Trans limo, for the same fares as Gray Line, but with regular pick-ups at most hotels every half hour (on the half-hour and hour), and always available outside the baggage claim at the airport; tel. 385-LIMO. A taxi ride should run no more than $6-7 to south and central Strip hotels, $8-9 for Convention Center and upper Strip hotels, and $10-12 for downtown.

BY TRAIN

Amtrak's *Desert Wind* passes through Las Vegas once a day in each direction on its way between Los Angeles and Salt Lake City, and to points east. The depot, which was built on the site of the original Union Pacific station, is at 1 Main Street downtown (head straight back from the main entrance of the Union Plaza Hotel casino). The train pulls out of L.A. at 1 p.m. daily, arriving Las Vegas at 7:55 p.m., $63 one-way and $109 round-trip. The first 30 percent of round-trip tickets between L.A. and Las Vegas go for $75, and the next 30 percent are sold for $99; reserve early for the best deal. The train pulls in from Salt Lake City at 7 a.m., departs a few minutes later, and arrives back in L.A. at 2 p.m.; the fare is $82 one-way, and $164 round-trip. For ticket and schedule information, call (800) 872-7245.

On the drawing board are plans for a mag-lev (magnetically levitated) high-speed bullet train which will complete the one-way trip between Los Angeles and Las Vegas in just under an hour. You could almost live in Las Vegas and commute, round-trip weekdays, to L.A.—which would finally and officially render Las Vegas what it's been considered, by some, since the 1940s: the largest subdivision of Los Angeles. Look for a completion date around 1996.

BY ROAD
Las Vegas crowds around the intersection of Interstate 15, US 95, and US 93. The Interstate runs from Los Angeles, 272 miles (437 km), four to five hours at 65 mph (100 kph) to Salt Lake City, 419 miles (674 km), six to eight hours. US 95 meanders from Yuma, Arizona, on the Mexico border, up the western side of Nevada, through Coeur D'Alene, Idaho, all the way up to Golden, British Columbia. US 93 starts in Phoenix and hits Las Vegas 285 miles (459 km) later, then merges with I-15 for a while, only to fork off and shoot straight up the east side of Nevada, and continue due north all the way to Jasper, Alberta.

The Greyhound depot is right next door to the Union Plaza Hotel (south side), at 200 S. Main St.; tel. 382-2640. These buses arrive and depart frequently throughout the day and night from and to all points in North America, and are a reasonable alternative to driving or flying. Advance purchase fares are extremely inexpensive, and with extended travel passes you can really put the miles on.

■ GETTING AROUND

BY BUS AND TROLLEY
Las Vegas Transit System operates 13 routes around the Las Vegas metropolitan area, from Henderson and North Las Vegas to the University and Strip. All buses depart from the modern Downtown Transportation Center (DTC), at Stew-

art Street and Casino Center Boulevard behind the post office, tel. 384-3540. A fairly convenient way, during the week at least, to get up and down the long hot Strip is on the "Strip Shuttle," which services Las Vegas Boulevard South from the Hacienda to the Desert Inn, then turns up Convention Center Drive to the Hilton, and returns to the Strip via the Sahara. Buses are supposed to run every 15 minutes from 8:30 a.m. to 1 a.m. Over the weekend, however, they're slow and crowded. Bus route 6 connects the Strip with downtown, leaving the DTC every 15 minutes from 7 a.m. to 12:45 a.m., and every 30 to 60 minutes for the rest of the early morning. All fares are $1.10, exact change; ask about commuter cards, senior citizens' and children's fares; transfers cost 15 cents.

Two trolleys also serve the Strip and downtown. The downtown trolley, run by Las Vegas Transit, departs the Downtown Transportation Center every 15 minutes from 8 a.m. to 10 p.m., making an 18-block loop in roughly 25 minutes. Fares are 50 cents for adults, 25 cents seniors; tel. 799-6024. The Strip

Hot wheels and high stirrups.

trolleys (tel. 382-1404) are operated privately, and follow the same route as the Strip shuttle buses, but they pull right up to the front door of 25 hotels. Five trolleys are running at any given time, passing your stop roughly every 30 minutes, from 9:30 a.m. to 2 a.m., $1, exact change. A good alternative to public buses, especially from Friday afternoon to Sunday night.

BY TAXI

Except for peak periods, taxis are numerous and quite readily available, and the drivers are great sources of information, and often entertainment. They cost $1.70 for the flag drop, then 20 cents every seventh of a mile. Waiting time is 30 cents a minute.

BY LIMO

With a local fleet of over 200 limousines, Bell Trans can handle anything you might dream up. Their rates are most reasonable too: $22 an hour for a standard limo, and $30 for a stretch with a one-hour minimum. They also do the airport limo transfers; tel. 385-LIMO. Presiden-

This limo is no stretch of the imagination.

tial Limousine, tel. 731-5577, charges $40 an hour for a six-seater, and $60 an hour for an eight-seater; both include TV/VCR, mobile telephones, champagne, and roses for the ladies.

"Longride" is Villa Roma's 32-foot-*long* limo, a modified 1978 Lincoln that's been "stretched" twice, complete with twin rear axles, red velvet interior (called the "lounge"—bartender optional), color TV, two stereo systems—one for the lounge, the other for the rumble seat, which overlooks the hot tub. The limo sleeps nine comfortably, and rents for $120 an hour. It sits next to Villa Roma Motel and Wedding Chapel on Convention Center Drive across from the Paddle-wheel; tel. 735-5211.

BY RENTAL CAR

Renting a car provides an opportunity to experience some real thrills while you travel around town. If you're visiting Las Vegas for the first time on a package deal at a Strip hotel and don't plan on going off the beaten track, you probably don't need a car; just ride the Strip shuttles or trolleys, or grab a cab. But if you've been here before and want to peel out a little, or see more of stunning southern Nevada, why not do it in the style to which you've always wanted to become accustomed? You can rent everything from a Corvette to a Cadillac, from a Fiero to a 4WD Bronco, from a Subaru station wagon to a 16-passenger van. Most rentals have mileage charges, but some offer unlimited. If you're going to be in town for four or even three days, ask about weekly rates; with the extra mileage and discounted charges, it might save you money off the cumulative daily cost. Check with your insurance agent at home about coverage on rental cars; often your insurance covers rental cars (minus your deductible) and you won't need the rental company's.

Be aware that morning and evening **rush hours** are brutal all over Las Vegas, and the Strip can turn into a sweltering and tense parking lot, especially at the traffic lights in front of Circus Circus, the Fashion Show Mall, Flamingo, and Tropicana. In fact, the Strip is an absolute zoo from Friday afternoon till Monday morning. Pick up a map and learn the Paradise Road, Industrial Road, and back-street shortcuts.

TOURS

The ubiquitous **Gray Line**, tel. 384-1234, as always, is representative of the ground sightseeing available in the area. They offer tours of the daytime city and nightclubs after dark, to Hoover Dam with connections to Lake Mead cruises, to Valley of Fire and Lost City Museum, and to Mt. Charleston, Red Rock Canyon, and Laughlin.

Ray and Ross Transport, tel. 646-4661 or (800) 338-8111, covers the same general territory, with city, nightclub, Hoover Dam, Colorado River, and Laughlin tours.

Cultural Focus, tel. 382-7198, is a non-profit tour agency which focuses on the history, environment, and people of southern Nevada, narrated by specialists.

■ EMERGENCY MONEY

Anybody reading *this* section is either 1) a victim of lost or stolen cash, 2) a degenerate gambler, or 3) a die-hard guidebook finisher. It wouldn't have been inappropriate, perhaps, to place this section at the end of the gambling chapter. But for one thing, while all degenerate gamblers are victims of lost or stolen cash, all theft victims aren't necessarily degenerate gamblers. For another, there's something somewhat inevitable about the closing statement of a Las Vegas guidebook addressing the eventuality of being broke and wondering what to do. After all, Las Vegas is the ultimate magnet for currency. Its attraction is directly proportionate to the action. The more money you bring to Las Vegas, the stronger its pull. As the money departs your possession, Las Vegas loosens its grip. In a way, this place is the ultimate con. It's like the devil, tempting the mind to abandon all logic, with every seduction of the flesh, in order to instigate the final agony, or ecstasy—surrender of the will. It's a palpable moment. It's when the house insinuates its nimble fingers into the wallets of hope, and gently removes all available cash, without guilt. It instantly pinpoints and imprints all suckers and losers.

Luckily, only a small minority of visitors arrives already weak enough for their little remaining will to atrophy. Most abide by limits and enjoy themselves. But this section is not for the winners and recreational players. It's for the suddenly lost, the newly dropped, the first-timer from Anywhereville who mounted a fearsome bucking bummer and rode it out till the bitter end, and now finds himself suckered and plucked. Even after his wife, hovering nervously, pleaded, "Please don't, honey...That's the gas money." Even as he watched, from a ringside seat, that manicured, jeweled, and hypnotic hand slowly, inexorably, like fate itself, pick him completely clean. Immediately, he's no longer of any use to the house, and he stumbles out into the darkness of midnight or noon—either. And as his will gradually returns on the wings of instinct, he repeats the wayworn words of the first question ever asked, "Well, what now?"

Carrying any personal checks? It's not difficult to cash personal, out-of-state checks in Las Vegas. Simply go to the cage (main cashier) in any casino and present your driver's license, major credit card, and a check for up to the house limit (usually between $100 and $300). The hard part, if you're in this situation, is walking into the clear through the casino without succumbing to the foolhardy notion that your luck has turned and now's the time to win back all the losses.

Got any credit left? There are Automatic Teller Machines (ATMs) in nearly every casino nowadays, but the fees are steep, from $9.75 for $50 to $50 for $1,000. It's better to take a cash advance off a credit card at a local bank. The service fee isn't quite so high, and you're not faced with carrying cash through the casino.

No checks or credit cards? You can try applying for a "card"—casino credit. The amount of credit supplied is usually the same amount as in your checking account back home, which the casino can confirm. If that fails, rumor has it that the casino is sometimes good for a few bucks for gas money or bus fare, especially if you've dropped a good portion of your bankroll there. Talk to the shift manager, who'll refer you to the casino manager.

If that doesn't work, a number of pawn shops will hock your possessions for cash. On South First Avenue and East Carson downtown, directly across the street from the side of the Golden Nugget, are **Stoney's Lucky Money** and **John's Loan.** Stoney's is one of the biggest, busiest, and oldest pawnbrokers in Las Vegas. **Pioneer Loans** is just down First Street across Fremont. At **Capital Leasing Co.,** 2501 Meadow Avenue, you can get "cash in a flash" by using your automobile as collateral. Go straight from there to the Greyhound depot. **Instant Auto Pawn,** 1613 North Boulder Highway in Henderson, provides the same service, and will hock your RV and houseboat to boot.

As an absolute last resort, you'll simply have to telephone your parents, children, siblings, or friends and have them wire you money through Western Union, one of the busiest telegraph offices in the world. Pick up your cash at 517 Fremont Street, downtown, tel. 382-4322, open 24 hours—then go home, lick your wounds, think it over, and be better prepared, with both will power and bill power, when you find you're back in Las Vegas, with cards, dice, or a handle in your hand.

Another million dollars.

(opposite) Road to Mouse's Tank at Valley of Fire park.

USEFUL ADDRESSES

■ MAJOR HOTELS

B = BUDGET; M = MEDIUM; E = EXPENSIVE

Aladdin	3667 LV Blvd. S. L.V., NV 89109	(702) 736-0111 (800) 634-3424	M
Alexis Park	37 E. Harmon Ave. L.V., NV 89109	(702) 796-3300 (800) 223-0888	E
Arizona Charlie's	740 S. Decatur Blvd. L.V., NV 89107	(702) 258-5200 (800) 342-2695	B
Bally's	3645 LV Blvd. S. L.V., NV 89109	(702) 739-4111 (800) 634-3434	E
Barbary Coast	3595 LV Blvd. S. L.V., NV 89109	(702) 737-7111 (800) 634-6755	B
Best Western Royal	99 Convention Center L.V., NV 89109	(702) 735-6117 (800) 634-6118	B
Boardwalk	3750 LV Blvd. S. L.V., NV 89109	(702) 735-1167 (800) 636-4581	B
Bourbon Street	120 E. Flamingo L.V., NV 89109	(702) 737-7200 (800) 634-6956	B
Caesars Palace	3570 LV Blvd. S. L.V., NV 89109	(702) 731-7110 (800) 634-6661	E
California	12 Ogden Ave. L.V., NV 89101	(702) 385-122 (800) 634-6255	B
Circus Circus	2880 LV Blvd. S. L.V., NV 89109	(702) 734-0410 (800) 634-3450	B
Continental	4100 Paradise Rd. L.V., NV 89109	(702) 737-5555 (800) 634-6641	B
Desert Inn	3145 LV Blvd. S. L.V., NV 89109	(702) 733-4444 (800) 634-6909	E
Dunes	3650 LV Blvd. S. L.V., NV 89109	(702) 737-4110 (800) 634-6971	M
El Cortez	600 Fremont L.V., NV 89101	(702) 385-5220 (800) 634-6703	B

El Rancho	2755 LV Blvd. S.	(702) 796-2220	B
	L.V., NV 89109	(800) 634-3410	
Fitzgeralds	301 Fremont	(702) 382-6111	M
	L.V., NV 89101	(800) 274-5825	
Flamingo Hilton	3555 LV Blvd. S.	(702) 733-3111	M
	L.V., NV 89109	(800) 732-2111	
Four Queens	202 Fremont	(702) 385-4011	M
	L.V., NV 89101	(800) 634-6045	
Fremont	200 Fremont	(702) 385-3232	B
	L.V., NV 89101	(800) 634-6182	
Frontier	3120 LV Blvd. S.	(702) 794-8200	M
	L.V., NV 89109	(800) 634-6966	
Gold Coast	4000 W. Flamingo	(702) 367-7111	B
	L.V., NV 89103	(800) 331-5334	
Gold Spike	400 E. Ogden	(800) 634-6703	B
	L.V., NV 89101	(702) 384-8444	
Golden Gate	111 S. Main	(702) 382-6300	B
	L.V., NV 89101	(800) 426-0521	
Golden Nugget	129 Fremont	(702) 385-7111	E
	L.V., NV 89101	(800) 634-3454	
Hacienda	3950 LV Blvd. S.	(702) 739-8911	M
	L.V., NV 89119	(800) 634-6713	
Holiday	3475 LV Blvd. S.	(702) 369-5000	M
	L.V., NV 89109	(800) 634-6765	
Horseshoe	128 Fremont	(702) 382-1600	M
	L.V., NV 89101	(800) 237-6537	
Imperial Palace	3535 LV Blvd. S.	(702) 731-3311	M
	L.V., NV 89109	(800) 634-6441	
Lady Luck	206 N. Third	(702) 477-3000	M
	L.V., NV 89101	(800) 523-9582	
Landmark	364 Convention Center	(702) 733-1110	B
	L.V., NV 89109	(800) 458-2946	
Las Vegas Club	18 Fremont	(702) 385-1664	B
	L.V., NV 89101	(800) 634-6532	
Las Vegas Hilton	3000 Paradise Rd.	(702) 732-5111	E
	L.V., NV 89109	(800) 732-7117	

MGM Marina	3805 LV BLvd. S.	(702) 739-1500	M
	L.V., NV 89109	(800) 634-6169	
Maxim	160 E. Flamingo	(702) 731-4300	M
	L.V., NV 89109	(800) 634-6987	
Mirage	3400 LV Blvd. S.	(702) 791-7111	E
	L.V., NV 89109	(800) 627-6667	
Nevada	235 S. Main	(702) 385-7311	B
	L.V., NV 89101	(800) 637-5777	
Paddlewheel	305 Convention Center	(702) 734-0711	B
	L.V., NV 89109	(800) 782-2600	
Palace Station	2411 W. Sahara	(702) 367-2411	M
	L.V., NV 89102	(800) 634-3101	
Park	300 N. Main	(702) 387-5333	B
	L.V., NV 89101	(800) 782-9909	
Rio	3700 W. Flamingo	(702) 252-7777	E
	L.V., NV 89103	(800) 888-1808	
Riviera	2901 LV Blvd. S.	(702) 734-5110	M
	L.V., NV 89109	(800) 634-6753	
Sahara	2535 LV. Blvd S.	(702) 737-2111	M
	L.V., NV 89109	(800) 634-6666	
Sam's Town	5111 Boulder Hwy.	(702) 456-7777	M
	L.V., NV 89122	(800) 634-6371	
San Remo	115 E. Tropicana	(702) 739-9000	M
	L.V., NV 89109	(800) 522-7366	
Sands	3355 LV Blvd. S.	(702) 733-5000	M
	L.V., NV 89109	(800) 634-6901	
Showboat	2800 E. Fremont	(702) 385-9123	B
	L.V., NV 89104	(800) 826-2800	
Stardust	3000 LV Blvd. S.	(702) 732-6111	M
	L.V., NV 89109	(800) 634-6757	
Tropicana	3801 LV Blvd. S.	(702) 739-2222	M
	L.V., NV 89109	(800) 468-9494	
Union Plaza	1 S. Main	(702) 386-2110	M
	L.V., NV 891011	(800) 634-6575	
Vegas World	2000 LV Blvd. S.	(702) 382-2000	B
	L.V., NV 89104	(800) 634-6277	

(opposite) Vegas Vickie kicks a blackjack.

■ WEEKLY MOTEL ROOMS

Barker, 2600 LV Blvd. N., (702) 642-1138, $120 plus $35 deposit with kitchen.

Crest, 207 N. Sixth, (702) 382-5642, $150 with kitchen, VCR, cable, breakfast.

Desert Hills, 2121 E. Fremont, (702) 384-8060, $110 with hotplate and refrigerator.

Dynasty, 4223 LV Blvd. S., (702) 798-5055, $110 without kitchen, $135 two-bedroom apt., keep calling.

Ferguson's, 1028 E. Fremont, (702) 382-3500, $149 without kitchen, $169 with.

Full Moon, 3769 LV Blvd. S., (702) 736-0055, $195 with kitchen.

Fun City, 2233 LV Blvd. S., (702) 731-3155, $125 with kitchen.

Glass Pool, 4613 LV Blvd. S., (702) 739-6636, $179 with kitchen downstairs, $194 with kitchen upstairs.

Hialeah, 1924 E. Fremont, (702) 384-1911, $125 with kitchen.

High Hat, 1300 LV Blvd. S., (702) 382-8080, $120 without kitchen, $140 with kitchen.

Knotty Pine, 1900 LV Blvd. N., (702) 642-8300, $115 without kitchen, $120 with.

La Palm, 2512 E. Fremont, (702) 384-5874, $115 without kitchen, $130 plus $25 deposit with kitchen.

Liberty, 2212 E. Fremont, (702) 383-7062, $112 without kitchen, $120 plus $15 deposit with kitchen.

New West, 801 LV Blvd. S., (702) 382-3700, $85 without kitchen.

Safari, 2001 E. Fremont, (702) 384-4021, $120 without kitchen, $125 with kitchen; same management as Hialeah.

Town Lodge, 225 N. Seventh, (702) 386-7988, $120 without kitchen.

■ RESTAURANTS

OLDEST

Alpine Village, 3003 Paradise Rd., tel. 734-6888, open 11:30 a.m. to 2:30 p.m., 5 p.m. to midnight, casual.

El Sombrero, 807 S. Main, tel. 382-9234, open 11 a.m. to 10 p.m., 3 to 10 p.m. Sunday.

Fong's, 2021 E. Charleston Blvd., tel. 382-1644, open 11 a.m to 11 p.m.

Golden Steer, 308 W. Sahara, tel. 384-4770, open 5 p.m. to midnight, neatly casual.

Green Shack, 2504 E. Fremont, tel. 383-0007, open 5 p.m. to closing.

Macayo Vegas, 1741 E. Charleston Blvd., tel. 382-5605, open 11 a.m. to 11:45 p.m., Fri. and Sat. till 1:45 a.m.

Sultan's Table, Dunes Hotel, 3650 Las Vegas Blvd. South, tel. 737-4110, open 6-11 p.m., jacket required.

The Flame, 1 Desert Inn Road at the corner of the Strip, tel. 735-4431, open 24 hours, casual.

The Venetian, 3713 W. Sahara, tel. 876-4190, open 11-11 Tues.-Sun., casual.

Wimpy's, 2437 Las Vegas Blvd. North, tel. 642-5710, open 11 a.m. to 10 p.m., closed Monday.

HOTEL FOOD
■ **Pageantry And Panorama**

Bacchanal, at Caesars Palace, tel. 731-7731, dinner seatings at 6-6:30 and 9-9:30 p.m., reservations a must, jacket.

Benihana, at the Las Vegas Hilton, tel. 732-5455, open 5:30-11:30 p.m., reservations essential, casual.

Centerstage, at the Union Plaza, tel. 386-2512, open 5-10 p.m., casual.

Dome of the Sea, Dunes Hotel, tel. 737-4110, open 6-11:30 p.m. Friday to Tuesday, reservations, jacket required.

Kokomo's, at the Mirage, tel. 791-7111, open 11 a.m. to 2:30 p.m. and 5:30-11:30 p.m., casual.

Moongate, at the Mirage, tel. 791-7111, open 5:30-11:30 p.m., casual.

Ristorante Italiano, at the Riviera Hotel, tel. 794-9363, serving from 6-10:30 p.m., reservations, jacket required.

Skye Room, on the 24th floor of the old Mint tower (now the Horseshoe), tel. 382-1600, restaurant open 6-10:30, bar 5:30 p.m. to 1 a.m., casual.

Visko's of New Orleans, on the 27th floor of the Landmark Hotel, tel. 733-1110, open 6-11 p.m., casual.

■ **Gourmet**

Burgundy Room, at the Lady Luck downtown, tel. 477-3000, open 5-11 p.m., reservations, dressy.

Delmonico's, at the Riviera, tel. 794-9363, serving from 6-10:30, jacket.

Le Montrachet, at the Las Vegas Hilton, tel. 732-5455 (9 a.m.-5 p.m.), 732-5111 (5-11 p.m.); open 6-11 p.m., reservations, jacket required.

Michael's, at Barbary Coast, corner of Flamingo and the Strip, tel. 737-7111, open at 3:30 p.m. for reservations, first seating 6-6:30 p.m., second seating 9-9:30, reservations a must, jacket.

Pegasus, at the Alexis Park Hotel, 375 E. Harmon Ave., tel. 796-3300, seating 6-8:30 p.m., till 9:30 weekends, reservations, jacket appreciated.

Regency, at the Sands, tel. 733-5292, open 6-10:30, reservations, jacket would be nice.

Rhapsody, at the Tropicana, tel. 739-2440, open 6-11 p.m., closed Mon. and Tues., reservations, dressy.

■ Steakhouses

All-American Bar and Grille, at the new Rio Hotel, 3700 W. Flamingo, tel. 252-7777, open 5-11:30 p.m., casual.

Diamond Lil's, at Sam's Town, tel. 459-8009, open 5:30-11 p.m., reservations, casual.

Steakhouse, at Circus Circus, tel. 794-3767, open 5 p.m. to midnight, casual.

Steakhouse, at the Horseshoe, tel. 382-1600, open 6-11, reservations, casual.

The Charcoal Room at the Hacienda Hotel, tel. 739-8911, open 5:30-11 p.m., Fri. and Sat. at 5, reservations, casual.

Wellington's at the Aladdin, tel. 736-0427, open 5-10:30 reservations, casual.

William B's, at the Stardust, tel. 732-6111, open 5-11 p.m., Fri. and Sat. till midnight, nicely casual.

■ Italian

Andiamo's at the Hilton, tel. 732-5455 (9-5), 732-5111 (5-11), open 6-11 p.m., reservations, casual (no shorts).

Chicago Joe's at Fitzgerald's, tel. 388-2400, open 11 a.m. to 10 p.m. daily except Sunday, reservations, casual.

Pasta Pirate at the California Hotel downtown, tel. 385-1222, open 5:30-11 p.m. Sun.-Thurs., till midnight Fri. and Saturday.

Portofino at the Desert Inn, tel. 733-4495, open 6-11 p.m., reservations, dressy.

Primavera at Caesars Palace, tel. 731-7568, open 9-11 a.m., noon to 3 p.m., and 6-11 p.m., reservations a must for dinner, casual (no shorts).

■ **Oriental**

Ah So, Caesars Palace, tel. 731-7731, open 6-11 p.m., reservations, jacket optional.

Empress Court, Caesars Palace, tel. 731-7731, open 6-11 p.m., reservations and jackets required.

House of Szechwan, Sands Hotel, tel. 733-5000, open 5 p.m. to midnight (closed Tues.), reservations, casual.

Lillie Langtrey's, Golden Nugget, tel. 385-7111, open 5-10:30 p.m., reservations, jacket optional.

A R O U N D   T O W N

■ **Breakfast**

Bagelmania, 855 E. Twain, tel. 731-6664, open 6:30 a.m. to 5 p.m. daily.

Bagels 'N' More, 2405 E. Tropicana, tel. 435-8100, open 7 a.m. to 4 p.m. daily.

Jamie's, 4725 S. Maryland Pkwy., tel. 736-8122, open 7 a.m. to 11 p.m. daily.

Poppa Gar's, 1624 W. Oakey Blvd., tel. 384-4513, open 5 a.m. to 9 p.m., Sat. 5 a.m. to 2 p.m., closed Sun.

■ **Brazilian**

Yolie's Steakhouse, 3900 Paradise Rd., tel. 794-0700, open 11:30 a.m.-11 p.m., casual.

■ **Chinese**

Chin's, 3200 Las Vegas Blvd. South in the Fashion Show Mall, tel. 733-8899, open 11 a.m-10:30 p.m, reservations, casual.

Golden Wok, 4670 S. Eastern, tel. 456-1868, open 2-10 p.m., casual.

Chinese Gardens, 5485 W. Sahara, tel. 876-5432, open 11:30 a.m.-10 p.m. casual

Szechwan, 3101 W. Sahara, tel. 871-4291, open 11:30 a.m.-midnight, casual.

■ **Continental/Cajun**

Cafe Michelle, 1350 E. Flamingo Rd. near Paradise in the Mission Center, tel. 734-8686, open 11-11 (Sun. till 6 p.m.), casual.

Ferdinand's, 5006 Maryland Pkwy. in the Camelot Center, tel. 798-6962, open 24 hours, casual.

The Tillerman, 2245 E. Flamingo, tel. 731-4036, open 5 p.m.-midnight, no reservations (be prepared for a wait), casual.

Vegas Bayou, 1290 E. Flamingo Rd., tel. 796-1314, open 11 a.m. till dawn, casual.

■ **Italian**

Battista's Hole In The Wall, 4041 Audrie across the street from Bally's, tel. 732-1424, open 4:30-11 p.m. daily, casual.

Bootlegger, 5025 S. Eastern Ave., tel. 736-4939, open 11:30 a.m.-11 p.m., 5-11 Sun., reservations, casual.

■ **Japanese**

Ginza, 1000 E. Sahara, tel. 732-3080, open 5 p.m.-1:30 a.m., casual.

Osaka, 4205 W. Sahara, tel. 876-4988, open 11:30 a.m.-3 p.m. weekdays, 5 p.m.-midnight nightly, casual.

■ **Mexican**

Dona Maria's, 1000 E. Charleston, tel. 786-6358, open 9 a.m-10 p.m, 8 a.m.-midnight Sat. and Sun., casual.

El Burrito, 1919 E. Fremont, tel. 387-9246, open 11 a.m.-10 p.m., daily.

Ricardo's, 2380 E. Tropicana, tel. 798-4515, open 11-11, noon-10 p.m. Sun., weekend reservations, casual.

■ **Pizza**

Battista's, 4041 Audrie, tel. 733-3950, open 11-11.

Brooklyn's Best, 4722 E. Flamingo, tel. 456-2974, open 10:30 a.m.-11 p.m.

Terina's, 1401 E. Charleston, tel. 459-6122, open 3 p.m.-1 a.m.

■ **Vietnamese**

Saigon Restaurant, 4251 W. Sahara in Sahara West Village just beyond the Statue of Liberty, tel. 362-9978, open noon-10 p.m. Thurs.-Tues., casual.

■ MUSEUM ADDRESSES

BLM Visitor Center, Red Rock Canyon, tel. 363-1921, open 9 a.m. to 4 p.m.

Ethel M's, Cactus Garden Dr. (head out E. Tropicana, right on Mountain Vista, left on Sunset Way, quick left onto Cactus Garden Drive), tel. 458-8864, open 9 a.m. to 5:30 p.m; they make the chocolate weekday mornings.

Guinness World of Records Museum, Las Vegas Blvd. S. behind Arby's next to Circus Circus, tel.792-3766, open 9 a.m. to midnight.

Imperial Palace Auto Collection, Imperial Palace Hotel, fifth floor of the parking structure, open 9:30 a.m. to 11:30 p.m.

Las Vegas Art Museum, 3233 W. Washington at Lorenzi Park, tel. 647-4300, open 10 a.m. to 3 p.m. Tues. to Sat., noon to 3 p.m. Sunday.

Liberace Museum, 1775 E. Tropicana just east of Maryland Pkwy., tel. 798-5595, open 10 a.m. to 5 p.m. Mon. to Sat., 1-5 p.m. Sunday.

Lied Discovery Children's Museum, 833 Las Vegas Blvd. N., tel. 382-3445, open 9 a.m. to 5 p.m. Tues., Wed., Thurs., and Sat., 9-9 Thurs., 12-5 Sun., closed Mon.

Lost City Museum, Box 807, Overton, tel. 397-2193, open 8:30 a.m. to 4:30 p.m. daily.

Marjorie Barrick Museum of Natural History, UNLV campus—head east on Harmon Ave., which dead-ends at the arena parking lot just beyond the museum, tel. 739-3381, open 9 a.m.to 5 p.m. weekdays, 10 a.m. to 5 p.m. Saturday.

Nevada Banking Museum, 3800 Howard Hughes Pkwy. in the First Interstate Building, tel. 385-8011, open banking hours.

Nevada State Museum and Historical Society, 700 Twin Lakes Dr. in back of Lorenzi Park, tel. 486-5205, open 11:30 a.m. to 4:30 p.m. Mon. and Tues., 8:30 a.m. to 4:30 p.m. Wed. to Sunday.

Old Fort, corner of LV Blvd. N. and Washington (in the northwest corner of the Cashman Field parking lot), tel. 382-7198, open 8 a.m. to 2 p.m. Sat. and Mon., noon to 4 p.m. Sunday.

Ripley's Believe It Or Not, inside the Four Queens casino at Fremont and Second.

Southern Nevada Museum, 1830 S. Boulder Hwy., tel. 455-7955, open 9 a.m. to 9:30 p.m. daily.

Southern Nevada Zoological Park, 1775 N. Rancho Dr., tel. 648-5995, open 9 a.m. to 6 p.m. Mon. to Sat., till 5 p.m. on Sunday.

Valley of Fire State Park, Visitor Center, Box 515, Overton, 89040, tel. 394-3088.

■ INFORMATION ADDRESSES

Amber Unicorn, 2202 W. Charleston near S. Rancho by the Baskin and Robbins, tel. 384-5838.

B. Dalton, Meadows Mall, 4300 Meadows Lane, tel. 878-4405; Boulevard Mall, 3528 Maryland Pkwy., tel. 735-0008.

Barnes and Noble, Moyer Student Union, UNLV, tel. 736-3955.

Chamber of Commerce, 2301 East Sahara just east of Eastern, tel. 457-4664.

Front Boy Maps, 3340 W. Sirius St., tel. 876-7822.

Gambler's Book Club and Shop, 630 S. 11th near the corner of E. Charleston or Box 4115, L.V., NV 89127, tel. 382-7555, or (800) 634-6243 to order, open 9 a.m. to 5 p.m. Mon. to Saturday.

Readmore Books and Magazines, Commercial Center, 953 E. Sahara, tel. 733-8155, plus four other locations around town.

Waldenbooks, Meadows Mall, tel. 870-4914, Fashion Show Mall, tel. 733-1049, and right across the street from the Boulevard Mall, tel. 369-1996.

■ LAUGHLIN HOTELS

B = BUDGET;   M = MEDIUM;   E = EXPENSIVE

Colorado Belle	2100 Casino Dr.	(702) 298-4000	M
	Laughlin, NV 89029	(800) 458-9500	
Edgewater	2020 Casino Dr.	(702) 298-2453	M
	Laughlin, NV 89029	(800) 257-0300	
Flamingo Hilton	1900 Casino Dr.	(702) 298-5111	M
	Laughlin, NV 89029	(800) 445-8667	
Golden Nugget	2300 Casino Dr.	(702) 298-7111	M
	Laughlin, NV 89029	(800) 237-1739	
Harrah's Del Rio	2900 Casino Dr.	(702) 298-4600	E
	Laughlin, NV 89029	(800) 447-8700	
Pioneer	2200 Casino Dr.	(702) 298-2442	B
	Laughlin, NV 89029	(800) 634-3469	
Ramada Express	2121 Casino Dr.	(702) 298-4200	M
	Laughlin, NV 89029	(800) 2-RAMADA	
Riverside	1650 Casino Dr.	(702) 298-2535	M
	Laughlin, NV 89029	(800) 227-3849	
Sam's Town	2700 Casino Dr.	(702) 298-2242	M
	Laughlin, NV 89029	(800) 835-7903	

RECOMMENDED READING

■ BIBLIOGRAPHY

Gardner, Jack. *Gambling Bibliography*. Gale Research Company, 1980. The definitive bibliography on books about gambling—games, systems, bookmaking, probability, history, ethics, cheating—compiled by an administrator for the Clark County libraries.

Paher, Stanley. *Nevada—An Annotated Bibliography*. Nevada Publications, 1980. One of, if not *the*, most useful books for any researcher into Nevadana, with over 2,000 listings and descriptions of books about the state. Hundreds of entries about Las Vegas alone.

■ BIOGRAPHY

Berman, Susan. *Easy Street*. The Dial Press, 1981. The incredibly poignant story of a young girl growing up in Las Vegas in the late 1940s and early 1950s as the only child of Davie Berman, boss gambler from Milwaukee, front man for the eastern mob, and colleague of Bugsy Siegel, Gus Greenbaum, etc. In this book, Susan Berman, as good as orphaned at 12, reclaims her father from mob mythology, and imbues the difficult transition made by the illegal gamblers to Las Vegas legitimacy with humanity and sensitivity.

Garrison, Omar. *Howard Hughes in Las Vegas*. Lyle Stuart, 1970. Everything about this troubled, mysterious billionaire is gripping. But this book, centered around the four years Hughes spent sequestered on the ninth floor of the Desert Inn, is especially eye-opening, shedding light on the public events and private life of the recluse, as he set about to buy and redesign the city that may well have been "his true spiritual home."

Glass, Mary Ellen. *Lester Benny Binion*. Oral History Project, University of Nevada, 1973. One of many outstanding personal remembrances recorded by researchers and historians for the U. of Nevada collection. Highly informed questions and uninhibited answers make for an entertaining read about this legendary gambler and hotel owner.

Hoffa, James and Oscar Findlay. *Jimmy Hoffa—The Real Story*. Stein and Day, 1975. Told by the Teamster leader himself, this chronicles his blood feud with Robert F. Kennedy, whom Hoffa describes as a vicious, vindictive, immature, incompetent, spoiled brat of a gangster, and who spent 10 years railroading Hoffa into prison.

Linn, Edward. *Big Julie of Las Vegas*. Fawcett, 1974. The fast-paced and fascinating story of high-roller junkets, as conceived, organized, and chaperoned by Jules Weintraub, an irrepressible promoter who achieved legendary status as Junket King of Las Vegas.

Torgerson, Dial. *Kirk Kerkorian—An American Success Story*. The Dial Press, 1974. A beautifully written, rags-to-riches biography of one of Las Vegas's biggest names—and biggest hotel builders. Among the myriad fascinating stories herein are how Kerkorian was forced to sell out the International and Flamingo hotels to Hilton, primarily due to Meyer Lansky's 20-year hidden ownership in the Flamingo, and Howard Hughes's strange competition with Kerkorian when they were both commandeering Las Vegas in the late 1960s.

■ FICTION

Anderson, Ian. *The Big Night*. Simon and Schuster, 1979. About a notorious gambler who assembles a team of five women to beat Las Vegas out of a million bucks in one night. A quick page-turner, enjoyable as long as you suspend most of your disbelief. Also see *Turning the Tables on Las Vegas*, in which "Anderson," a pseudonym for R. Kent London, describes one of his dreams: training a squad of women to stick it to macho Las Vegas. The September 1987 *Blackjack Forum* reported that London was convicted in New York in the Wedtech fiasco.

Brown, Harry. *The Wild Hunt*. Harcourt, Brace, Jovanovich, 1973. This wild and rollicking tale, written in a style that seems combined from Pynchon, Fariña, and Joyce, follows Pfc. Beaudin P. Black as he kills the prized geese of his CO colonel, who chases him across the country—including a short stop in Las Vegas.

Chandler, David. *Father O'Brien and His Girls*. Appleton-Century, 1963. Based on the true story of Father Crowley, who responded to Las Vegas's unique challenges by, for one, holding Mass in a showroom at 4 a.m. The priest and his nuns battle the forces of evil for lost Las Vegas souls.

Demaris, Ovid. *The Vegas Legacy.* Dell, 1983. By a co-author of the *Green Felt Jungle,* this story is very loosely based on Nevada history, about a presidential convention taking place in Las Vegas at which the Nevada powers-that-be attempt to install their corrupt favorite son as the candidate.

Dunne, John Gregory. *Vegas—Memoir of a Dark Season.* Random House, 1974. Quirky first-person narrative about a troubled writer who gravitates to Las Vegas to weather a mild breakdown, and becomes involved with an assortment of characters: hooker, private eye, lounge comic, apartment manager.

Haase, John. *Big Red.* Pinnacle Books, 1980. Towering novel about the building of Boulder-Hoover Dam, from the point of view of Frank Crowe, the dam's chief engineer. As monumental and epic a book as the dam itself.

Kantor, Hal. *The Vegas Trap.* Beeline Books, 1970. One of a *legion* of pulp novels centered around "the Great Las Vegas heist." Here, a casino enforcer, the nephew of an underworld owner, runs a counterfeit-chip scam, fronted by an old Army buddy. Characters have some dimension; a couple of good plot twists; fair writing.

McMurtry, Larry. *The Desert Rose.* Simon and Schuster, 1983. An affectionate and poignant character study of an aging showgirl and her ties to Las Vegas—men, daughter, neighbors, co-workers—that McMurtry penned during a three-week lull in the writing of his epic *Lonesome Dove.*

Puzo, Mario. *Fool's Die.* Putnam, 1978. A sprawling, semi-autobiographical novel about a writer who starts out as an orphan, gets married and raises a family in New York, makes a pilgrimage to Las Vegas, and publishes a blockbuster novel which is turned into a box-office smash. Contains some of the best writing in fiction about a Las Vegas hotel owner and his right-hand assistant, scams on both sides of the gaming table, and casino color.

Ross, Sam. *Fortune Machine.* Delacorte Press, 1970. Hair-raising roller-coaster ride taken by a novice card-counter, hitting Las Vegas for $200,000 to "buy" his girlfriend from her rich and rough father. Gripping style: first person, short tight sentences, terse dialogue; you really *feel* the action. Good characters, affirming conclusion.

Silberstang, Edwin. *Snake Eyes.* Thomas Congdon Books, 1977. Attention-holding and spare story of a card-counter, a chip hustler, a compulsive and suicidal gambler, a cheating blackjack dealer and his dope-running confederate, a hotel owner, his underworld backers, and a has-been household-name entertainer. Money, as is true throughout this genre, is a character of its own, a ping-pong ball bouncing among, and gluing together, the people, then finally settling right back where it comes from and belongs—the house. The protagonists are left with nothing but their affection for each other and their faith.

■ GAMBLING

Anderson, Ian. *Turning The Tables On Las Vegas.* Vintage Books, 1976. "Ian Anderson" was a pseudonym for R. Kent London, a highly successful and anonymous card counter. Goes into extraordinary detail about playing and betting strategies, camouflage, interaction with the pit personnel, and maintaining a winning attitude. Required reading for aspiring counters.

Bass, Thomas. *Eudaemonic Pie.* Houghton Mifflin, 1985. A true hippie adventure story about a group of physicists at UC Santa Cruz who invented a computer that fit in a shoe to beat the casino at roulette.

Eadington, William R. *The Evolution of Corporate Gambling in Nevada.* University of Nevada-Reno, 1980. A brief, incisive survey of the challenges faced since the mid-1950s by the casino industry and the state to achieve popular legitimacy, conventional financing, federal tolerance, and control of undesirables.

Eadington, William R. and James Hattori. *Gambling in Nevada: Legislative History and Economic Trends.* University of Nevada-Reno, 1980. Reports on legislation passed by Nevada lawmakers since gambling was legalized to control the casino industry, on court challenges to determine the constitutionality of the legislation, and on the gradual acceptance of corporate ownership.

Eadington, William R., editor. *Gambling Papers: The Card-Counter Controversy.* University of Nevada-Reno, 1982. A compelling collection of articles and court briefs about the conflict among Atlantic City casinos, the New Jersey Casino Control Commission, and the blackjack card counters, spearheaded by Ken Uston, one of the all-time great blackjack players and writers.

Findlay, John. *People of Chance—Gambling in American Society from Jamestown to Las Vegas.* Written by a Pennsylvania State U. history professor, this incredible book is not only *the* best book on the evolution of American gambling, but also one of the great books on American history itself.

Gambler's Book Club Catalog. This 28-page tabloid lists and describes more than 1,000 titles on every aspect of gambling, from baccarat to video slots. The catalog itself provides enjoyable and highly informative reading, and helps pinpoint exactly what kind of book you're looking for. Write: Box 4115, Las Vegas, Nevada 89127, or call (800) 634-6243.

Humble, Lance, and Carl Cooper. *The World's Greatest Blackjack Book.* Doubleday, 1980. A college course covering all aspects of blackjack, from memorization aids for basic strategy and card counting (Hi-Opt I and II systems) to cheating dealers and the best places to play. Has useful comparison charts on the different counting systems.

Miller, Len. *Gambling Times' Guide to Casino Games.* Gambling Times, 1983. One of a slew of how-to books about craps, roulette, keno, blackjack, and the Wheel of Fortune. Covers the usual rules, odds, and etiquette.

Ortiz, Darwin. *On Casino Gambling.* Dodd, Mead & Company, 1986. One of the best-written and most useful how-to books for playing casino games.

Patterson, Jerry, and Eddie Olsen. *Break The Dealer.* Another book for serious blackjack players, which tracks the subtle changes in casino blackjack strategies to maintain, without fanfare, an edge over card counters. Introduces the shuffling aspect.

Regan, Jim. *Winning at Slot Machines.* Citadel Press, 1985. Written by the slot manager at Bally's Reno, this small book dispels some myths about slots, goes into detail about theoretical odds, describes the differences between the many reel machines, and discusses etiquette.

Riddle, Major, and Joe Hyams. *Weekend Gamblers Handbook.* Random House, 1963. Another casino how-to, but with a twist: Riddle was a congenital gambler and a long-time owner of the Dunes. Fascinating perspective about gambling from the percentage side of the pit, and great anecdotes about gamblers, streaks, and the Dunes.

Scarne, John. *Scarne's Guide to Casino Gambling.* Simon and Schuster, 1978. One of a score of books written by one of the world's great experts on gambling. Scarne lived, breathed, dreamed, and *was* gambling. He invented games and systems. He traveled around the world tracking down obscure stories and history, consulting with casinos, catching cheaters. He calculated odds and percentages and basic strategies long before computers. And he wrote and published prolifically, and encyclopedically.

Skolnik, Jerome. *House of Cards—Legalization and Control of Casino Gambling.* Little, Brown & Co., 1978. The most in-depth look at the sociology of control within the casino industry. Covers everything from chip-transfer and fill-slip procedures in the pit to the potential for corruption of Gaming Commission members. A must-read for anyone looking behind the scenes.

Snyder, Arnold. *Blackbelt in Blackjack—Playing 21 as a Martial Art.* RGE, 1983. Snyder, one of a core group of successful blackjack card counters and writers, has a thorough facility with the game and the language, as well as an active and unusual imagination. He devised the Red Seven unbalanced count, that combines the running count and true count. He established the First Church of Blackjack. He also publishes *Blackjack Forum,* a quarterly full of blackjack articles, issues, editorials, and general ranting and raving.

Soares, John. *Loaded Dice—The Story of a Casino Cheat.* Taylor Publishing, 1985. Incredible story of one of, if not the, greatest crews of "crossroaders" ever to rip off Las Vegas, with elaborate dice and slot scams. Takes a very hard look at all the cheating and stealing from outside *and* inside the casino.

Solkey, Lee. *Dummy Up and Deal.* Gamblers Book Club, 1980. Written by a Las Vegan who earned a degree in urban ethnology and dealt blackjack for seven years as part of her "field study." Talks with great authority about the dealer culture, language, territorial domains, and the dealer relationship with the casino.

Thorp, Edward. *Beat The Dealer.* Vintage Books, 1966. This was the book that launched a thousand brains. Thorp was the first to publicize a card-counting system, and though the years have proved it nearly inoperable, it stimulated the whole idea that casino blackjack could be beaten, and therefore played as a profession, and therefore analyzed to the nth degree.

Wykes, Alan. *Complete Illustrated Guide to Gambling.* Doubleday, 1964. Exhaustively researched, beautifully written, and profusely illustrated book on the history (with a little psychology) of gambling.

■ HISTORY

Best, Katherine, and Katherine Hillyer. *Las Vegas—Playtown U.S.A.* David McKay and Co., 1955. This snapshot of Las Vegas, by a travel-writing pair of Virginia City residents, remains the all-time most incisive, insightful, and humorous portrait of the boomtown during its most exciting boom. Could easily inspire a novel about Las Vegas that takes place in the critical year of 1955.

Cahlan, Florence Lee, and John F. Cahlan, *Water—A History of Las Vegas.* Las Vegas Water District, 1975. Written by the long-time publisher of the Las Vegas *Review-Journal* and his reporter-wife, this is a sprawling, two-volume history of Las Vegas which "shows how its evolution as a city closely paralleled the development of its water."

Demaris, Ovid, and Ed Reid. *Green Felt Jungle,* Trident Press, 1963. The classic and ultimate "Diatribe" book—a savage indictment of Las Vegas and its mobsters, payoffs, cheating, and prostitution. Though highly sensational, it was lively, authoritative, and a veritable desk reference for many exposé writers to come.

Ehrlich, Fred. *Chinese Restaurants in Las Vegas.* Term paper, University of Nevada-Las Vegas, 1981. Good effort to record the history of Chinese restaurants in the city, and relate their development to the history of the Chinese people in Nevada.

Kaufman, Perry Bruce. *Best City of Them All—Las Vegas: 1930-1960.* Thesis, UC Santa Barbara, 1979. An exhaustive survey of the 30-year period following legalized gambling, and all of its conditions, controversies, and conclusions.

Kelley, Ralph. *Liberty's Last Stand.* Pioneer Publishing, 1932. An exciting and vivid contemporary account of the Las Vegas underworld around 1929, with marvelous descriptions of Block 16 clubs and Boulder Highway roadhouses.

Meyers, Sid. *The Great Las Vegas Fraud.* Mayflower Press, 1958. This was the first title in a long series of books that came to be called the Diatribe, and is perhaps the most vicious, with several score of examples and comments that project Las Vegas as a greedy, ruthless, and treacherous booby trap.

Moehring, Eugene. *Resort City in the Sunbelt.* University of Nevada Press, 1989. An amazingly dense—comprehensive, academic, heavily footnoted—description of Las Vegas's development since the 1930s as "typical not only of a sunbelt, resort, and casino city, but of all cities in general." Indispensable for Las Vegas researchers.

Moldea, Dan. *Dark Victory—Ronald Reagan, MCA, and the Mob*. Viking, 1986. A highly detailed investigative report on the Reagan-Hollywood-underworld connection, with startling revelations about Las Vegas: the Parvin-Dohrman story, the Chicago mob's preeminence and its connection to the Teamster Pension Fund, and Reagan's intervention to circumvent the FBI and Justice Department's probes of organized crime.

Murphy, Don R. *The Role of Changing External Relations in the Growth of Las Vegas*. Thesis, University of Las Vegas, 1970. A comprehensive overview of the various social, political, economic, and environmental factors, mostly originating outside of Las Vegas, that contributed to the city's great growth.

Paher, Stanley. *Las Vegas: As It Began—As It Grew*. Nevada Publications, 1971. This outstanding history, with hundreds of fascinating black-and-white photographs and half a dozen historical maps, covers in detail the popular history of Las Vegas from the Old Spanish Trail up through the building of Hoover Dam.

Paher, Stanley, editor. *Nevada—Official Bicentennial Book*. Nevada Publications, 1976. A collection of historical stories and vignettes. Clark County articles include a fascinating look at Las Vegas as a "Temperance Town" by Charles "Pop" Squires, a fascinating look *at* Squires, and a visit to the rough-and-tumble town during Christmas in 1905, among others.

Ralli, Paul. *Nevada Lawyer*. Mathis, Van Nort & Co., 1946. Unusual cases, characters, and local color that this Las Vegan since 1933 ran across during his first 10 years. An expanded second edition was published by Murray & Gee in 1949.

Ralli, Paul. *Viva Vegas*. The sequel to *Nevada Lawyer*, with hometowny sketches, events, and short bios of prominent men in the community.

Reid, Ed. *Las Vegas—City Without Clocks*. Prentice Hall, 1961. Written by a reporter for the Las Vegas *Sun*. By comparison, a slightly more affectionate and less sensational look than *The Great Las Vegas Fraud* that preceded it, and *Green Felt Jungle* that followed, of which Reid was a co-author.

Reid, Ed. *Grim Reapers—Anatomy of Organized Crime in America*. Henry Regnery Co., 1969. Reid departed Las Vegas already a top organized-crime reporter. The Las Vegas chapter details the sordid story of how Caesars Palace arose from the desert, federal wire-tap revelations, skimming operations, and the like.

Roske, Ralph. *Las Vegas—A Desert Paradise.* Continental Heritage Press, 1986. A large pictorial history, which covers many aspects of Las Vegas from past to present. The backmatter celebrates roughly 60 local companies instrumental in the growth of Las Vegas.

Sifakis, Carl. *Mafia Encyclopedia.* Facts on File Publications, 1987. Biographies of scores of top underworld personalities and locales, including Las Vegas, Moe Dalitz, Bugsy Siegel, Gus Greenbaum, Virginia Hill, and Johnny Roselli.

Taylor, Dick and Pat Howell. *Las Vegas—City of Sin?* Naylor Company, 1963. Written by two casino executives, this book was another semi-Diatribe-style exposé, like *City Without Clocks,* that combined a wide-eyed view of Las Vegas's glittery surfaces with a peek at its slimy underbelly. It reprinted feature articles about Las Vegas that had appeared in *Reader's Digest, Saturday Evening Post, Life,* and even *Sports Illustrated.*

Turner, Wallace. *Gambler's Money—A New Force in American Life.* Houghton Mifflin, 1965. Written by a reporter for *The New York Times,* this is an insightful, negative interpretation of the Nevada "experiment" in legalized gambling, with a detailed investigation into the business practices of Las Vegas bosses, specifically Moe Dalitz and the Desert Inn group.

■ DESERT ROOTS

Alley, John. *Las Vegas Paiutes—A Short History.* Las Vegas Tribe of Paiute Indians, 1977. A short but extremely informative, well-written, and sensitive story of the southern Nevada Tudinu. The best history of Las Vegas from the Paiute perspective.

Benioh, Travis. *The Paiute Language for Beginners.* Multi-Cultural Center, Southern Utah State College, 1980. Brief guide to the pronunciation and important vocabulary of the local Indian dialect.

Fiero, Bill. *Geology of the Great Basin,* University of Nevada Press, 1986. An attractive, profusely illustrated, and comprehensive title in the University Press's Great Basin series. A highly accessible and readable survey of the forces that shaped the great Nevada desert, from the beginning of time to the present.

Geology and Mineral Deposits of Clark County, Nevada. Nevada Bureau of Mines, Bulletin 62, University of Nevada. A highly specific, technical, though decipherable, report on the geology, mineralogy, stratigraphy, and hydrology of the individual basins and ranges surrounding Las Vegas.

Lillard, Richard G. *Desert Challenge.* University of Nebraska Press, 1942. Interesting interpretive history of Nevada, with a great section on geology, and a look at Las Vegas as a divorce village.

Lyneis, Margaret, et al. *Archaeological Element, Historical Preservation Assessment and Planning Process, City of Las Vegas.* Department of Anthropology, University of Nevada-Las Vegas, 1978. A survey of archaeological and historical sites—remains, springs, cemeteries—in central Las Vegas.

McPhee, John. *Basin and Range.* Farrar, Straus, & Giroux, 1980. Another breathtaking book by this master nonfiction storyteller. Here he manages to relate the entire history of geology in the course of a drive along Interstate 80 in northern Nevada with a geologist who located an old unworked-over mine, and took a million dollars in metals from it.

Rafferty, Kevin A. *Cultural Resources of the Las Vegas Valley.* BLM Environmental Research Center, 1985. An authoritative and incisive description of the geology, ecology, hydrology, topography, and climate of the Las Vegas Valley. Also offers highly detailed coverage of the paleohistory, including fascinating speculation about the disintegration of the Anasazi society in a Mesoamerican context.

■ PROSTITUTION

Frey, James, et al. *Prostitution, Business and Policy: Maintenance of an Illegal Economy.* University of Nevada-Las Vegas, 1980. A report on the social organization of the illicit enterprise of prostitution as an extension of legitimate marketing activities.

Frey, James, et al. *Analysis of a Prostitution Network: Exchange and Illegal Economy.* University of Nevada-Las Vegas, 1980. A fascinating inside look at hotel prostitution operations centered around the bell desk: bell captain, bellmen, "bellgirls," and guest-tricks.

Gallagher, John, and John Cross. *Morals Legislation Without Morality.* Rutgers University Press, 1983. An academic exploration of Nevada's "puzzling criminal statutes" concerning drugs, gambling, prostitution, and divorce, which are based more on money than morality.

Kasindorf, Jeannie. *The Nye County Brothel Wars.* Linden Press, 1985. Spellbinding account of outsider Walter Plankinton, who tried to open a brothel in Pahrump, Nevada, and the harassment, arrest, arson, and attempted murder that he brought upon himself. Also the racketeering and white-slavery involvement of his competition, and the high-level corruption of local law enforcement.

Lane, Bert. *Las Vegas—Shelter, Food, Sex.* Tandem House, 1976. A guidebook from the mid-1970s, its value now is more historical, especially the coverage of sex for sale in Las Vegas at the time that the state outlawed it.

Prince, Diane. *A Psychological Profile of Prostitutes in California and Nevada.* Thesis: United States International University, 1986. An exhaustive study of attitudes of prostitutes: family and sexual histories, self-esteem, motivation, emotional relationships, and character traits.

Schwartz, J.R. *Best Cat Houses in Nevada.* Straight Arrow Publishing, 1989. A guide to 36 brothels in Nevada, including several near Pahrump, just over the Clark County line in Nye County, where brothel prostitution is legal.

Vogliotti, Gabriel R. *The Girls of Nevada.* Citadel Press, 1975. One of the best books written about Nevada, including the complete rundown of prostitution issues, a great bio of Joe Conforte, and a unique history of Las Vegas.

■ TRAVEL AND DESCRIPTION

Graham, Jefferson. *Vegas—Live And In Person.* Abbeville Press, 1989. This large format, profusely photographed book lives up to its name. Graham's brief history carries him right up to Las Vegas live— games, high rollers, movers and shakers, entertainers, waitresses, bellmen, maitre d's, wedding chapel owners, and signmakers. Las Vegas has needed such a book for a long time.

Knepp, Don. *Las Vegas—The Entertainment Capital.* Lane Publishing, 1987. This Sunset Pictorial is packed with hundreds of black and whites and color plates that illustrate Las Vegas's long, fascinating, and larger-than-life entertainment heritage—collected and captioned by a writer, photographer, and illustrator extraordinaire who works for the famous Las Vegas News Bureau.

Las Vegas Perspective. Nevada Development Authority and First Interstate Bank, 1990. Chamber of Commerce demographics for the Las Vegas and Clark County metropolitan statistical area.

Murray, Jack. *Las Vegas—Zoom Town, U.S.A.* 1962. Self-published and chatty little book that provides a bit of local color from the early 1960s.

Nevada magazine. Published continuously (though under several names) since 1936, this bi-monthly contains an extraordinary amount of coverage on the 36th state, with proportionate attention paid to Las Vegas. Good writing and photography, great production, and the "Events" section alone is worth the subscription price.

Pearl, Ralph. *Las Vegas Is My Beat.* Lyle Stuart. 1973. Similar to, though not self-indulgent as, *Zoom Town,* this book is loaded with descriptions of the mobsters, stars, high rollers, and low-life, among others, with whom the author, a long-time Las Vegas newspaperman and TV personality, came into contact.

Puzo, Mario. *Inside Las Vegas.* Charter Books, 1976. A humorous, sensitive, and insightful glimpse into the gambling life of Las Vegas. This book could only be written by Puzo, an inveterate though not degenerate gambler, and an intimate friend of the city who, in Stan Paher's words, "gently and lovingly pierced through the smut, glitter, and attendant myths to the patient personality waiting within for someone to understand the elusive city."

Thompson, Hunter S. *Fear And Loathing in Las Vegas.* Fawcett Popular Library, 1971. The famous account of a trip by the master of gonzo journalism to Las Vegas to cover the Mint 400 Desert Race for *Sports Illustrated,* with his 300-pound Samoan attorney, a red Cadillac convertible, and enough illegal and exotic drugs to hurtle the whole city toward a psychotic break.

Ventouri, Robert et al. *Learning From Las Vegas—The Forgotten Symbolism of Architectural Form.* MIT Press, 1977. A technical, though fairly readable, analysis of the shapes, sizes, and placement of Las Vegas signs, casinos, parking lots, and false fronts in the service of intensified communication of the commercial vernacular along the new American "strip."

Vinson, Barney. *Las Vegas: Behind The Tables, Parts I and II.* Gollehon, 1986. In the tradition of *Zoom Town* and *Las Vegas Is My Beat,* these books provide an entertaining, informative look at gamblers and gambling, casino management and procedures, amazing stories and statistics, with a little history, helpful hints, and trivia, by an insider of 25 years.

Wolfe, Tom. *The Kandy-Kolored Tangerine-Flaked Streamlined Baby.* Farrar, Straus & Giroux, 1965. The Las Vegas chapter in this big book of essays is perhaps the classic look at the city as the penultimate expression of the new culture—glamour, entertainment, art—style!—that emerged from 1960s' America.

I N D E X

■ ABOUT THE AUTHOR

Deke Castleman has been a dishwasher, laborer, short-order cook, gas station attendant, janitor, stagehand, electroplater, machinist, mechanic, school-bus, truck, and delivery-car driver, door-to-door vacuum-cleaner salesman, and locksmith; Alaskan seasonal tourguide, waiter, and bellman; typist, typesetter, editor, managing editor, senior editor, and video scriptwriter. Along the way he wrote *The Gentleman Caller* (an unpublished novel), *Alaska-Yukon Handbook, Nevada Handbook,* and Discover America's *Las Vegas.*

■ ABOUT THE PHOTOGRAPHER

San Francisco-born photographer, Michael S. Yamashita, has been shooting pictures for National Geographic Society magazines and books since 1979. He is a frequent contributor to *Travel and Leisure* and *Portfolio,* and his many corporate clients include the Mexican Tourist Board, Singapore Airlines, and Nikon Cameras. While on assignment for these clients and other publications, he has covered locations worldwide.

Mr. Yamashita's work has been exhibited at the Smithsonian Institution's Museum of American History, the National Gallery in Washington, and Kodak's Professional Photographer's Showcase at EPCOT Center in Florida. His work has received citations from the Pacific Area Travel Association, and the Asian-American Journalists Association.